Lives on the Line

T0323394

Lives on the Line

How the Philippines became the World's Call Center Capital

JEFFREY J. SALLAZ

OXFORD
UNIVERSITY PRESS

Oxford University Press is a department of the University of Oxford. It furthers
the University's objective of excellence in research, scholarship, and education
by publishing worldwide. Oxford is a registered trade mark of Oxford University
Press in the UK and certain other countries.

Published in the United States of America by Oxford University Press
198 Madison Avenue, New York, NY 10016, United States of America.

© Oxford University Press 2019

All rights reserved. No part of this publication may be reproduced, stored in
a retrieval system, or transmitted, in any form or by any means, without the
prior permission in writing of Oxford University Press, or as expressly permitted
by law, by license, or under terms agreed with the appropriate reproduction
rights organization. Inquiries concerning reproduction outside the scope of the
above should be sent to the Rights Department, Oxford University Press, at the
address above.

You must not circulate this work in any other form
and you must impose this same condition on any acquirer.

Library of Congress Cataloging-in-Publication Data
Names: Sallaz, Jeffrey J., 1974– author.
Title: Lives on the line : how the Philippines became the world's call
center capital / Jeffrey J. Sallaz.
Description: 1st Edition. | New York : Oxford University Press, [2019] |
Series: Global and comparative ethnography | Includes bibliographical references and index.
Identifiers: LCCN 2018058622 | ISBN 9780190630669 (pbk. : alk. paper) |
ISBN 9780190630652 (hardcover : alk. paper) | ISBN 9780190630690 (Oxford Scholarship Online) |
ISBN 9780190630676 (Universal PDF) | ISBN 9780190630683 (electronic publication)
Subjects: LCSH: Call center agents—Philippines. | Labor market—Philippines. |
Philippines—Social conditions—21st century.
Classification: LCC HE8789.P45 S35 2019 | DDC 381/.14209599—dc23
LC record available at https://lccn.loc.gov/2018058622

9 8 7 6 5 4 3 2 1

Paperback printed by Sheridan Books, Inc., United States of America
Hardback printed by Bridgeport National Bindery, Inc., United States of America

For Ging and Teej

They have been at a great feast of languages,
And stolen the scraps.
—WILLIAM SHAKESPEARE, *Love's Labour's lost*

Contents

Lives on the Line

PART I

Introduction

1

One Job, Many Lives

Ashley, Who Escaped

She was nineteen years old and still living at home when her father failed to return from work one Wednesday evening. There had been an especially clamorous fight between her parents the night before. Still, Ashley hadn't expected her dad, a U.S. Air Force veteran, to simply not pull into the driveway in his Ford pickup—the red one, the one with the "America: Love It or Leave It" bumper sticker—after his shift ended at the auto shop that day. As Thursday and Friday passed with no word from him, Ashley began rationalizing her dad's absence as a response to her mom's mental health issues—to the crying fits, to the tantrums—that had left her unable to work or to do much else for the past several years. One thing was certain. Dad's unexpected disappearance exacerbated these problems. "Right after dad left," Ashley calmly explained, "my mom went insane, okay? Like legit crazy. Like straitjacket crazy." Hence began a series of events that would lead Ashley first into and then out of the call center industry.

Her dad's disappearance triggered an instant shift in Ashley's outlook on life, in her way of being in the world. This was 2011. The year before, she'd graduated from high school and enrolled at a community college in her hometown, the southwestern American city where her father's military career had ended. The year before that, her older brother had dropped out of that very same college. "Screw school, I'm tired of it," he'd announced to the family before enlisting in the U.S. Army and being deployed to Afghanistan. Ashley would soon come to a similar view of postsecondary education: it was immaterial to who she was and what she wanted to become. "A diploma's just a fancy piece of paper," she liked to say. "It doesn't matter to me. I'm like soooo over people who need that kind of credibility."

Ashley's dream wasn't to strap on combat boots but, rather, to tie on an apron. She wanted more than anything else to earn a living doing what she loved most, which was baking. In her ideal world, she would own a pastry shop in Colorado, which she would describe as "the most scenic place on Earth." And how exactly would courses in algebra and French help her get there? After just one semester, Ashley dropped out of the community college, just as her brother had.

The path from her small bedroom in the back of her family's ranch-style home to the pastry shop in Colorado wasn't all that clear. But it hadn't been something that needed to be figured out right away. Since the age of sixteen, Ashley had been "working retail" at a women's clothing store—an Ann Taylor LOFT—in an upscale local mall. Though the job paid only the minimum wage (a little under $8 per hour at the time), it offered discounts on merchandise, meaning that Ashley could acquire designer skirts and blouses that were otherwise beyond her means. It gave her excuses to perfect the art of applying makeup, to spend a hundred dollars on a haircut, to hone a certain singsongy intonation of voice. And it allowed her to meet guys like Chad, a twenty-two-year-old golf coach at a nearby country club. He had asked for her telephone number one Sunday afternoon while his mom was perusing the LOFT's sale rack.

With no rent to pay, with a countenance beaming every time she looked into one of her store's mirrors or took a selfie, and with Chad now her boyfriend, it was only too easy to ignore the nightly feuds between mom and dad. Doors slammed and tempers flared in the three-bedroom home with two Saguaro cacti in front. But nineteen-year-old Ashley's sleep was peaceful, her future wide open.

It all changed that Wednesday evening. No dad at home meant no paycheck on Friday, no military pension coming at the end of the month. As her mother lunged from room to room in what Ashley could only assume were panic attacks, the reality hit her, like cold water to the face, that the bills would be due soon. Most of them could be put off for a month, but what if her dad didn't return before then? Would the city shut off the power and water? Would their cell phones stop working? Would they lose their home? As these "woulds" spiraled around in her head, Ashley developed a sort of tunnel vision. Her horizon for understanding herself and her world narrowed; long-term dreams took a backseat to immediate needs. This typical American teen—living at home, working a retail job for spending money—became a breadwinner.

Here is where my path crossed with Ashley's. In 2011, I began studying a U.S.-based company known to be a global leader in the $150 billion "business processing outsourcing" (BPO) industry.[1] The company manages other firms' "customer contact" jobs—mainly "voice work" in call centers—and for this reason I gave the firm the pseudonym "CallCo." For nine months from 2011 to 2012, I performed participant observation as a "call agent" at a CallCo facility in the American southwest. Ashley was one of twenty-one new agents in my "batch."[2]

My initial research question had been that of how outsourced call centers elicit effort and ensure quality service from their employees. They do so, I found, through a combination of work standardization, technical control, and simply relying on human beings to work hard in order to appear competent in their interactions with other human beings.[3] An equally important question that I came to confront was *why the relationship between American firms and American workers such as Ashley was so fragile*. CallCo and its corporate clients were constantly scheming ways to move accounts out of the country, while workers were constantly resigning from the call center. In short, while there was an initial attraction between CallCo and its employees, both parties fled the relationship as soon as possible.

Ashley's initial attraction to call center work was perfectly sensible, given her predicament. After sorting through various bills and bank statements on the Saturday after her father vanished, she realized that balancing the household budget in the weeks and months to come would require more income. Both her boyfriend Chad and her brother stationed in Afghanistan volunteered to chip in a hundred dollars every payday. But such largesse wouldn't cover all their expenses. Late that evening, around the kitchen table, Chad's mother, Vivian, mentioned to Ashley that her co-worker's daughter had once worked at CallCo. "Viv" recalled that the job paid eleven bucks an hour *and* guaranteed full-time work. This came out, Ashley quickly calculated, to at least $500 more per month than her $8 per hour retail job paid. At this moment, *a call center job represented a real way to get by*, a means by which to keep her family, diminished as it was, afloat.

The following day, Ashley logged on to CallCo's website and took its entry exam. She listened to audio clips of imaginary callers with challenging accents—a drawling Southerner, a belligerent Brooklynite—then submitted her own voice files of polite replies. Two days later, on Tuesday, a human resources (HR) rep phoned to offer Ashley a job. As I would come to learn, CallCo rarely has a problem finding qualified workers in this struggling

American city. The company offers a rare and rapidly disappearing species of jobs: *one that doesn't require a college degree yet pays a premium (of 30–40 %) above the minimum wage.* As long as applicants can carry on a basic conversation in English, they stand a good chance of being hired by CallCo. It doesn't take long to realize, however, that the resulting employment relationship is fundamentally flawed.

The call center where Ashley and I worked had been built in the late 1980s, and at its peak a few years later had hosted fifteen major corporate accounts. Over the following decades, as the technology to do so became widely available and grew ever cheaper, account after account was moved out of the country. By the time we arrived in 2011, there were only three accounts remaining. Each was still there only for reasons logistical or legal. One account handled calls from patients of a national pharmacy chain; another fielded fraud claims for a major credit card company; another answered queries from customers of a national package delivery firm. It was on this third account, for the firm "ShipIt," that Ashley and I worked.

Each morning we would walk through a cavernous warehouse, past row after row of empty cubicles and decrepit banners celebrating corporate accounts—for Microsoft, TurboTax, PayPal, and so on—that had long since been offshored. But it was not only firms that were fleeing this facility. By the time I finished my nine months of fieldwork as a CallCo/ShipIt agent, *I was one of the call center's most veteran employees.* Of the twenty-one members of our batch, seventeen had left within a year. Ashley was one of the few who remained as long as I did, though from early on, like most everyone else, she began plotting an escape route.

My field notes from this time catalogue a litany of complaints from Ashley. Compared to her Ann Taylor LOFT job, call center work, while trying at first, soon became monotonous and, in her words, "boring as hell." Customers were not middle-aged women silently shopping for scarves but, rather, frustrated and occasionally irate callers trying to track down packages containing those very same scarves purchased online. And the call center's constant supervision had no parallel in retail. Ashley grew to despise Kelsey, our "team leader" (CallCo's euphemism for a supervisor), and Frank, the account manager, both of whom she described as "terrible people with terrible attitudes." She bemoaned the myriad unseen personnel and programs constantly monitoring our work, quantifying our performance, and prodding us to shorten our "average handle times."

This feeling of animosity appeared to be mutual. ShipIt kept this account in the United States, CallCo managers would tell us matter-of-factly, only because the nature of the work required knowing idiosyncratic things about American geography, climate, and culture.[4] More generally, it was not difficult to perceive an antipathy from those CallCo managers who supervised us on a daily basis. In one memorable instance, we were suffering through a mandatory team meeting. Kelsey and Frank stood in front of the room, scrolling through a roster of employees and highlighting in red the names of agents who were frequently late to work or had high handle times. "It's slim pickings here," Kelsey muttered audibly, to which Frank laughed in agreement.

This workplace, it seemed to me, was a farce. Between the labor pool represented by Ashley and the few firms that continued to hire American workers to field calls, there was an initial attraction but no grounds for an ongoing attachment. We were all going through the motions in what felt like a prolonged yet inevitable breakup.

Most of Ashley's batch-mates quit CallCo within a few months of being hired. Why was she an exception? What bound her to the job for so long? Quite simply, the exceptional circumstances that had unexpectedly transformed her into a breadwinner. CallCo's $11 per hour wage *did* allow Ashley to make ends meet for her mother and her. "When my dad left, I was the one who was gonna have to support us, and the call center *was* supporting us," she admitted much later. "We were barely able to keep our house and after paying all our bills and [for] groceries, we literally had one hundred bucks left. But that was something."

Although it allowed her to keep her household afloat, employment at CallCo began to generate tangible problems for Ashley. These were emotional, embodied reactions to call center work of a negative sort. Suddenly she was bickering with Chad, her boyfriend, over "small things, meaningless things, just things I fight about because I'm stressed out." After her mother would go to bed she began sneaking off to nearby bars, where she would imbibe cheap vodka drinks and "bum cigarettes." Soon Ashley was struggling to get out of bed each morning. At work, it became harder and harder to make it to the smoking patio and back during her fifteen-minute breaks. She was rapidly accumulating disciplinary "points" for absences and tardiness, twelve of which trigger an automatic dismissal. Not wanting to be fired, but losing faith in her ability to keep things together, Ashley grew increasingly motivated to find a pathway out of the call center (figure 1.1).

By now, six months after her father had left, the desperation and disbelief that had blurred her perception like a veil began to lift. After work she would spend hours on the internet researching options available to someone in her situation. During an off day, she took her mother to a public clinic, where

FIGURE 1.1 Ashley, looking down.

a psychiatrist diagnosed anxiety and bipolar disorders. As the medications began to stabilize the mood swings, Ashley was able to talk her mother into granting her a general power of attorney. She then submitted paperwork on her mother's behalf for disability payments and short-term assistance via several state programs. And most significantly, Ashley began meeting with an attorney. Over the following months, he assisted her with tracking down her father and securing an agreement from him to remit money home monthly or else face legal action.

These new income streams released Ashley from the vice grip in which CallCo and its wage premium had held her. She took a job as a waitress at a local diner. That allowed her to be around pastries, her passion, and was less routinized and demoralizing than the call center. Looking back on her call center experience several years later, she said thus: "The entire situation was absolutely ridiculous. It was a hell of terrible people."

Mina, Not a "Call Girl"!

Mina, an eighteen-year-old woman living in Mumbai, India, is described at length in Reena Patel's excellent 2010 book, *Working the Night Shift.*[5] Like

Ashley, Mina found herself in quite a bind after her father abandoned her mother. He had decamped to Saudi Arabia, leaving Mina to look after her mother, who had long been a housewife, and her younger sister. And like Ashley, Mina turned to call center work as a way to keep her family intact. She was nearly finished with her college degree, her English was practically flawless, and she passed the entry exam with ease. Mina's wage was a fraction of what Ashley had been earning in the United States (at the time of Patel's study, new call center workers in India earned around $75 *per week*), but it allowed her to pay for her family's housing loan and her sister's school tuition. Nonetheless, Mina would also leave the call center industry, though for very different reasons.

The general story of when and why firms such as CallCo first set up call centers in India is well known. During the 1990s, new technologies allowed a good many business processes to be sourced from across oceans and national borders. Labor-intensive voice work was a prime candidate to be offshored.[6] And from the start, India was a logical place to send such work, as labor costs there are low, the country produces hundreds of thousands of college graduates each year, and English is an official language of the country.

Hence was born voice offshoring. The first call centers were established in India shortly before the year 2000; CallCo itself opened its first facility there in the early 2000s. That the voice industry took root and thrives in India quickly became a truism. When in 2010 NBC debuted *Outsourced*, a sitcom about call centers, it made perfect sense that the show would be set in India—in Mumbai, in fact. Twenty years after the first call centers opened there, the terms *India, voice*, and *outsourcing* continue to overlap in the popular imagination.

In truth, the voice business has struggled in India. The country's larger BPO industry has diversified into a wide range of technical fields, employment in which is highly desired by educated young Indians. Call centers, in contrast, have from the start scrambled to recruit and, in particular, to *retain* employees. Men cycle in and out of the industry, using call centers as steppingstones toward higher-status tech jobs. Women, meanwhile, face considerable headwinds when it comes to obtaining and keeping call center work. Mina's story illustrates well how this latter dynamic plays out.

When she first described to her extended family her plan to work in a call center, Mina was told that "a girl might get spoiled if earning her own money." Patel attributes such pushback to widespread "attitudes toward [Indian] women who defy gendered notions of place and space, be it [by] going out at night or entering a Hindu temple during their menstrual cycle."[7]

Call center work, in other words, threatens to spoil not just girls but also the whole social order.

For Mina, who worked each night from 6:30 p.m. to 3:30 a.m., these dispersed attitudes took far too tangible forms. Along with the rest of the country, she had been horrified in late 2005 to read in the newspapers about Pratibha Srikanth Murthy, a call center agent in Bangalore who was raped and murdered on her way to work one evening. After that terrible episode, call center firms began running shuttles to pick up and drop off female agents from the front gates of their housing compounds. Still, Mina and the other women in her building who had opted to try their lots in the call center industry could feel the eyes of their male neighbors upon them as they boarded the shuttles each evening. They heard rumors that the men were maintaining lists—"keeping names," as everyone called it—of which girls went out each evening and at what time they returned. Mina was thus not at all surprised when policemen eventually came to her front door, interrogating her mother and demanding to see Mina's work papers. From then on, she kept her employee ID close at hand while riding to and from work, to show the police squads who regularly pulled over her shuttle in the wee hours of the morning (figure 1.2).

Whereas for Ashley the problem had been that of maintaining her sanity at work, for Mina it was managing her reputation outside of it. As one of her colleagues put it, for too many men the equation was clear: "Call center

FIGURE 1.2 Mina, looking out.

job equals call girl job!"[8] From the start, patriarchal attitudes have made it extremely difficult for Indian women to do offshored voice work. In large part as a result, attrition rates from India's call centers mirror those from American ones.[9]

Daisy and Belle: a Near-Hire and a Socialite

Daisy was yet another young woman who both found herself in a dilemma and turned to call center work as a way out of it. She had been born in the northern Philippines in 1993. Her father abandoned her mother shortly after Daisy's birth; soon after that, her mother left the country to become a migrant worker in Hong Kong. There she married a Chinese man and, for reasons unknown, was never able to communicate with or send any money back to Daisy (there were persistent family rumors of a gambling problem).

At the age of three, Daisy was sent to live with her mother's sister in a small village on the eastern shore of Negros, a poor island-province in the central part of the Philippines. This aunt, *tita* Ching, had long been lonely. She'd married young, but had been unable to have children; her husband worked as a seaman and so was home but a few months each year. The money that he remitted allowed *tita* Ching and Daisy to live a materially secure life in their village. Even so, "modern" amenities such as home internet access, cable television, and even media such as books and DVDs were difficult to come by in this isolated region, regardless of how much foreign currency one had in one's pocket.

When Daisy finished high school, *tita* Ching pressured her to stay in the village. But Daisy could see in her aunt what such a future would entail, and so vowed to get out, to experience life in a real city. She would sit late into the night in her village's lone internet café, so as to Skype with another of her mother's sisters, *tita* Arlene. This *tita* had left for Germany a decade ago after marrying a tourist and obtaining a spousal visa. Now she offered to pay Daisy's tuition at her alma mater, a private university in Manila. The only condition was that Daisy would minimize expenses by living with her *lolo* (grandfather). Sixteen years old at the time, Daisy leapt at the opportunity to move from her isolated village to the country's capital, a bustling metropolis of millions.

As she boarded the ferry to Manila, Daisy was full of excitement, but also apprehension. Her primary tongue was Cebuano, the language of the central Philippines, whereas in Manila, situated on the northern island of Luzon, Tagalog and English (along with their portmanteau, Taglish) are used for speaking and writing.[10] Daisy had studied these languages in school and could understand them, but she'd had little practice speaking them. In fact, she had encountered a native English speaker only a few times in her life, via the occasional missionary or tourist off the beaten track. As she attempted to establish her life in Manila, the language issue remained a sticking point. At school, Daisy had no problem comprehending the lectures and textbooks, both of which were in English. She was shy and embarrassed to speak English in everyday interactions, however, and so made do with her rudimentary Tagalog.

It was at this point that *tita* Belle came into Daisy's life. Technically a distant cousin, Belle represented precisely the sort of person Daisy dreamed of becoming. Born and raised male, Belle today describes herself as "gay, proud, and *soshal* (i.e., living like an urban socialite)." What captivated Daisy most about her *tita* was her cosmopolitanism, her urbane way of presenting herself to the world.[11] Most days, Belle would dress in slim-fit Levis jeans, a brightly colored polo or graphic t-shirt, and black Chuck Taylor sneakers. She owned her own motorbike, a definite status symbol given the decrepit state of public transportation in Manila. When navigating the city's crowded sidewalks, she walked with a decidedly confident and feminine swagger. And Belle was, as would she often boast, "loud"—that is, she spoke English exclusively and even, one could say, ostentatiously.

Stylish, proud, and loud, Daisy's *tita* Belle embodies the successful performance of a gay identity in contemporary Philippine society.[12] Insofar as this mode of self-presentation entails speaking English well, gay persons such as Belle *represent ideal call center agents*. When the first foreign call centers opened in the Philippines in the early 2000s, firms did not know what to expect. Would this be a rehash of the Indian experiment? Would ambitious young men soon pull out of the industry and demure young women be pushed out of it? Those who managed the first Philippine call centers were by all accounts surprised to find that the industry acted as a magnet for the gay population dispersed throughout metro Manila. Here was a job that not only recognized a central component of their subculture—English fluency—but also rewarded it with a significant wage premium. Call centers soon became known as, in the words of one of my respondents, a "gay paradise." It was through employment in one that Daisy's *tita* Belle financed her branded clothing, her motorbike, her whole lifestyle (figure 1.3).

Tita Belle took a special interest in her relative recently arrived from "the province." She made it her mission to rid Daisy of her provincial dress, gait, and manner of speech. "When I first got [to Manila]," Daisy recalled, "the

FIGURE 1.3 Daisy, observing Belle.

one person who influenced me most is my *tita*, my gay *tita*. You see, she is a socialite and most of the time she speaks in English. When we're cooking she told me, 'You have to speak in English because I don't understand you. You have to speak English to me.'" As it would turn out, de-provincializing herself would become for Daisy an ongoing task of utmost importance.

As per her deal with *tita* Arlene in Germany, Daisy saved money by moving into her *lolo*'s small apartment in central Manila. Since *lola* (Daisy's grandmother) had passed away several years prior, *lolo* had been living alone, and so this setup seemingly worked for them both. It quickly became clear to Daisy, however, that this was not going to be a good arrangement for her. To *lolo,* she was less a companion than a servant.

At school she had declared a Tourism Management major and envisioned herself traveling the world as a supervisor on a cruise ship. At home, her room was hardly bigger than a broom closet, while *lolo* demanded that she daily do a wide range of chores—"cooking, washing, laundry, sweeping," she complained, "all of which I don't like"—in exchange for a small allowance of 500 pesos, or about $12, per month. Daisy suspected that this was not the full amount that *tita* Arlene was sending from Germany, that *lolo* was keeping most of it for himself. She badly wanted her own place to live.

Once again, Daisy leveraged her skill at social networking. At this time, she had three Facebook accounts, two cell phones, four SIM cards, and was active on multiple dating websites that specialize in connecting Western men and Filipina women. Before long, Daisy was communicating with a German man, Thomas. He was six years her elder and, judging from his pictures, *mataba* (overweight). Nonetheless, Daisy encouraged his attempts to "court her" by agreeing to Skype with him on a nightly basis.

After two months of online courting, Thomas made Daisy a proposal, which she readily accepted. Even though they had never met in person, she would pledge herself to him and he in return would pay for all her needs: her tuition, her living expenses, and even her own apartment. For Daisy, this seemed like a gift from above. She described feeling as though "I'm so blessed that there's someone to help me in my tough times." She went on, "Thomas told me, 'Okay, it's not a problem. I will work here for you. I will be the one to send you to school. I will pay rent for an apartment. I will send allowances every month.'" Freedom for Daisy seemed finally to be at hand. She left *lolo*'s small room and moved into a spacious one-bedroom apartment paid for by her German Thomas.

It was within the confines of this apartment that Daisy's hopes for an independent life were dashed. Thomas, it turned out, was an intensely jealous man and demanded to surveil her constantly. When not at school, she was to be at home with her webcam turned on at all times. She was to eat, sleep, and spend all her spare time on the couch, in front of it. Not surprisingly, Daisy experienced this arrangement as severely compromising her sense of self. "He wanted me to be with him always," she repined, "like he don't want me to go out even to buy my foods. He wants always the camera will be in front of me and I will sleep on the sofa. It's not comfortable and you know, even if he is sending me money. . . . I don't like it because I have my goal in my life to work and earn money by my own."

Hence how I met Daisy, in 2012. By this time CallCo, the company from which Ashley had escaped, was one of the largest private-sector employers in the Philippines. I was doing fieldwork in one of the firm's call centers in Manila by working as an HR officer. One of my duties was to evaluate the English proficiency of job applicants. Daisy was among eight young Filipinos whom I interviewed one afternoon. She and I sat facing each other in a small conference room, me with a clipboard, checklist, and pen in hand. I had no problem comprehending Daisy, but I duly noted on my score sheet that she pronounced big as "beeg," Jeff as "Jep," and made numerous grammatical errors typical of Filipino English speakers. A quick tally of these miscues classified Daisy as a "near-hire"—industry-speak for those who are conversa-tionally fluent in English but who need to improve their grammar and "neu-tralize" their accents.[13] I handed Daisy her score sheet and informed her that she was welcome to reapply in three months.

By coincidence I bumped into Daisy later that evening on a metro station platform. As we rode the train together, she confided her dilemma of being trapped between a local patriarch (her *lolo*) and a foreign one (the German Thomas). Neither situation offered her a chance for a dignified life, and I noted how she used terms such as "prisoner" and "inmate" to describe her predicament. Daisy recounted how the independent lifestyle of her gay *tita* had convinced her that a call center job was her best chance to escape. Her experience earlier that day at CallCo, it turned out, had been only the latest in a string of failed English exams at Manila's call centers.

The solution to Daisy's dilemma was deceptively simple: refine her English, become a call center agent, gain her freedom. She could not afford, however, to enroll in the remedial English courses offered by local training academies. And besides, how would she justify to Thomas so much time spent away from the webcam?

A week later, Daisy broke things off with jealous Thomas and moved back in with her *lolo*. This allowed her to spend more time with *tita* Belle and her circle of gay co-workers, all of whom had grown up in Manila and were ad-amant about speaking only English together. But most of this socializing took place during their after-work (early morning) drinking sessions. Daisy's schoolwork began to suffer accordingly. And then there was the stultifying life after school of endless chores and chit-chat with *lolo*, who spoke Tagalog exclusively.

Exactly three months after failing her initial test with me, Daisy again applied to CallCo. I was no longer administering the exams, but I met her outside of the testing room and wished her luck. To no avail, as she failed again.

At this point, Daisy took a job at a "local call center"—that is, a Philippine-owned facility handling calls from the domestic market. The breadth of her language skills made her a perfect fit for the job. On any given day, she would Skype with *tita* Ching in Cebuano, chat with *lolo* in Tagalog, then sing kar-aoke in English with Belle. The job, however, was far from perfect for her. It paid only the city's minimum wage of less than $10 a day—far from enough to move out of *lolo*'s house, from under its chores and curfews. And so Daisy diversified and intensified her strategies for hooking up with a foreign in-come source. She began inquiring about loans to pay the processing fees to go abroad as a migrant worker, and she reactivated her accounts on the online dating sites through which she'd met Thomas.[14]

Joy: a Nurse Deferred

Like Daisy, Joy grew up in a Philippine household cobbled together out of necessity, ingenuity, and an ethos of responsibility for one's kin. Joy's parents separated when she was young, after which both left the country to work abroad as migrant laborers. Her *nanay* (mother) became a domestic helper in Hong Kong, her *tatay* (father) a construction worker in Qatar. And like Daisy, Joy was raised by a *tita*, her mother's sister.[15] From the start, however, the two women's biographies diverged in significant ways.

Joy and her younger sister were sent not to a distant province but to her *tita's* crowded apartment in a bustling *barangay* (neighborhood) in central Manila. In this dense urban environment, Joy, her sister, and her three cousins were immersed in the English language from a young age—via Western pop music, cartoons, movies, and books such as the Harry Potter series. Furthermore, as "city girls," they were not content to get by speaking Taglish, the Tagalog–English hybrid that even the coarsest of Manila taxi drivers can converse in. By speaking English well, they came to imagine themselves as *arte* (artsy), *soshal*, and posh—much like the proud gays they saw preening around Manila's malls.

Fate further nudged Joy in a different direction. While Daisy had been an only child, Joy was her household's eldest daughter—what in Tagalog is known as an *ate*—and hence was expected to serve as a provider for her younger sister and cousins. As far back as Joy could remember, her destiny had been predetermined for her. She would attend a nursing college in Manila, fees for which would be paid by remittances sent home from her *nanay* in Hong Kong. Joy would graduate from nursing school, pass the board exam, then follow her parents overseas as a migrant worker herself, to serve as a breadwinner for her kin in the Philippines. To complete the cycle, to suppress the *arte* girl inside and embrace the traditional role of the *ate*: this was the path before her.

Joy never questioned her duty to labor and sacrifice for her younger kin. But something happened on the way abroad. I first met Joy in 2012, when she was twenty-one years old and shortly after she had finished nursing school. She was one of 80,000 aspiring nurses to have graduated that year in the Philippines, and she soon discovered that there was a backlog of 200,000 Filipino nurses waiting to be "sent out" for work.[16]

Although the nursing board exam is expensive, her mother had sent the money and Joy had passed it. Now began the period of awaiting replies to her applications to work abroad. For Joy, this meant entering that dreaded state known by the Tagalog slang *itambay* (basically a play on the English word standby), in which one is no longer a student but yet has no job and no disposable income. Her mother offered to send her a regular allowance, basically some spending money, until an opportunity to migrate presented itself. But Joy, fiercely independent, was steadfast in refusing such support. "I didn't want my *nanay* to give me any more money," she reasoned, "because she had already paid so much for my schooling and my exams. I wanted to be my own person."

Without any spending money or classes to attend, however, Joy's life soon felt very limited. "All I could do was stay at home, watch TV, sleep, and eat," she recalled. "That was my routine. . . . It was impossible to go out because I didn't have my own money. I was feeling more and more like a burden to [my] *tita*. And I missed my school friends, the camaraderie."

Unsure of how long she would have to wait to begin her nursing career, and growing increasingly restless sitting at home all day, Joy began considering some stopgap options. "That," she explained, "was when I thought, *Maybe I can get a job, you know, like a part-time job while I was waiting, so that I would have my own money*. That was my motivation at the time." She submitted applications to a fast-food franchise and a Starbucks. Then it occurred to her that her ex-boyfriend's roommate worked at a call center in Makati, Manila's financial district. She got in touch with him on Facebook, and "he told me what to do. This is the building name, this is the floor, the name of the company and everything. You should try it."

Try it she did. And unlike Daisy, Joy breezed through the mandatory English exam. Her two decades of living in a global city coupled with her four years of intense nursing instruction, all of which was in English, prepared her well to answer questions such as "What type of animal would you roast at a birthday party here in the Philippines?" (A "pig," Joy answered, rather than a "peeg"). She was now a call center agent.

At first she assumed that call center work would be a temporary gig. "I was thinking," she reasoned at the time, "that I could stay here for three months, six months, and then I would go out [i.e., migrate abroad] to work in a hospital and be a nurse. That's what I studied for." On her first day on the job, however, she had an epiphany: "The first time I set foot in my company, I was in jeans and I said I would take calls. But then I saw those people in smart casual attire and they had laptops with them. It was so different than in nursing, where you just wear your uniform, your scrub suit, every single day. I looked around at everyone and I just thought, *I could be like that one day*."

Three years later, in 2015, Joy was still on the phones, answering calls from users of PayPal. By now, a few of her former schoolmates had managed to secure lucrative nursing jobs abroad—in countries such as the United States, Canada, and Australia—while others were laboring for next to nothing in local hospitals or clinics. A good many, however, had taken the same path as Joy, by trading in their nursing scrubs for the telltale business-casual attire and corporate-logoed lanyards that mark one as a call agent in Manila to this day (figure 1.4). The most notorious drawbacks of call center work—the night shifts and the difficult customers—are precisely what these "nurses deferred" were trained to handle.

While working the phones does not pay as much as tending patients abroad, Joy was earning a salary of 24,000 pesos (about US$600) per month—substantially more than Manila's minimum wage. When I last interviewed her, in the summer of 2015, she reported that she no longer needs

FIGURE 1.4 Joy, beaming.

allowances from her mother. In fact, she now pays half her aunt's rent and covers the tuition bill for her younger sister to attend a private high school, hence fulfilling the expectation that she, as *ate*, serve as a breadwinner for her kin. In contrast to the forlorn nursing grad she'd been three years before, Joy now beamed with confidence. Wearing designer sunglasses and holding a Starbucks Frappuccino, she told me that her plans of migrating abroad to work in a hospital were on permanent hold. "Nursing," she stated bluntly, "is out of the picture."

2

Assembling a Labor Market

AT SOME POINT in the year 2010, a call center agent was hired in the Philippines. The person very well may have been someone like Joy—an educated female breadwinner—or Belle—a cosmopolitan gay person. The hiring of this individual was significant because it meant that the Philippines had supplanted India as the world's "capital of call centers," as the *New York Times* put it.[1] Though it has less than a tenth of India's population, the Philippines now had more call center employees.

As recently as the year 2000, the Philippine call center industry was inconsequential. It employed about 3,000 people and generated just over $40 million in revenues annually. By 2015, the industry had been growing at a 30% annual clip for over a decade. It now provided jobs for *a million* Filipino workers, generated $25 billion in annual revenues, and constituted *8% of national GDP*. As of this writing, revenues from call centers are overtaking remittances from migrants as the largest source of foreign exchange flowing into the country. Just as Britain, at the height of the industrial revolution, was dubbed "The Workshop of the World,"[2] the Philippines today, in the midst of our transformation into a global service economy, can be called the world's "voice capital."[3]

It would be easy to be cynical about this development. Industrial workshops were spaces wherein things were produced, unions were forged, and good jobs were made. To be the world's call center, in contrast, seems a dubious distinction. For academics and critics in wealthy countries, call center work represents the "archetypical low-end job in the new economy."[4] They argue that such work is *precarious*, since firms can easily pick up and relocate elsewhere; highly *routinized*, with managers and algorithms predetermining what workers say and do on the phones; and *emotionally taxing*, insofar as it entails dealing with callers who are often irate and uncooperative.[5] More generally, offshored call centers, unlike the factories of the manufacturing era, are a shaky foundation upon which to ground a national economy. They generate few spin-off effects beyond shopping malls and drinking establishments; they are susceptible to nationalist sentiments in wealthy countries; and there is the omnipresent danger that artificial intelligence will evolve to the point that we no longer need real human beings to track our packages and field our complaints.[6]

This pessimistic view did not resonate with those whom I came to know during two years of fieldwork in the Philippines. Apart from the occasional newspaper editorial worrying that call centers transformed young people into caffeine-addicted zombies, most scholars and journalists were pragmatic in their assessments of the industry. Given that the country has long exported its best and brightest as migrant laborers, keeping at least some of them at home by allowing them to earn a decent living in call centers can only be a good thing.[7] That the emergence of an offshored call center industry in the Philippines has coincided with a period of sustained economic growth—as of 2017, it was "one of the fastest-expanding economies in Asia"—further buttresses the argument that call centers may be a boon for, and not a drag on, the Philippine economy.[8]

The narratives in the previous chapter also refute the assumption that call center jobs are inherently synonymous with bad jobs. While Ashley, the young American woman, felt this way, it was not at all clear that Mina, the young Indian woman, did. It was not the nature of the work that pushed Mina out of the industry but, rather, pushback from men in her neighborhood. And it certainly was not the case that young Filipinas such as Daisy, Belle, and Joy interpreted call center jobs as bad jobs. As desperate dependents, as ambitious gay persons, as responsible daughters, they daily battle poverty, patriarchy, and the residue of decades of failed social policy. They are pragmatic—strategic even—when evaluating things like language, college majors, and careers. Their experiences seemingly support Winifred Poster's argument that "global work sites," such as call centers, "can become unique sources of personal and community empowerment for women"[9] (and, I would add, gender minorities). For many of the workers whom I studied, these jobs are veritable lifelines.

It is not my intent to issue some final pronouncement upon the burgeoning call center industry in the Philippines. My goals are more modest—and twofold. First, I wish to take the country's recent emergence as the world's voice capital as something interesting, as something that warrants explanation. Second, I intend to use it as a launching point from which to explore some more general questions about the state and fate of work in the twenty-first century. As industry expert Rosemary Batt has written, call center "operations are representative of what is new in the globalization of service work . . . they are emblematic of the uncertainties created by globalization."[10] Call centers offer a service—facilitating routine communication between firms and their clients—that is essential to contemporary capitalism. Yet ongoing advances in various technologies—faster and cheaper fiber-optic communication channels, new database-management software, evolving techniques of supply-chain management—constantly reshape the global voice industry. The birth and evolution of this industry tell a fascinating tale with implications for how we think about global labor markets, job quality, and the gendering of work.

A Puzzle

Invariably when I describe my call center research to colleagues, they express surprise to learn that global investment patterns have shifted so dramatically to the Philippines. Almost as invariably, this leads to some impromptu theorizing. The logical starting point is to wonder if this is a simple *cost story*. Are Filipino workers cheaper than their counterparts in India? The answer is no. Salaries for front-line employees and floor-level managers in the two countries have long been roughly the same, as have office space rents and telecommunication service fees. In 2010, the year that the Philippines overtook India as the world's voice capital, total operating costs per employee ranged from $15–16,000 per annum in the Philippines and from $14–17,000 in India.[11] A variety of other basic operating expenditures, as I will document later, are basically the same in the two countries.

What about a *policy-centered explanation*? Did the Philippine government produce a novel set of incentives making the country a qualitatively better place to operate call centers? Let's look at what exactly the state did during the early 2000s. In 2008, it directed the country's main telecommunications firm to upgrade its fiber-optic network to put it on a par with other nations competing for offshored services.[12] The Philippines Export Zone Authority (PEZA) classified foreign-owned call centers as export zones, wherein firms are granted various benefits and exemptions. These include duty-free importation of equipment, a six-year "income tax holiday," and automatic permanent resident status "for foreign investors with initial investments of US $150,000 or more."[13] The Philippine national legislature passed industry-friendly data privacy laws and repealed old limits on night work.[14] In 2004, the Business Process Association of the Philippines (BPAP) was established to represent the interests of the service offshoring industry in the Philippines—just as the National Association of Software and Service Companies (NASSCOM) does in India. By 2009, BPAP had honed a message for potential investors: "The risks are low, talent is high, and the government support is great!"[15]

Ultimately, these policy innovations by the Philippine state were reactive rather than proactive. They largely mimicked those already in place elsewhere, and they were usually instituted *in response to* inflows of investment from foreign capital. These various incentives did not mark the Philippines as a superior place to operate call centers. Of course, states fundamentally shape the larger landscape in which firms, workers, and other key players interact. But, I argue, industry-specific policies did not differentiate the Philippines from other potential investment sites for call centers during the 2000s.

When the booming Philippine voice industry is discussed in the media, it is framed as a *cultural-compatibility* story. As one report put it: "the Philippines has overtaken India in running call-centres, helped by an affinity for the language, culture and work ethic of the United States, its former colonial master."[16] The assumption here is that the industry's success is an unintended but fortuitous result of the Philippines having been colonized by America a century earlier. These stories typically go on to enumerate specific traits that supposedly differentiate Filipino workers in the eyes of American firms. Sometimes this is a particular accent. "The English spoken by Filipinos," a *Los Angeles Times* article explained, "is closer to Americans' than in India."[17] Sometimes it is (pop) cultural knowledge: "Filipinos are exposed to MTV from their teenage years . . . when engaging U.S. callers in small talk, it helps to know who's winning in the NBA."[18] And sometimes it is an innate personality trait, such as empathy or forbearance. "Only Filipinos," a BBC reporter reasoned, "have the patience for [call center] work, which is why U.S. companies are here."[19]

I am skeptical of such accounts. To explain evolving patterns of investment in the global voice industry through reference to a people's innate "patience" is simplistic at best, essentialist at worst. The idea that familiarity with MTV or the NBA permits Filipino call center agents to make small talk doesn't accord at all with the reality of working in a call center insofar as *the call center labor process is structured precisely to eliminate opportunities for small talk.*[20] There may be a kernel of truth in the accent story. Speaking English well and with a "neutral" accent hold unique meanings in Philippine society. As the cases of Daisy, Belle, and Joy illustrated, they are key to the successful performance of particular class, gender, and family identities. And it may well be the case that some firms were initially intrigued by the idea of finding a bottom-less pool of perfect English speakers in the Philippines.

It is hard, however, to find evidence that such a pool of talent exists. The data suggest the opposite. Consider that the main metric used by firms to identify "talent" is a standardized English exam like the one I administered to Daisy and Joy. Exam failure rates in the Philippines are three to four times *higher* than in India,[21] with 90% of applicants to Philippine call centers being rejected owing to poor language skills.[22] I saw this play out daily at the CallCo facility in Manila. For every Joy who breezed through the English exam, there were eight or nine interviewees like Daisy who could not pass it.

A more nuanced version of the culture/accent story would compare successful applicants such as Joy not to Daisy but to Mina, the Indian call agent described by Reena Patel. That is, perhaps those Filipinos who *do* pass the voice exam deliver clearly superior customer service—superior enough, at least, to offset the higher search costs that screening so many more applicants entails. In the following chapter, I examine consulting reports written by and for outsourcing firms in the key 2000–2010 period. I find that firms lacked (and still do) tools to reliably collect and compare data on service quality.[23] Caller surveys ("Please press 1 if you'd like to participate in a brief customer service survey after the completion of your call") are notoriously unhelpful. As one analyst put it: "A perennial challenge in [customer service] polling is gathering responses from enough people to support meaningful conclusions. . . . [P]eople who have the time and the inclination to fill out long, boring surveys aren't necessarily representative customers."[24] As far as I can tell, during this key period of industry formation, potential investment sites were evaluated through rather blunt instruments. Years of education and performance on the standardized English exams served as proxies for human capital, while easily gathered metrics such as agents' average handle time (AHT) were used to measure quality and performance.

To be clear from the outset, I am *not* claiming to have discovered some single and unequivocal "independent variable" that explains the emergence of the Philippines as the world's voice capital during the past fifteen years. In fact, when I began grappling with this puzzle, I was struck by how unexceptional the Philippines looks if we consider metrics such as wages, industrial policy, and human capital. As my research progressed, however, one particular metric began to stand out as distinguishing the voice industry in the Philippines: what are by industry standards *remarkably low turnover rates*. Although firms do not routinely publish data on turnover rates for specific jobs, various surveys suggest that attrition from Philippine call centers is only

10 to 20% annually.[25] At the CallCo facility in Manila where I performed field-work, the number was under 10%. Such figures are far "less than . . . what call centres in India face,"[26] and but a fraction of those plaguing outsourced call centers in the United States and other rich nations.[27] "Turnover," marveled one review of the global voice industry, "appears manageable for most firms" in the Philippines.[28] And so an initial puzzle—how the Philippines became the world's voice capital—morphed into a straightforward question: Why are turnover rates in Philippine call centers so low?

Once again, I found that outside observers tended to offer essentialist accounts. Fealty toward one's superiors, one journalistic account implied, is just an innate and unchanging characteristic of Filipinos: "Philippine workers tend to be more *loyal* to employers, and, thus, attrition rates tend to be much lower than competing nations."[29] And once again, we are wise to disregard such essentialism. For we have by now a multitude of empirical studies documenting Philippine workers exercising *voice*, such as Steven McKay's study of a union campaign among electronics workers in the industrial parks south of Manila,[30] and *exit*, such as Pei-Chia Lan's study of Filipina housekeepers in Taiwan going on the run rather than put up with abusive bosses.[31] Staying in a job, like deciding to find or leave one, is, I argue, less an expression of some innate essence than *a strategic and sensible maneuver made in the context of specific labor-market institutions.*

A Mutually Strategic Attachment

It is easy to see why it is that for firms, a stable workforce is preferable to one that rapidly turns over. The costs of having to constantly advertise for, evaluate, train, and socialize new employees, along with processing the resignations (or dismissals) of current ones, can be significant. These costs are "hidden" insofar as it is a tricky endeavor to quantify them and integrate them into more general metrics such as "labor costs."[32] More generally, high turnover makes it difficult to establish and maintain an organizational culture over time. Relationships among employees and between employees and managers will be ephemeral and can easily sour, as they did for Ashley, the young American who eventually escaped from CallCo and today remembers the company as "a hell of terrible people."

This is not to say that workplaces with high turnover rates are inherently dysfunctional. Fast-food outlets, Robin Leidner demonstrated in her classic study *Fast Food, Fast Talk*, serve millions of people every day despite continuously churning through front-line staff.[33] Outsourced and offshored call centers have long operated along this same model. Like McDonalds, they standardize the labor process and pay low wages; in return, they accept that they will have to constantly hire and train new employees—a dynamic I have labeled "permanent pedagogy" and others a "sacrificial HR strategy."[34] The tradeoff is not unlike that suggested by an old adage among engineers: "Good, fast, or cheap. Pick two." Call center work is standardized so as to ensure a baseline level of speed and quality; otherwise, it's long been considered an inevitable choice: "Cheap labor or low turnover. Pick one." Hence, what made the Philippines a remarkable discovery, a veritable nirvana for call center firms. Here they discovered a pool of workers who were qualified, who were cheap (compared to American workers), *and* who remained attached to the industry (unlike their American and Indian counterparts).

This leads us to consider the very meaning, or meanings, of attachment *for workers themselves*. A workplace's attrition rate is but a statistic aggregating myriad individual exits from that workplace. Scholars dating back to Albert Hirschman have interpreted these exits as signals of dissatisfaction with how an organization is being run.[35] If one is unhappy in one's job and unable to effectively voice one's complaints, quitting (voluntary attrition, as it's called) is a way of "voting with one's feet."

The act of not leaving, of *staying in one's job*, has in contrast long eluded a single, satisfactory interpretation. It may be that those who stay are also voting with their feet—by not leaving, they are implicitly endorsing the organization and its working conditions. Organizational scholars call this loyalty, or *affective commitment*: employees stay because they "buy in" to the organization's mission and become emotionally invested in its success.[36] In general, however, scholars have been reluctant to assume that "staying" necessarily signals contentment at work. Surely there can be other motivations for and meanings associated with staying in a job. Low turnover can be the result of desperation and even coercion; unskilled workers laboring in a sweatshop would be the embodiment of such a *coerced attachment*. Nor do affective and coerced attachments cover the gamut of potential motivations for staying. Labor scholar Steven McKay, for example, describes *bargained commitment*, in which employment stability is anchored by collectively bargained agreements between firms and labor unions,[37] while the Hirschmanian tradition has long posited a form of *neglectful commitment*, in which workers are vaguely dissatisfied with their jobs but nonetheless drift along with minimal enthusiasm.[38]

These concepts capture neither the *attraction* that pulled individuals like Joy (the nurse deferred) into the Philippine call center industry nor their ongoing *attachment* to it. Here there was no coercion. Speaking English well is what the sociologist Pierre Bourdieu would call a form of cultural capital, a scarce and hence valuable resource for those in the Philippines (and most of the world).[39] It ultimately affords English-fluent Filipinos other options—in particular, opportunities to work abroad at much higher salaries. To the extent that Joy *could* resume her nursing career, for instance, it is hard to label her choice to stay in the call center an entirely coerced one. On the other hand, her attachment to her employers—to CallCo and to its client, PayPal—reflected neither deep-seated loyalty nor mindless drift. As with just about all the call center agents whom I studied, Joy was initially attracted to the call center for pragmatic reasons: to earn some spending money, to support a sibling, to make her family happy. Such workers then stay not because they are seduced by an organizational culture or they lack the motivation to further improve their lots but, rather, because *sticking with call center jobs continues to make sense for them within the contexts of their lives.*

We could label this a pragmatic or, better yet, *strategic attachment.* Just as call center firms stumbled upon the Philippines and found it to be the best investment option relative to other sourcing locales, many educated young Filipinos stumbled upon the call center industry and found that it offered the optimal career strategy given their obligations, aspirations, and identities. Becoming *and remaining* a call center agent is perfectly sensible, given the wider milieu of their lives.

What is this milieu that makes attachment so sensible? How do we see it, how do we describe it, and how do we explain precisely why it matters? Here we encounter a barrier, a limit inherent to so much of the literature in organization studies, labor-process theory, and political economy. McKay defines this barrier and lays out a path around it as follows:

> [T]heories of organizational commitment . . . need to *understand the constituent elements of commitment in a more dynamic and multidimensional way.* [S]*tudies of commitment should go beyond the shopfloor . . . to put workers' commitment attitudes into a broader socioeconomic context.* [They should] address what seems to be a growing but evident *paradox of high worker commitment despite tightly controlled working conditions.*[40]

In other words, individual stories and organizational dilemmas are fine starting points, but neither individuals nor organizations are where we want to end up. Seeking out and staying in a given employment relationship are strategic maneuvers that must be explained through reference to wider forces and flows. It is not a matter of *moving beyond* individual stories such as those of Ashley, Mina, Daisy, Belle, and Joy, but of *situating them* in relation to other actors, technologies, and processes. These, I argue, are the "broader socioeconomic context" that McKay speaks of. They constitute a labor market—the ultimate conceptual and empirical object of this study.

Establishing an Object

"The act of constructing a basic object of analysis," writes Matthew Desmond, is "indispensable to ethnographic methodology."[41] Too often, however, the very strength of ethnography—its commitment to getting up close and personal with individuals so as to document their lives—makes it all too easy to neglect this initial act. Without some basic conception of what the individual stories that the ethnographer collects add up to, an ethnographic work (and she who reads it) risks getting stuck in the proverbial weeds. Thinking from the outset about what constitutes one's "basic object of analysis" is a way to identify and resolve puzzles. It is a means to tie theoretical concepts, field methods, and empirical data into a coherent whole.

At its root, this study is about how firms find workers, how workers find jobs, and why, in some circumstances, the two sides stay attached to one another. It is about why, in the contemporary Philippines, there seems to exist between call center firms and their employees an affinity, "an attractive force . . . that causes them to *enter into and remain in* combination."[42] At first approximation, then, the basic object of this study is a particular sort of *market for service labor*.

To label something a market, however, is to fall short of defining precisely what that thing is. This is because the term operates differently across various domains of knowledge. In the everyday vernacular, a *market* is any place where people go to buy things that are for sale (a supermarket, a farmers' market, a stock market, etc.). In the field of economics, markets are defined more precisely, to delineate explicit acts of barter regulated by the forces of supply and demand.[43] Sociologists in turn, while they acknowledge that markets are "arenas that exist for the production and sale of some good or service," generally insist upon situating market behavior within some larger social context.[44] Economic sociology, the subfield within which I work, has developed a repertoire of concepts with which to contextualize markets, including labor markets.

The lay, or commonsense, view of markets derives from and reflects the power of economics as a field.[45] This field takes as its first principle that explicit bartering is the default way to structure exchange. Markets, in this view, arise spontaneously from an innate human "propensity to truck, barter, and exchange one thing for another," in the Scottish philosopher Adam Smith's famous phrase.[46] Of course, market participants, as human beings, may fall prey to cognitive biases that generate suboptimal decisions and short-term inefficiencies; deception, profiteering, monopolies, and other predatory behaviors are a constant menace to healthy market functioning.[47] In the long run, however, explicit bargaining in a market arena efficiently coordinates the exchange of goods and services—including labor—because it allows buyers and sellers to pursue their own interests *independent of any larger context or constraint*. As a standard contemporary economics textbook explains, "The coordination that occurs through markets takes place not because of some central plan but because of Adam Smith's 'invisible hand.' "[48] In short, within mainstream economic thought, markets emanate from an *ex ante* human instinct to barter and are best understood as a process whereby aggregate levels of supply and demand are discovered and coordinated spontaneously.

Economic sociology makes different assumptions about exchange, one of which is that explicit barter in a market is not the only way to accomplish it. As the Austrian historian Karl Polanyi argued, throughout most of human history exchange occurred through either *reciprocal* gift-giving or centralization followed by coordinated *redistribution*.[49] Anyone who has donated blood or paid taxes can attest that these two forms of exchange remain with us today. It follows that any empirical study of a market must consider how nonmarket forms of exchange coexist with and influence the workings of that market. As an illustration of this point, consider the stories of Daisy (the near-hire) and Joy (the nurse deferred) described in the opening chapter. Both wanted to sell their labor to call centers in order to escape the sense of dependency engendered by having to rely upon the largesse of others (Daisy's *lolo*; the German Thomas; Joy's mother abroad). The fact that both women live in a poor country lacking a social safety net to redistribute resources to those in need constitutes an underlying constraint upon all their choices. Markets, in short, are not the sole means to accomplish exchange; people in real-world situations typically find themselves enmeshed in various hybrid exchange systems.[50]

On a more fundamental level, economic sociologists tend not to conceptualize markets as entities *separate* from things noneconomic. If markets work best when they are allowed to self-regulate, then it follows that "social" things—from individual emotions to cultural traditions, to policies and regulations of all sort—should be treated as pollutants of normal market functioning.[51] Many economic sociologists argue the contrary: markets are so intertwined with their surrounding environments that to analytically separate the two domains—the "economic" from the "social"—is a fool's errand.[52] Decoupling the economic from the social is particularly hard to justify when dealing with markets of labor.[53] Here the seller and the good being sold are one and the same—"the human activity which goes with life itself," in Polanyi's words—while labor markets entail ongoing and "*actual contacts* between buyers and sellers" of labor.[54] As I have written elsewhere, the manner in which market society "transforms a vast mass of human beings into commodities" is an ongoing accomplishment that cannot be explained outside of its historical, political, and cultural context.[55] States are typically key actors in these explanations; about this I will have more to say.

To study markets as empirical objects, economic sociologists have developed a variety of *metaphors*. As sociologist Mitchell Stevens and colleagues write, metaphors are useful to scholars as "imaginative interpretations and summaries of reality [which] illuminate features of a phenomenon that more mundane descriptions would not reveal."[56] More than mere rhetorical flourishes, metaphors are theories of the larger world that guide our ongoing efforts to study it empirically.

The most well-known metaphor for studying markets sociologically is that of *embeddedness*.[57] To embed one thing within another is "to enclose [it] closely in" it, "to make [it] an integral part of" that surrounding thing.[58] Think of a fossil embedded in stone, a PDF file in an email, or a journalist within a combat unit. To say that markets are embedded in society is to say, at a minimum, that the two are linked in such a way as to make an analysis of one in isolation from the other incomplete. The embeddedness metaphor dates back to Karl Polanyi's 1944 masterpiece *The Great Transformation*, though it entered sociology mainly via Mark Granovetter's 1974 book *Getting a Job*, along with his 1985 *American Journal of Sociology* article "Economic Action and Social Structure: The Problem of Embeddedness."[59] All three of these works used empirical analyses of labor markets to illustrate the idea of embeddedness. Granovetter's key finding was that firms and workers use personal networks rather than formal channels to find one another, such that when it comes to getting a job, "economic man is hardly an object for emulation."[60] Subsequent studies have used the embeddedness metaphor to show how interpersonal ties and the resulting trust that they generate structure the exchange of a wide range of goods, from used cars to credit cards.[61]

A distinct and still developing metaphor for studying markets imagines them as *fields*. Some scholars use this metaphor to depict arenas of exchange as analogous to sporting fields or even battlefields. Markets are less spaces of bartering between buyers and sellers than games won by influencing policy, establishing barriers to entry, and cultivating niches—in short, by subordinating economic forces to the logic of an autonomous field game.[62] Other scholars use the field metaphor to show how markets overlap with broader spaces of meaning-making, such as cultural, linguistic, and semiotic fields. Market exchange, for example, is not possible without money: a historically specific set of techniques for valuing things and giving meaning to them through quantification.[63] Trade and exchange require categories of thought that commensurate a wide variety of disparate things into market inputs and outputs.[64] And a substance can be bought and sold in the first place only if it can be made to fit within larger moral and cultural frames, as demonstrated by attempts to establish markets in life insurance (successfully), reproductive material such as sperm and eggs (successfully), Buddhist temples (only somewhat successfully), and human blood (unsuccessfully).[65]

Regarding labor markets specifically, we have a spate of recent studies conceptualizing them as analogous to *romantic connections*. Employment relationships, according to this metaphor, look less like negotiations between calculating agents and more like encounters sparked by attraction, flirtation, and seduction. This metaphor has proved useful for portraying the gendered character of emergent global labor markets. Research has shown how (male) managers in the rich world become consumed by the fantasy of docile and "nimble-fingered" women workers in Latin America and Asia, but also how these same workers become infatuated with the new lifestyles and identities offered by foreign employers.[66] Studies of labor markets in the contemporary United States suggest that it is not the desire for an exotic "other" that attracts workers and firms to one another but, rather, homophily (i.e., the desire to be with others like oneself). Unemployed professional workers experience job hunting as analogous to dating, with "chemistry" rather than qualifications being the defining factor in their ultimate success; white managers are more likely to call back white job applicants than more qualified applicants of color; corporate hiring committees and students from Ivy League universities "seduce" one another during the interview process.[67]

Labor Markets as Assemblages

Markets as embedded, markets as fields, markets as sites of seduction: this is by no means an exhaustive list of metaphors that sociologists use to study arenas of trade and exchange. Nor do I intend to adjudicate among those that

I have summarized, to pronounce one as correct and the others as misguided. A metaphor is useful to the extent that it allows one to delineate one's object of study in a productive and coherent way. To explain the uniqueness of the call center labor market in the Philippines—in particular, *the affinity between workers and firms* as symbolized by low employee attrition rates and ongoing investment in the country—I conceptualize it as an *assemblage*. Its constituent elements are mediators and flows.

My use of the assemblage metaphor draws upon three distinct yet cognate lineages. The first is the branch of economic sociology associated with Neil Fligstein's work, and in particular his book *The Architecture of Markets*.[68] This line of research emphasizes "the political structuring of labor market institutions"—that is, the ways in which states intervene to stabilize the potentially contentious relationship between firms and workers, buyers and sellers of labor.[69] The second is the research program associated with Bruno Latour and his colleagues in the field of science studies, who study various systems, including markets, as actor-networks.[70] To analyze a labor market as an actor-network is to explain how webs of heterogeneous actors and technologies come together and adhere—or not. The third is the tradition of global ethnography associated with Michael Burawoy, which has long argued that social structures such as labor markets are best understood as manufactured phenomena.[71] Here especially are metaphor and method unified: one begins by taking a case study as an interesting finding, then extends one's focus outward, across space and time, to assemble a compelling explanation of that finding.[72]

I do not mean to gloss over the many significant differences among these research traditions. I do contend that each is broadly consistent with what I have elaborated elsewhere as a "critical economic sociology of labor" insofar as each treats a given market as a phenomenon to be *explained* rather than *assumed*.[73] Each adopts some variant of the assemblage metaphor to generate such explanations. And each is committed to a realist ontology. In other words, to conceptualize markets as assembled constructions is not to treat them as "social constructions of reality" as the term has come to be defined in the subjectivist tradition.[74] The object of this study—an emergent global labor market—is not some fiction that exists and has efficacy in the real world only insofar as enough people believe it to be true. My use of the construction metaphor is much more tangible: markets are real entities whose initial assemblage and ongoing durability (or lack thereof) demand explanation via detailed empirical analysis. I will here lay out what I see to be four general principles for doing an architecture of a labor market.

First Principle

The first is to *depart from a discovery*—and it need not be a paradigm-shifting one. If the "social construction of reality" metaphor promotes a vision of the scholar as an omniscient observer who unveils the reality behind some fiction, my more concrete use of the metaphor entails thinking of researchers as more humble and empiricist—as normal scientists in the Kuhnian sense.[75] They have peered into the world and discovered something unexpected: a puzzle of some sort that holds interest for others in their epistemic community.[76] Think of an astronomer who has detected an extragalactic planet, an archaeologist who has unearthed a hitherto unknown style of mosque, or a team of chemists who have isolated a new molecular compound. The initial questions to be confronted are clear: What is this thing made of? How does it work? Is this a solid and durable phenomenon, or something brittle and ephemeral? In short, where did this thing come from and what holds it together?

The example from the field of chemistry can assist to help visualize this book's initial discovery. The nature of the affinity between Western call centers and Filipino workers is not unlike that which constitutes a covalent bond between atoms. As first-year chemistry students well know, covalent bonds are puzzling. Because the two atoms involved have similar electronegativities, there are between them forces of attraction but also of repulsion. Explaining their subsequent bonding requires further elaboration on the nature of the relationship between the two sides—in this case, how the sharing of electrons results in a more stable atomic assemblage. While there is no obvious analogue to the sharing of electrons when we're discussing labor markets, the larger puzzle of an unexpected bonding is similar. For employees, outsourced and offshored call centers represent a mix of attractive forces (high wages relative to other local job opportunities) and repulsive ones (demanding working conditions). In the United States, India, and most other places where this model has been implemented, the result has been high rates of employee turnover and/or capital flight.[77] Yet in the Philippines, these seemingly unstable forces result in what seems to be a stable bond, an affinity between the two sides.

Figure 2.1 models this affinity. The top line depicts the flow of material resources—mainly wages—from firms to workers. For workers, this would appear to be a source of attraction. Wages paid by firms to Filipino workers such as Belle and Joy are significantly higher than for other forms of entry-level, white-collar work in the Philippines. The bottom line depicts the flow of effort from workers to firms—that is, the satisfactory performance by call

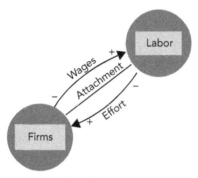

FIGURE 2.1 Chart showing a singular affinity.

center agents of strict standards regarding the pace and quality of phone work. This would seem to be a source of repulsion for workers. Unlike elsewhere, however, in the Philippines these two contradictory flows result not in a splitting of bond participants but, rather, in a seemingly stable connection (the middle line). To explain this singular attachment, I argue, requires considering other flows and other actors. The questions are where to locate and how to document them?

Second Principle

The second principle I offer, concerning how we extend out from our initial discovery, is primarily prophylactic. It is well summarized in the book *Reassembling the Social* by Bruno Latour: "*Clamp down your fieldsite*"![78] Resist, that is, the temptation to explain your discovery by immediately zooming out to some larger context or structure. This is not to make a radical argument about ontology, to deny the existence of social-structural entities of a *sui generis* nature. "Culture," "capitalism," "patriarchy," "the state," "social fields"— entities of these sorts undoubtedly exist and influence our everyday worlds in countless ways. More often than not, however, instinctively designating these entities as major players in our models produces suboptimal accounts. It is to fall prey to what Pierre Bourdieu called the "short circuit fallacy"—that tendency to produce "interpretations which, though a *short circuit*, go directly from what happens in the [real] world to what happens in the [social] field" writ large.[79]

Take, for example, the young Indian woman Mina discussed in the opening chapter. She initially desired call center work but found it difficult to sustain employment in the industry, insofar as it led to accusations that she was a "call girl." Right off the bat, it would be tempting to nominate patriarchy—"a system of society in which men hold the power"—as the reason why a bond fails to form between call center firms and a key subset of potential workers in India.[80] One problem with doing so is that this account would likely make little sense to Mina herself. It was a series of more mundane realities—the fact, for example, that the men in her apartment complex monitored its front gate and wrote down her name every evening when she left for work—that troubled her and nudged her away from the job. Another problem is that patriarchy seemingly plays the opposite role in the Philippines where, rather than repel workers from the industry, it attracts them to it. Daisy, for instance, intensely desired call center work as a means to escape the surveillance of both her grandfather and her European boyfriend. It offered her a hope of independence and freedom from the men controlling her life. All of this is not to deny that patriarchy exists and has powerful effects. It is to say that the ethnographer who grasps instinctively for a macro-level concept to explain puzzles emanating from field data risks leaping from the concrete too soon.

Third Principle

"Clamping down" an initial discovery is a way to keep from prematurely short-circuiting to some macro structure. Our third principle directs that we instead *trace real connections* emanating out from our fieldsites and linking them to other actors and spaces. Rather than seize a short circuit, this principle directs us to dig under the floors and look behind the walls to see how a given structure is buttressed and wired.

Of what do these connections undergirding a given assemblage consist? They may be interpersonal ties of the sort that social-network studies document, but they needn't necessarily be. Latour in fact proposes the term "work-net" to clarify that the myriad connections making up a given assemblage cannot be reduced to interpersonal ties alone. "*Work*-nets," he writes, "allow one to see the labor that goes on in laying down *net*-works . . . [they] designate flows" of various sorts.[81] Furthermore, while these flows may consist of money and other material resources, we must exercise care not to prioritize these over other, more ideal and even symbolic entities. "Connections," Burawoy writes in *Global Ethnography*, "create new regimes or sets of social relations in which the 'material' and 'discursive' moments are inextricably linked."[82]

The connections underlying a given market assemblage needn't be confined to interpersonal ties or material exchange, but they must be conceptually meaningful and empirically traceable. We can define them broadly, as *flows carrying materials, people, ideas, and symbols*, including those flows that generate relations of power and domination. What matters is that the flows we trace help us to understand our initial discovery, that they advance our knowledge of our fieldsites and their underlying architecture. And as this specification of connections makes clear, the flows that they carry must leave some sort of footprint that can be documented empirically. It is imperative to say plainly which connections are evidenced by particular empirical traces; their existence cannot be presumed.

Our initial modeling of the bond between foreign call centers and Filipino workers delineated three connections. The first represented a flow of material resources from the former to the latter. This flow is easily traceable, as reliable estimates of wage rates and ranges are routinely reported in the press and readily provided by workers themselves. The flow of energy and effort from call agents to firms is less easily traced. As I discussed earlier, firms typically assess this flow via blunt metrics such as average (call) handle times. For our purposes, it is defensible to argue that because call center work is so thoroughly routinized, any successful call center operation will generate an acceptable level of effort from employees. And then there is the literal connection of attachment as measured by attrition rates—the puzzle worth explaining.

These three connections—of remuneration, effort, and attachment— are in no way an exhaustive list of those that connect firms and labor in the Philippines. The standardized English exams administered to potential employees are an important means of regulating flows of people into the workforce. Firms, as I will show, utilize a variety of instruments to monitor and evaluate the Philippine labor force in relation to other labor forces in other nations. And the call center job advertisements that cover metro stops throughout Manila represent a flow of communication from firms to potential workers. The two sides, in short, are connected in myriad ways.

In all these examples of connections between firms and workers, the content of these flows has been hard to separate conceptually from the connectors themselves. It's difficult, for example, to say what the average starting salary for call center agents in Manila means without first knowing what this salary means for the firms that pay it (especially relative to average wages in other locales) and for workers themselves (relative to other income-earning activities available to them). Furthermore, both these connectors, firms and labor, are connected to other entities outside the dyad-qua-bond. To treat a complex system such as a labor market as an assemblage is both to deepen our understanding of its two constituent parties and to identify other entities of interest. This leads me to put forward a final principle.

Fourth Principle

It is to *identify and unpack mediators*. If the flows coursing through a market architecture constitute its underlying scaffolding, then what are its pillars? Who are the core actors anchoring the work-net? These entities we shall designate as mediators. Their defining characteristic is that *they do not passively receive and pass along flows; they actively modify them in significant ways*. They are akin to an experienced translator who transforms a text from its original language into a new one, skillfully preserving by subtly modifying its meanings, or to an organization within a large production chain that receives and improves a good so as to add value to it.

Burawoy writes that a given "global force makes itself felt through *mediators* that transmit it as their interest."[83] Fligstein argues that an actor becomes an interested (and interesting) mediator to the extent that it exercises "social skill." It may reframe flows of ideas, information, and investments; set agendas for future action; and/or broker to whom flows are directed.[84] For Latour, mediators are those entities that "transform, translate, distort, and modify the meaning or element they carry." Their defining characteristic is that "their input is never a good predictor of their output."[85] The key insight across all these elaborations of the mediator concept is that the workings of a given social architecture cannot be adequately understood without taking special account of some subset of actors within it.

How precisely are mediators identified? The key is to establish the proper balance of inductive (mediators discovered) and deductive (mediators assumed) research strategies. As any ethnographer knows, fieldsites are replete with tacit knowledge as to "who is important around here," "who is really pulling the strings," who is consequential and who is not. The risk inherent in taking such accounts at face value is that we thereby let folk knowledge inductively identify our study's key players for us. A study's full conceptual object, Bourdieu once wrote, must be won "against the illusion of immediate knowledge"; it certainly should not be crowd-sourced.[86]

Departing deductively carries risk as well. One can easily, at the commencement of a study, march onto the stage a stable of actors presumed to be dramatis personae. In studies of labor markets and employment systems, the initial roll call is usually predictable in advance. There are trade unions, managers, shareholders, state regulators, and education systems; they meet around bargaining tables, in the policy arena, on the shop floor, in the courtroom; and they are almost always located in a wealthy country of the Global North.[87]

It seemed clear from the outset of this study that not all these standard actors were present as players. General state and industry-specific regulators, for instance, who typically are charged with monitoring firms to ensure compliance with various employment and labor laws, are absent from the Philippine BPO industry. As soon as they are operational, call centers and other BPO facilities are classified as export processing zones, meaning they are largely allowed to self-regulate. Firms perform self-audits that they can choose to share with the government or the press; but really, there is no regular state presence in the ongoing operation of the industry. The same holds for trade unions, who have had little to no success in organizing offshored call center workers in the Philippines or elsewhere.[88] It is interesting to pose counterfactuals such as how the industry would look if employees were to collectively organize (which I do in part IV of this book). But to treat a labor market as an assemblage is to initially bracket such counterfactuals: no real effects, no mediator.

Other standard players, though they *were* physically present, were not worthy of mediator status. They possessed insignificant power, that is, to transform the various flows they touched; their inputs predicted their outputs.

Human resource (HR) personnel and front-line managers ("team leaders") were cases in point. In some studies of labor markets, they serve as key actors by selectively disseminating information about job opportunities, prejudicing the hiring process, and regulating the intensity of effort expected at the point of production.[89] In the Philippine call center industry, however, they do none of these things and so they do not play a large role in my account. Information about employment opportunities is not a scarce resource; call center job advertisements literally wallpaper public spaces throughout Manila. Applicant screening is highly standardized so as to reduce to a modicum any discretion on the part of the screener. (CallCo gave me a script, a rubric, and a checklist to evaluate applicants like Daisy and Joy; I was as much an instrument of these tools as vice versa). The labor process as well is standardized via scripting, software flows, and electronic monitoring.[90] The result is what A. Aneesh has termed an algocracy, or a system of technical control via code that largely renders redundant in-person supervision.[91] The work done by team leads (who are paid but marginally more than the agents they supervise) to compile reports, coordinate schedules, and the like are accomplishments. They are just not ones that fundamentally alter or redirect underlying flows of voices, effort, and authority. I bracket HR personnel, line managers, and other actors who are present in the industry but who are largely ineffectual. They are *intermediaries* rather than full-fledged mediators.

Some of the standard players assumed by the literature *were* present as mediators. The existing system of postsecondary education in the Philippines, for example, is a dynamic and consequential sector. Access to it largely determines whether one is a call center hire, near-hire, or non-hire. More generally, by reading and reacting to global labor market trends, this education system (in tandem with the state migration bureaucracy) structures the larger array of job options available to educated young Filipinos. If intermediaries can be bracketed—that is, a brief summary can locate them in an assemblage and describe what flows through them—mediators cannot. Once we discover one, we will want to learn more about it: where it came from, how it works, how exactly it transforms which flows. Mediators, in short, require unpacking.

One advantage to conceptualizing actors as mediators is that it allows us to pre-screen some of the usual candidates; another is that it allows us to discover them in unexpected places. Research, in this approach, is a casting call for mediators. In the pages to follow I will thus have little to say about line managers and state regulators, but a great deal to say about the Catholic church, consulting firms, divorce laws, and doting aunts. Each of these latter entities transforms, redirects, or blocks flows. At the same time, we must recognize that they are somewhat idiosyncratic to the Philippine call center's market architecture. I label them *secondary mediators*, so as to distinguish them from those actors whom we must presume to be present in *all* labor market assemblages.

These *primary mediators* should be kept to a minimum, so I shall posit only three. There is widespread agreement across theoretical traditions that firms, states, and workers are essential to the construction of contemporary labor markets. To thus understand our initial discovery—a stable attachment between call center firms and workers in the Philippines—requires that we not only clamp it down but also begin by unpacking these three mediators and tracing the flows among them.

Organization of the Argument

Part II of this book consists of a trio of chapters unpacking the main mediators within the emergent global market for voice labor. Chapter 3, "Firms: Seeing Like a Call Center," focuses upon the firms that control the technology necessary to operate offshore contact centers (represented by point A in figure 2.2). I conceptualize them as active mediators directing investment flows globally. A history of the industry is in fact a history of firms' ongoing search for cheap,

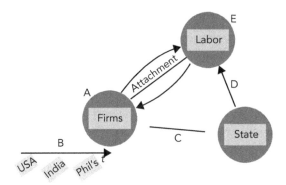

FIGURE 2.2 Chart showing architecture of the labor market.

English-speaking, and "loyal" workers. Initial forays in the United States and India were failed experiments (point *B*). Chapter 4, "The State: Making a Middle Path," picks up the story in the Philippines. Drawing upon two years of fieldwork in Manila, I explain how the city functions as a perfect node for connecting flows of foreign investment and local labor. The Philippine state, I argue, adopts a "hands off" approach to BPO firms (point *C*). What makes it a mediator worth unpacking is how it structures employment opportunities for Filipino college graduates (point *D*). A broad net of policies regarding migration, welfare, and reproductive health has long offered them a dismaying choice between migrating for money and living at home in poverty. Chapter 5, "Labor: Seeking the Philippine Dream," considers the most interesting element in the entire assemblage: workers themselves (point *E*). Qualitative and quantitative analyses of a sample of sixty call center agents in Manila reveal why taking a call center job is a strategic *and sustainable* decision, given the other options available. Key here is understanding the broader contexts of the call center agents' lives—how they manage their obligations, resources, and opportunities.

Part III zooms in on the Philippine call center labor force (see figure 2.3). It identifies three distinct pathways by which college graduates enter the industry and then find it sensible to remain in it. Chapter 6, "Responsible Women," describes the archetypical call center agent: a young female who has committed herself to such employment as a way to enact the role of the "breadwinner." Joy is a perfect example of a worker who tolerates stressful call center work because it pays well and allows her to stay near her kin. Chapter 7, "Restless Gays," describes a highly visible minority in the industry. Young gay persons such as Belle, for whom speaking English well is a marker of status in the Philippine gay community, are initially attracted to call centers. For them

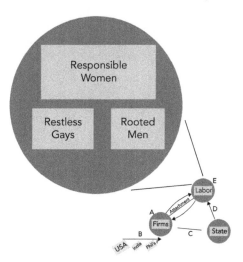

FIGURE 2.3 Chart showing the three employee archetypes used in this study.

the initial allure fades, but discrimination in the larger labor market coupled with the industry's good salaries essentially tie them to call centers. Chapter 8, "Rooted Men," describes how a select segment of cisgender Filipino men come to feel comfortable speaking English and in turn use call center wages to strengthen their roots in the Philippines.

In Part IV, I conclude by using my findings to engage two prominent debates about the present and future of work. The first, addressed in chapter 9 ("Gone, Baby, Gone"), concerns the fate of service jobs in the United States given globalization and ongoing advances in information technology. The case of offshored call centers suggests that the relationship between firms in this field and American workers is over for good. Call center (and, increasingly, other white-collar) jobs, despite the rhetoric of politicians, are not coming back. The second debate, addressed in chapter 10 ("The Relativity of Work"), is about whether American firms, by offshoring work, create sweatshop-like conditions in poor countries and transform their workers into a desperate precariat. Here I argue that not all offshored jobs are the same. The call center industry in the Philippines is less an electronic sweatshop than a new, if unexpected, form of Fordism. The long-term durability of this "assemblage," however, is by no means assured. Following this concluding chapter comes a methodological narrative describing my fieldwork in the Philippines—especially the sample of sixty remarkable individuals whose life histories constitute the backbone of this book.

PART II

Mediators Unpacked

3

Firms

SEEING LIKE A CALL CENTER

IN HIS BEST-SELLING book, *The World Is Flat: A Brief History of the Twenty-first Century*, the journalist Thomas Friedman wrote that:

> Columbus accidentally ran into America but thought he had discovered part of India. I actually found India and thought many of the people I met there were Americans. Some had actually taken American names, and others were doing great imitations of American accents in call centers and American business software labs.
>
> Columbus reported to his king and queen that the world was round, and he went down in history as the man who first made this discovery. I returned home and shared my discovery only with my wife, and only in a whisper.
>
> "Honey," I confided, "I think the world is flat."[1]

Freidman goes on to recount reading *The Communist Manifesto* and finding himself "in awe at how incisively [Karl] Marx detailed the forces that were flattening the world . . . and how much [Marx] foreshadowed the way these same forces would keep flattening the world right up to the present."[2] Friedman ultimately twists Marx's critical analysis of capitalism as a dynamic but ultimately flawed system into a utopian vision of freedom and universal prosperity. The fall of the Soviet Union, rapid advancements in information technology, and other "flatteners" now allow capital, labor, goods, and services to flow freely around the world. Eliminating frictions to free trade eliminates inefficiencies of all sorts, delivering us to a productive and harmonious global society not at all dissimilar to Francis Fukuyama's earlier depiction of neoliberal capitalism as the "end of history."[3] Significantly, Friedman uses American investment in India's business process outsourcing sector, especially its call centers, as evidence of the world's flattening.

Scholars have by now launched a great deal of ammunition at Friedman's thesis. The world is not flat, they argue, insofar as power and inequality continue to determine how and where capital, people, goods, and ideas flow. Wealthy metropolises in the Global North are "spiky,"[4] while poor regions of the Global South remain in the world economy's "shadows."[5] Others argue that poor nations, in order to attract foreign investment, suppress workers' rights in a pernicious "race to the bottom";[6] meanwhile, in wealthy countries, neoliberalism generates material insecurity for the vast majority of citizens who then become susceptible to demagoguery, nativism, and calls to close borders and restrict flows of capital and labor.[7] The sociologist Tamara Kay has shown that free trade agreements themselves—the ultimate "flatteners"— result from power struggles among various interest groups, each seeking to define the terms of these agreements so as to benefit their constituencies.[8]

My issue with Friedman's flat-world thesis is that it renders firms flat as well. They are denied mediator status, meaning that they no longer represent actors of interest within the various structures constitutive of the global economy. Scholars today, Friedman infers, can safely bracket firms—and states, too, for that matter.

In his historical account, the first era of globalization was that of European colonization of the globe (from 1492 to approximately 1800). In this era, "the *dynamic process* driving the process of global integration was how much brawn . . . your *country* had and how *creatively* you could deploy it."[9] In "the second great era, Globalization 2.0, [which] lasted roughly from 1800 to 2000 . . . the *key agent of change*, the *dynamic force* driving global integration, was *multinational companies*."[10] Globalization 2.0 was in turn felled by personal computing, fiber-optic cable networks, and new workflow software. "While . . . the dynamic force in Globalization 2.0 was *companies* globalizing, the dynamic force in Globalization 3.0—the force that gives it its unique character—is the newfound power for *individuals* to collaborate and compete globally."[11] In short, the dynamic actors in the new global economy are neither states nor firms. They are individuals sitting at their laptops connected to the World Wide Web.

I'm not yet ready to give up on states and firms as mediators, as entities which skillfully transform and redirect flows. Both states and firms, I will show, have been instrumental in assembling a global labor market in voice. In the following chapter, I'll discuss how the Philippine state created a domestic labor force for the global call center industry. The present chapter unpacks the multinational firms that make decisions about where to locate call centers and how to operate them.

First, I provide a framework for understanding such firms as "voice capital." A call center is a set of technologies for producing value by handling service queries, and I trace the historical evolution of these technologies. But voice capital is also a social relationship between firms and employees, a relationship that is characterized by liquidity and lust. The second part of this chapter draws upon primary data such as consulting reports to illuminate how voice capital sees the world and decides where to direct flows of investment. I show that firms imagine not a flat terrain but, rather, a landscape graded so as to channel investment toward two reservoirs of labor: India and the Philippines. For various reasons, India was the first landing spot for voice capital. However, a review of the ethnographic literature on India's outsourcing industry suggests that the experiment to build a call center industry there achieved mixed results. While Indian call agents are qualified and cheaper than their American counterparts, they too rapidly cycle in and out of the industry. The underlying market architecture was and is infirm.[12]

Voice Capital

Multinational firms (or divisions thereof) that specialize in communicating with clients over the phone are the buyers in the emergent (and increasingly global) market for voice. They have invested in, developed, and subsequently manage the technologies to perform this business service. These technologies include some means for facilitating instantaneous talk across space, repositories of information (such as computer databases of past sales) needed to resolve clients' issues, and strategies for managing the labor process of employees who interact with clients. These firms and the technologies they deploy I designate as voice capital. A short recounting of its history reveals that voice capital actively organizes flows of investment, knowledge, and language; in its neoliberal (primarily American) variant, it lusts for an idealized form of labor.

A Brief History of Voice Capital

Voice capital has a definite genealogy linked to that of the telephone itself, which was patented by Alexander Graham Bell in 1874. For over half a century thereafter, telephone systems were used mainly as *professional and commercial instruments*—as a means by which a salesperson could stay in touch with the head office while traveling, for instance, or for different regional offices to stay in contact throughout the day.[13] As the Nebraska state telephone phone book directed in 1914: "Business . . . calls shall at all times have preference over social talk."[14] Such directives certainly reflected the prioritization of corporate over individual interests, given a scarcity of lines and bandwidth, especially during peak business hours.

By the early 1950s, a majority of American households had at least one telephone.[15] Sociologist Claude Fischer, in his landmark social history of the telephone, describes widespread concern at the time that residential telephone service had "sapped Americans' moral fiber" and "undermined neighborhood solidarity."[16] Fischer argues persuasively that rather than isolate us, the telephone strengthened and extended connections among friends, neighbors, and kin. *And the same held true for relations between large organizations, such as firms, and their customers.*[17] Prior to the mass availability of residential telephone service, the two sides could communicate only in person (as when a traveling salesman visited a home or a shopper traveled to a store) or via post (through catalogues, letters of inquiry, written complaints, etc.).[18] With a telephone in the home, individuals could, for the first time, directly contact businesses from afar, and vice versa.

At first, American businesses of all sizes assigned existing staff such as secretaries and stock boys to answer the phones and make outgoing calls.[19] By the 1960s and 1970s, however, large organizations such as mass retailers, banks, polling agencies, data-management companies, and telecom firms were establishing business units whose sole purpose was making calls to and receiving them from clients.[20] Personnel in these units pioneered the field of what was then called "telematics"—essentially, the "integration of communications and software technologies."[21] We can designate these developments as the real origin of voice capital, that is, of a dedicated set of technologies for creating value via the rationalization of an organization's means of communicating with its clients.

In the decades to follow, these technologies became a standard component of just about all contemporary organizational forms. In the United States today, dialing 1-800-HELP-NOW will direct you to the nearest Red Cross blood bank, 1-800-MY-IPHONE will connect you with Apple's genius bar, 1-800-TAX-1040 will direct you to an assistant with the Internal Revenue Service, while 1-800-BE-ALERT will allow you to report "illegal aliens" to Immigration and Customs Enforcement.

One key driver of this diffusion was a steep decline in long-distance call costs. The breakup of the Bell monopoly by the U.S. Department of Justice in the early 1980s allowed new firms to enter the industry and made price competition the norm. Between 1984 and 2000, according to the Federal Communications Commission, "the price of long distance service fell [from 17.26 cents to 1.9 cents per minute] and the volume of long distance calling surged."[22] The advent of cellular internet telephony during the 1990s further slashed the cost of long-distance calling, often to a negligible expense. By the end of the twentieth century, "call centers [were] the ubiquitous means by which utilities, healthcare providers, transportation and freight companies, social service agencies, travel and entertainment providers, and sales firms conducted" their routine business activities.[23]

To this point I have defined voice capital in a technical and rather narrow sense: as a factor of production, as equipment and technologies that given certain inputs (e.g., a customer query) will produce a predictable output (the relevant information). How does this square with the argument just given— that the firms which control these factors of production are full-fledged mediators? That there is something about the way they manage themselves and their environments that establishes them as key players in the construction of a larger market architecture? It's necessary to expand our understanding of voice capital.

Voice Capital as Liquid Capital

It is no coincidence that truly global voice capital has from the start been mainly American private capital. This is due in part to the widespread use of English as the world's default language of business. Still, the United States, whose economy constitutes around a fourth of the world's gross domestic product, accounts for three-fourths of the global market for outsourced voice services.[24] Other countries have been far less aggressive when it comes to restructuring call center operations so as to maximize short-term profitability. I am in agreement with those scholars who view the modern, offshored call center as both an offspring and a symbol of neoliberalism, the political-economic movement that swept much of the world in the latter decades of the twentieth century.[25] Governments broke up monopolies and sold off state assets so as to stimulate competition across a broad array of markets. Corporate executives and managers adopted a shareholder mentality that treated firms as collections of assets to be managed so as to bolster stock prices. Business units were rigorously analyzed to distinguish core from non-core functions, with the latter being reorganized, subcontracted out, or sold off. *Call center operations were a prime candidate for such neoliberal restructuring.*

Social theorist Zygmunt Bauman describes neoliberal capitalism as a form of "liquid modernity."[26] In the *Communist Manifesto*, Marx, referring to the early industrial era, described capital as a force that "cannot exist without constantly revolutionising the instruments of production, and thereby the . . . whole relations of society"; the result was and is a world constantly in flux, one in which "all that is solid melts into air."[27] Bauman extends Marx's allegory to depict neoliberal capitalism as, at root, a *liquid* system. "The present day liquefied, flowing, dispersed, scattered and deregulated version of modernity," he writes, "augurs the advent of light, free-floating capitalism."[28] Liquidity at the system level is logically driven by liquidity on the part of key mediators within the system. Capital is certainly one such mediator. With neoliberalism, firms and business units began to regularly self-examine, quantifying their activities in monetary terms and comparing current with past and future courses of action.[29] They are today compelled, to paraphrase Marx, to constantly calculate, and it is this act of calculation that grants contemporary capital its mediator status.[30]

From this perspective, *voice capital is a paragon of liquid capital.* There is nothing inherent in a phone line or a computer database that entails developing the call center labor process in a certain direction, locating call centers in a certain location, or pursuing particular sorts of call center workers. Under neoliberal conditions, however, call center operations are interpreted as noncore to firms' primary business functions and so are constantly remade and/or spun off. To survive, voice capital must be willing to remake itself and how it engages with the world around it. It must long—even actively lust—for new means of making profits and be willing to bend and flow accordingly.

From this perspective, the origins and subsequent development of voice capital were dominated by two trends, neither inherent to the technology itself. The first was self-transformation via the rigorous application of Taylorist principles to the call center labor process. These principles included scripting as much of workers' speech as possible, designing workflow software to eliminate autonomous decision-making by employees, electronically tracking call times, and secretly auditing calls to ensure acceptable service quality. The "integration of computers and telephones," Jamie Woodcock argues, "opened up the potential for detailed supervision and data collection" inside the call center.[31]

It is true, as I discovered by working as an outsourced call agent myself, that in practice complete work routinization is imperfect and likely impossible.[32] No call center could function if its agents did not mobilize their own competencies and improvise various "work arounds." Nonetheless, a professionally run call center today should be able to maximize call volumes while maintaining a basic threshold of service quality. It is also true, as I documented in the opening chapter, that the call center's standardized labor process does not necessarily make it a "bad job." Depending on the larger field of possibilities in a worker's life, "working the phones" may be a source of personal satisfaction, if not basic survival. Most workers, however, find outsourced call center work to be stressful and stultifying, a result of which has been that high employee turnover rates have long been a bugbear for call center managers.[33]

The second defining trend in the life cycle of (neoliberal) voice capital is the avid pursuit of what geographer David Harvey refers to as a spatial fix.[34] Firms and business units seized the opportunity to use new information technologies to physically uncouple call centers from the larger businesses they serve.

Intra-national movement of voice capital had begun by the 1980s, as firms headquartered in large American cities moved their call center operations to small cities and towns in the United States where the cost of living—and thus the average wage—was lower.[35] In some cases to this day, the flow of voice capital remains constrained by national boundaries. This can be due to linguistic reasons (a Japanese supermarket chain, for instance, would find it difficult to locate a sufficient number of Japanese speakers in a given locale outside Japan) or legal ones (privacy regulations in U.S. health-care law may bar organizations from routing certain medical information outside of the United States).

By the mid- to late 1990s, however, most firms were free to site customer contact centers wherever in the world they wished. It quickly became conventional wisdom, as Ruth Buchanan recounts, that call center operations can and *should* "be segregated from the rest of a firm's operations and relocated to a suburban *or offshore* location."[36] Firms had the option to set up their own call centers in non-American locales (known as offshore captive operations) or to contract with a specialized firm to run their call centers outside the United States (thereby both offshoring and outsourcing). Either way, offshoring a firm's voice operations increasingly became the default option. By the early 2010s, business service offshoring, the larger industrial grouping of which call centers are a part, was a $300 billion industry growing at a 10% clip yearly.[37]

Two Grades, Two Pools

By the late 1990s and early 2000s, the question for voice capital was not "to offshore or not to offshore?" but "where to offshore?" This was a key moment in the history of the industry, and one that requires further unpacking. The skills needed to perform adequately as a call center agent are not the same as those required to be a basic manufacturing worker, and so voice capital could not simply follow Ford or Apple to Mexico or China. What was needed was a *new* set of techniques for surveying the global landscape so as to then *direct flows of investment* in call centers.

How exactly did voice capital "see" the world in the early twenty-first century? When it looked out upon the horizon, did it see a flat terrain or one that was in some way graded? Toward what regions and what sorts of workers was it drawn? To address these questions, I analyzed an emergent genre of management literature that I'll call "source destination rankings." These are attempts by firms and consulting agencies to order various regions of the world according to their desirability as places from which to source labor for business services such as call centers. On the whole, these reports are remarkably consistent in terms of how they depict the global landscape of investment opportunities. This landscape is not flat but, rather, graded in two fundamental ways, channeling voice capital toward two reservoirs of labor.

"A World to Choose From"

The demand side of the global market for offshored business services, this literature assumes, is Western in general and *American in particular*. Consulting reports always give important figures, such as labor costs or tax incentives, in dollars rather than in some other national currency. Specific business needs are in turn assumed to be those of Western firms. The consulting firm Tholons, for example, dedicates a section of its "Top 50 Emerging Global Outsourcing Cities" to various regions' "cultural affinity to North America."[38] As I have explained, this is not a misleading assumption about the global demand for offshored business services. From the start, American firms have accounted for between 65 and 75% of the global service offshoring industry, and an even higher percentage of offshored call centers.[39]

The procedures by which firms should evaluate whether to offshore or not are clearly spelled out in the sourcing literature. Managers are entreated to look long and hard at themselves—via, for instance, a "capability sourcing health check," as recommended in a 2010 briefing from Bain & Company[40]—in order to identify which of their firms' functions are *location sensitive*—that is, tethered by their very nature to a particular place. The work of engineers who deal with proprietary design information, for instance, might not be a good candidate for offshoring. In contrast are services that are "not constrained by the need for [direct] customer contact, local knowledge or complex interactions,"[41] and which the wise manager turns to the global labor market to procure. Handling routine customer calls is an "obvious example" of such a globally sourceable service.[42]

On the whole, the consulting literature suggests that firms have long been *overly conservative* about looking abroad for labor. "A gap exists," states a 2005 McKinsey and Company report, "between the number of service jobs that [firms] *could* locate remotely and the actual number of jobs that [firms] *have* located offshore."[43] This particular report goes on to fault "managers unwilling to become more involved overseas" and who thus end up being too "reluctant to offshore."[44] Such timidity is a dangerous thing, for it allows more daring firms to race ahead and outcompete them. Corporate decision-makers must thus be bold; they must come to grasp that they have a "wealth of choices,"[45] "literally . . . a world to choose from."[46]

Capital Channeled

To depict this new field of labor sourcing opportunities, the consulting literature draws upon a rhetoric rich with *liquid imagery*. The "*contours* of the global offshoring landscape" have generated "deep *pools* of qualified labor"[47] ripe for "companies to start *tapping*,"[48] while firms pursuing such investment opportunities constitute a "BPO *wave*"[49] of "foreign [capital] *inflows*."[50] "*Test the waters*," Bain & Company advised firms.[51]

Ultimately, *two fundamental grades* should channel capital flows abroad from the West. In evaluating the pros and cons of various potential investment locales, the reports typically enumerate a wide range of factors—a "plethora of variables"[52]—that decision-makers should consider: currency fluctuations, tax incentives, protection of intellectual property rights, the risk of natural disasters, and so on. There is usually some caveat that firms should "place their own importance weights on each criterion and sub-criterion."[53] A German firm looking to offshore its programming work, for example, should evaluate Poland more positively than would an American firm, owing to overlapping time zones. Over and over, however, the reports filter out the majority of such variables in favor of two particularly: the *cost* and the *quality* of labor available in a given locale. The opportunity to both achieve "*cost* arbitrage" and tap "a large *talent* pool" is thus how the research firm A. T. Kearney ranks various offshore destinations;[54] while an analyst for the consulting company CB Richard Ellis summarized: "The needs of BPO companies are simple: *qualified* and *cheap* labor."[55]

It is along an axis of cost that the world is first and foremost tilted. Consider McKinsey and Company's 2005 report, "The Emerging Global Labor Market."[56] It describes the global sourcing landscape as one in which investment flows from "high-wage countries" to "low-wage countries." The company vends a proprietary metric—the "Location Cost Index" (LCI)—to assist firms in the former countries in differentiating among investment opportunities in the latter. Labor costs, alongside other operating expenses such as office rents, tax rates, telecommunication services, and utilities, are a key component of the LCI. As do other firms, McKinsey emphasizes that labor costs are not identical to headline wages. The "true cost" of labor, it contends, must take into consideration payroll taxes, mandated benefits, and the like.[57] A. T. Kearney, in its Global Services Location Index, uses its own metric, "financial attractiveness," which agglomerates each country's average costs for labor, infrastructure, and regulatory compliance.[58] Although individual reports make a big fuss over their own proprietary metrics for capturing various costs, one gets the sense that many of the individual measures are redundant. As McKinsey admits: "Cost factors tend to move together."[59]

By any means, classifying countries, regions, and cities according to cost creates *a world tilted sharply toward East, South, and Southeast Asia* (see figure 3.1). India, the Philippines, China, and Malaysia invariably cluster at the top of various cost indices, with occasional appearances from Mexico, Brazil, Poland, and Hungary.[60]

The world of offshored business services is tilted along a second gradient, that of *skill*. Manufacturing capital, requiring as it does mainly physical labor (simple labor power, in Marx's terms), can flow directly to large pools of cheap labor in low-wage regions (such as coastal China).[61] Voice and other forms of service capital, in contrast, must ask whether pools of potential labor possess certain specialized skills. In other words, while manufacturing capital may chase cheap hands and nimble fingers, voice capital must filter for particular minds and voices. This means that when evaluating potential investment sites, it cannot look only at population size and labor costs: "Multinational [BPO] companies," McKinsey advises, "should focus specifically on the suitable talent supply . . . rather than relying on the size of a country's population."[62]

Ascertaining a population's "talent supply" is trickier than it appears. Whereas data on wages, real estate, and the like are generally commensurable

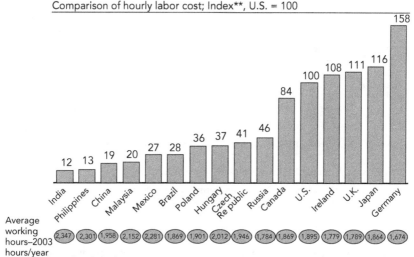

INDIA AND PHILIPPINES ARE THE MOST ATTRACTIVE
COUNTRIES IN TERMS OF LABOR COST*

Comparison of hourly labor cost; Index**, U.S. = 100

FIGURE 3.1 How McKinsey and Co. grades the world according to labor costs.

Source: McKinsey Global Institute, "Emerging Global Labor Market," 47.

across nations (expressed as they are in U.S. dollars), indicators of human capital are much less so. Is a bachelor's degree in computer science from a university in Kuala Lumpur equivalent to one from a university in Bangalore? How can a manager evaluate from afar the English fluency of an employee in Hyderabad versus one in Manila?

Within the genre of consulting reports there are multiple systems for measuring and comparing human capital across regions. Suitability, hirability, quality, talent competitiveness, and employability are common labels for these metrics. But most of these systems hinge on a few basic indicators.

Because offshored services almost always entail working with computers, firms must consider whether a given labor force will possess "entry-level IT skills"—that is, the ability to type quickly, navigate an internet browser, and work within basic word processing and spreadsheet programs.[63] In poor countries, however, computers are not present in a majority of households, primary schools, and secondary schools.[64] Postsecondary education—in particular, the absolute number of bachelor's degrees in a given population—is thus widely taken to be a valid indicator of a labor pool's technical skill set. And so McKinsey lauds the "suitability of labor" in the Philippines, given that the country "produces roughly 350,000 college graduates each year."[65] Other

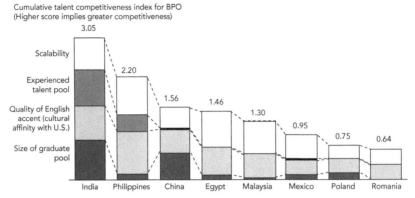

FIGURE 3.2 A sample "Talent Competitiveness Index."

Source: Alejandor P. Melchor III, "The Perfect Storm and the Next Wave Cities Program," presentation at Negros Oriental IT Expo, Dumaguete, Philippines, 2012.

reports attempt to distinguish more finely among college graduates in a given region. Tholons, for instance, bases its rankings not only upon the number of college graduates but also the number of "technical graduates" in IT-related fields.[66] Figure 3.2 presents one firm's sophisticated index for evaluating the competitiveness of different countries' populations of college graduates. Note how the Philippines, despite having a small "graduate pool," outperforms China and even approaches India's level when it comes to cumulative "talent."

Two Pools

Taking into account *both* costs and skills, the global landscape of service sourcing opportunities reveals three *potential* pools of labor. Consider figure 3.3, a chart used by a major American outsourcing firm to assess investment locales. The *x* (horizontal) axis represents a country's labor costs relative to the United States; the *y* (vertical) axis depicts how well a country's population scores on the firm's metric for "IT Skills." According to the executive who shared this chart with me, his company considers only countries on the right side of the *x*-axis (i.e., Egypt, Vietnam, Thailand, the Philippines, India, China, and Romania) to offer worthwhile cost savings. Furthermore, only countries higher along the *y*-axis can be counted on to provide a sufficient number of college graduates with acceptable IT skills. China, India, and the Philippines are the sole occupants of this "ideal" quadrant of the chart.

    Western BPO firms—and call centers specifically—have so far eschewed China as a site of investment. The obvious explanation for this is the low level

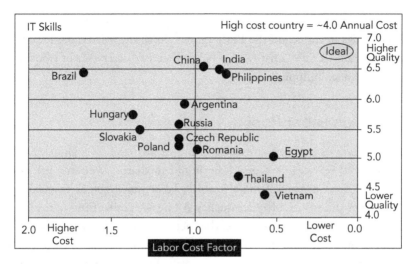

FIGURE 3.3 One firm's investment map.

of English proficiency among Chinese college graduates. GlobalEnglish, a software firm, publishes a "Business English Index" to "track competency across . . . geographies in business communication using English."[67] It groups Chinese workers among those who "cannot understand most [English] presentations, take a leadership role in [English] discussions or perform relatively complex tasks."[68] ATKearney similarly concludes that "without a tradition of English-language education," China is not competitive as a global sourcing destination for Western firms: "most customers of Chinese BPO service providers are likely to be domestic [or] other Asian countries seeking nearshore options."[69]

This means that the majority of "offshore [service] delivery centers . . . narrow their global operations to . . . only two countries": India and the Philippines.[70] The global landscape of service offshoring, in other words, is dually graded. The desire for *cheap* labor channels voice capital, much as it does for manufacturing firms, to Asia. Once there, voice capital further seeks pools of *skilled* labor. Only India and the Philippines can satisfy both longings. Average per capita income in both countries is significantly lower than in the United States, while English and technical literacy are assumed to be high.

Within the managerial literature, these two countries are referred to as the "titans"[71] and "powerhouses"[72] of service outsourcing. As the head of a New York–based outsourcing firm stated, they are the "only countries in the world that can offer such services at a high quality and at affordable prices."[73]

One well-regarded ranking of top outsourcing cities in fact gave *all eight top spots* to cities in India and the Philippines.[74] In short, voice capital looks at the world and sees not a flat terrain but, rather, two reservoirs of labor: one Indian and one Philippine.

The Indian Labor Pool

Voice capital was not a passive actor in the construction of a global market for offshored services. It was a fully liquid mediator. Western (primarily American) firms organized the call center labor process so as to maximize call volumes and ensure adequate quality. Along with other firms in the larger business process outsourcing space, they actively pursued a spatial fix to the pressures of neoliberalism by proactively evaluating offshore investment locales. Their techniques for doing so identified two potential pools of qualified yet cheap labor: India and the Philippines. This section draws upon the extensive ethnographic literature on the BPO industry in India to document what came next. I argue that voice capital's attempt to build a stable labor market in India was only partially successful. Indian call center workers are cheaper than their American counterparts, but no more committed and so are as likely to leave. The Indian labor pool, in other words, was shallower and more turbulent than it appeared. Women find call center work to be stigmatizing, while men treat it as a steppingstone toward more technical fields.

BPO Capital Splits

Although India and the Philippines overlap on a two-dimensional matrix of labor cost and talent, it is easy to see why the former was more attractive to potential investors as of the late 1990s. The sheer magnitude of its labor pool—a population of a billion plus—tantalized BPO firms. Here was an unprecedented opportunity to leverage what Xiang Biao terms "*transnational surplus value . . .* measured as the disparity between the input for producing IT labor in India and the prevailing wages in the global market"[75] And whereas the Philippines during the 1990s was recovering from two decades of martial law, India was implementing a program of economic liberalization.

India's "dramatic shift in development strategy"[76] repealed longstanding impediments to foreign investment. It established export processing zones wherein foreign BPO firms could set up operations with minimal taxation and regulation.[77] The state established a business association (NASSCOM) to represent the nascent interests of foreign outsourcing firms, and reformed longstanding labor laws to allow flexible shift scheduling and work during nighttime and holidays.[78] India furthermore had by now established a global reputation as an emerging IT powerhouse. A 1961 Act had created multiple Indian Institutes of Technology (IITs), modeled after the world-renowned Massachusetts Institute of Technology (MIT) and dedicated to training students in technical fields such as programming, engineering, and information technology.[79] The country was also supposedly awash in "Argonauts":[80] Indians who had studied abroad but then returned home to establish "software, customer service, and back-office outfits."[81]

Western BPO firms (and journalists such as Thomas Friedman) rushed in to India in the late 1990s and early 2000s. Here, however, something curious happened, as the fates of the two species of BPO capital—voice and non-voice—diverged.

Firms seeking technical skills such as programming or database management found a solid enough foundation of labor in major Indian cities. The primary qualification needed to work in knowledge process outsourcing, or KPO, is expertise in at least one programming language or advanced computer program. There were certainly not enough IIT graduates and repatriated Argonauts to meet the growing demand for such labor. Xiang Biao, however, in his 2006 book *Global "Body Shopping,"* described how an "IT mania" swept through southeastern Indian while he was performing ethnographic work among aspiring KPO workers.[82] Hyderabad and Chennai, two major outsourcing hubs in the region, were booming. Families in turn began to recognize the opportunities to be afforded by sending their children—and sons, in particular—into the IT industry. In fact, Biao found that parents of so-called IT grooms were demanding double the size of a typical dowry from potential brides' families.

In response to this IT mania, a new and for the most part unregulated breed of for-profit institutions arose in India. Schools offering quick and inexpensive college *degrees* and *technical* certifications became known as D-shops and T-shops, respectively. Biao found that while some of these schools offered real training, others "notoriously sold degrees without imparting any practical knowledge."[83] Even so, Western tech firms found—and continue to find—India to be a good value proposition. There remains an abundance of applicants from reputable colleges and universities, while even those with substandard computer skills can often be trained on the job. By 2015, the IT-BPO sector in India employed around 3 million people and accounted for a quarter of total national exports.[84]

The story was different for voice offshoring. Western call centers found India's labor pool to be shallower than it appeared. To start, there has been no English-language equivalent to an IT mania among the masses. Speaking English well has long been a mark of class and caste distinction in India. Only the wealthy can send their children to private schools that teach English from an early age (as opposed to public schools where English instruction begins after the eighth grade). Well-off families are also more likely to speak English to their children and to have a television or internet connection in the home (which exposes children to English-language media).[85]

Employability at a call center, as the opening chapter documented, is determined by a standardized test of an applicant's English fluency, grammar, and accent. By the time one has reached one's late teens or early twenties, however, it is far more difficult to learn a new tongue than it is to master a computer program. Call centers thus quickly developed a reputation as spaces accessible only to affluent young Indians from privileged backgrounds. As Shehzad Nadeem, who interviewed and surveyed call center workers across India for his 2010 book *Dead Ringers*, found, 82% are from high castes; as he wrote, the call center "industry draws its workforce from the *privileged* castes and classes, not landless peasants scouring scrap heaps for recyclables."[86]

Call Center as Stigma

Call center firms also discovered that India's labor market is stratified and thus is limited by gender. Nath's 2011 interview project with Indian call center workers estimated that 77% are male;[87] Aneesh's 2015 ethnographic book, *Neutral Accent*, found that "most [call center] applicants were men";[88] while surveys of outsourcing workplaces throughout India consistently find very high percentages of male workers.[89] This is not the outcome of any state policy or legislation. In fact, as the outsourcing boom began, the Indian state removed legal barriers to women's' employment, such as a 1948 Act prohibiting women from working at night.[90] Nor do call center firms discriminate against female applicants. Reena Patel's 2010 book *Working the Night Shift* (introduced earlier) describes how employers make special efforts to recruit women workers and to provide for them needed amenities such as transport to and from work. Still, men compose the large majority of call center applicants and workers in India.

Longstanding patriarchal norms—and their manifestation in particular *practices*—constitute headwinds for women seeking work in India's call center industry. Existing studies enumerate three such headwinds. The first Patel traces back to the "historical practice of purdah," or veiling, in Muslim and Hindu communities of South Asia.[91] All evidence suggests the persistence to this day of a widespread belief that the family patriarch who allows his wife or daughters to venture out for work risks being stigmatized; the man of status and honor shields his female kin from public view and even confines them to the house. Concretely, this translates into internal policing by families of aspiring female call agents. The ethnographic literature is replete with examples of this dynamic. For instance, one of Patel's case studies described how her father was "furious" at her choice to seek work in a call center.[92] And one of Nadeem's respondents explained that working in a call center can make a young woman unmarriable: "Nowadays, you can't get married [if] you work in a call center. The name BPO shouldn't be written anywhere in your [marriage negotiations]."[93]

A second headwind derives from a highly gendered division of labor in Indian households. Even in middle and upper class families, women are obligated to do the bulk of household chores and to personally serve their fathers, husbands, and other male kin.[94] Consider how Patel describes the daily routine of her respondent Anan, who defied gender norms to work as a manager in a call center: "Despite her success as a Senior Quality Assurance Manager, [Anan] is expected to awaken before her husband every morning to get his clothes ready, prepare his tea, and get their three-year-old son ready for preschool. . . . [H]er husband is the only son and has been pampered all of his life." One can imagine the nearly superhuman effort that it must take for women such as Anan to fulfill their domestic obligations *and* work full time in the call center industry. Kiran Mirchandani, who interviewed hundreds of call center workers in New Delhi, Bangalore, and Pune for her book *Phone Clones*, concluded that phone work "is gendered [i.e., male-dominated] . . . because of women's primary responsibility for domestic work and childcare."[95]

These two headwinds that Indian women face—the stigmatization of work outside the home and the heavy demands of labor within it—are not unique to the call center industry. They surely go a long way toward explaining India's very low rate of female labor force participation (at *only 27%*) as a whole.[96]

The third and perhaps most significant headwind *is* specific to the voice industry. To be a call agent in this part of the world is to be at work when the West—and America, in particular—is awake. It is to work the night shift. In the context of the patriarchal norms just discussed, traveling to and from work late at night or in the early morning hours raises the specter of impropriety. Hence, Patel's research subjects had to constantly deal with the accusation: "Call center job equals call girl job!"

The result is a generalized *and not unfounded* fear among female call agents for their physical safety on a day-to-day basis. As part of his study, Nadeem catalogued hundreds of assaults upon female call agents, including molestations, rapes, acid attacks, and murders.[97] While thousands of Indian women muster the strength to overcome these headwinds, we must conclude that the numerical overrepresentation of men in the industry is due precisely to longstanding patriarchal norms, along with the behaviors, sensibilities, and practices they generate.

Call Center as Steppingstone

Voice capital found that the potential labor pool in India was shallower than it appeared. English proficiency is highly correlated with social class, while women face so many headwinds that they are de facto excluded from the labor market. Who steps forward to take calls? Well, it seems to be mainly young, urban men possessing college degrees (often in an IT-related field) who apply to call centers, and all indications are that they do well enough on the standardized English exams. However, these individuals constitute a turbulent labor pool insofar as they do not stay attached to the call center industry. This translates into high turnover, "the most serious human resource problem" that call centers confront in India.[98]

Existing research suggests that there are both pull and push factors at work. On the pull side is the allure of better jobs in the KPO field, toward which call center work can serve as a steppingstone. The ethnographic literature describes how there is often an initial attraction between foreign call centers and potential workers. Winifred Poster, who spent years conducting case studies of call centers throughout India, describes how many new college "grads" interpret call centers as instant "employment opportunities, upgraded pay, and comfortable working conditions."[99] Patel emphasized that during the early 2000s, call center starting salaries were three to five times those offered in more traditional occupations such as teaching, engineering, and government work.[100]

Before long, however, the attraction fades as these (primarily male) workers begin to reinterpret call center work. They situate it—and themselves—in relation to opportunities in the larger BPO field. As a worker interviewed by Patel explained, "for qualified youth like engineering grads . . . call center jobs [are] viewed as transition jobs."[101] Biao describes call center work as it exists in the minds of young (male) Indian workers as the first step on an "escalator."[102] Working in a call center becomes less an end than a means to a better job in the non-voice (IT, or KPO) sector of the BPO field. It allows workers to buttress their résumés with experience working for a foreign firm, refine their English, build networks, and gain familiarity with standard business software. Regardless of whether non-voice jobs pay more than their voice counterparts, they are higher status. They offer the opportunity to become what one of Nadeem's respondents called a "publicly admired techie."[103] Beyond that, there is the allure of building and then leveraging the skills needed to reach the top of the escalator and become an Argonaut oneself. A call center job can help ambitious Indian men find work in the IT industry, which then can enable them to migrate on a skilled-worker visa to Australia, Singapore, or Malaysia initially, and ideally then on to the United States.[104]

In addition to these opportunities *pulling* Indian men out of the call center are *push* factors. If they interpret call center work as a mere steppingstone, as a purgatory to be endured until better opportunities arise, then it makes sense that they will come to view it as a "low skill job," in the words of one of Patel's respondents.[105] Then there is the longstanding requirement that call center workers speak English with a neutral accent, assume an American name, and tolerate abuse—even nationalist and racist abuse—from callers.[106]

Nearly all empirical studies of India's call center industry have documented that these requirements are perceived as offensive by a substantial number of agents.[107] "Americans think they can put down other nations," call agent Kaushik told researcher Vandana Nath,[108] while one of Nadeem's respondents complained that American call centers are just "foreigners using you for a few years."[109] Tellingly, multiple researchers have documented how Indian call agents describe themselves using the self-deprecating phrase "cyber coolie," referencing a nineteenth-century racial slur toward South Asians.[110] Eventually, Aneesh found, call center agents, "unlike employees in other [BPO] industries, show a lot less . . . loyalty for their companies"; they come to adopt "an utter disregard, even contempt, for call center operations."[111] The end result is that turnover in India's outsourcing/offshoring industry is mainly a call center problem. Estimates of annual attrition rates in call centers are 50% and higher, while only around 15% in IT fields.[112]

Voice capital's project to build a stable labor market in India achieved mixed results. Labor costs were lower, but the overall labor pool was shallower and more turbulent than their two-dimensional maps suggested. Indian workers, we can say, proved to be active mediators. They interpreted call center work in relation to existing gender norms and other opportunities in the larger labor market—as, that is, a stigma and a steppingstone. While the IT/KPO side of the BPO industry has flourished in India, call centers continue to be haunted by the specter of attrition. By the early 2000s, firms began to experiment with the other main sourcing locale identified by their reports: the Philippines. There they would find a labor pool that interprets call center work very differently. In the following chapter I describe the broad contours of this pool, with a special emphasis on how the Philippine state created an entire generation of young people for whom working in a call center is a sensible and sustainable decision.

4

The State

MAKING A MIDDLE PATH

FOREIGN ARRIVALS TO what is today the Philippine archipelago have long been fraught affairs. Ferdinand Magellan, the famed Portuguese explorer, arrived in the eastern Visayas in 1521 and swiftly planted the flag of the Spanish crown, which had sponsored his endeavor to be the first to circumnavigate the globe. Magellan received a warm welcome from a local *datu* (chieftan), whom he successfully converted to Catholicism. A week later, Magellan sailed to the nearby island of Mactan, where he and most of his men were slaughtered by the Visayan warrior-chieftan Lapu-Lapu.

Nearly four centuries later, Spain ceded the Philippines to the United States. American administers arrived in Manila only to encounter a revolutionary movement that would take three years—from 1899 to 1902—and terrible violence to suppress. Yet just four decades after that, in 1944, the Philippine people cheered the return of U.S. General Douglas MacArthur as he waded ashore on the island of Leyte during the height of World War II. MacAarthur and his forces swiftly ended two years of brutal occupation by Japanese forces, shortly after which, in 1946, the United States lowered its flag in Manila and granted the Philippines its independence (figure 4.1).

In the decades to follow, the country and its economy would stagnate. Its economy remained mire in a low productivity trap, unable to industrialize or diversify beyond agriculture. Political dynasties translated into a string of ineffective and corrupt national governments. While billions of dollars in foreign direct investment (and millions of tourists) flowed into East and Southeast Asia, the Philippines failed to attract much interest from outsiders. In a region of tiger economies, the Philippines became known as "the stray cat."[1]

FIGURE 4.1 Magellan and MacArthur receive different welcomes in the Philippines.
Source: Left: Mactan Shrine painting in Cebu City, by Carl Frances Morano Diama.
Right: MacArthur's landing at Leyte, photograph by Gaetano Faillace.

This was the situation when, in 1994, the American firm Andersen Consulting (now Accenture) opened a small servicing center in Manila's financial district. Over the next decade, a handful of other firms followed suit. Sykes, PeopleSupport, eTelecare, Convergys, SITEL, AOL, and Texas Instruments were among those to dip their proverbial toes in Philippine waters. Undoubtedly, many of these firms were looking to diversify their portfolio of offshore suppliers. "An overconcentration of assets in a particular country," one of the consulting reports analyzed in the prior chapter warned, "expose[s] providers to a variety of location-specific risks," including currency fluctuations, natural disasters, and labor actions.[2] For a firm that had initially located its voice work in India, the Philippines surely represented an opportunity to shift some risk to new shores, especially if the price and quality of labor were assumed to be identical across the two countries. And some American firms must have been intrigued by the idea that a "cultural affinity" made Filipinos more employable and their accents more pleasing to American callers. By the year 2000, the call center industry in the Philippines had established a modest presence; it employed around 3,000 people and produced around $40 million in revenues annually.

At this point, the initial trickle of foreign investment turned into a flood. Ten years later, in 2010, there were 600,000 Philippine call agents and $9 billion in revenues. The numbers have continued to grow ever since. Such a sea change is too large to be explained by the need to diversify investments or by slightly different accents in Manila relative to Mumbai. Clearly, for voice capital, a paradigm shift occurred when it came to evaluating the Philippines as an offshore sourcing locale.

The overarching metaphor guiding this study imagines labor markets as emergent architectures. The previous chapter argued that call center firms, by pioneering new technologies for managing various flows of information, opened up the entire world as a potential investment site. In this chapter, I analyze the Philippine state as another *key mediator* in the shaping of the global market for voice. The Philippine state mattered not because it offered novel incentives to lure firms but, rather, because it produced—and continues to produce—particular sorts of workers who are initially drawn to call center work *and* who subsequently remain attached to it. These workers are based mainly in Manila, a chaotic mega-city home to thousands of college graduates who face an agonizing choice: migrate out as a contract laborer or stay at home as an impoverished professional. Call center work, in this context, becomes a sensible and sustainable "middle path" for many. How did such a bifurcated labor market come to be? Why has the Philippine state failed to foster economic development and advance public welfare to the point that obtaining a call center job serves as a lifeline for so many? To address such questions, I consider how colonial legacies produced a largely ineffectual and captured state apparatus in the Philippines.

Anti-Development as Colonial Legacy

It can be a knotty endeavor to explain key features of contemporary societies through reference to events that took place in the past. When studying former, or post, colonies, the short-circuit fallacy discussed in chapter 2 is a particular hazard. It is only too easy, that is, to posit a *direct* link from, say, widespread poverty in the Philippines today to Spanish occupation of the archipelago hundreds of years ago. More convincing are accounts that trace pathways and mechanisms through which a colonial legacy, over time, shapes a postcolonial society.

Most convincing are accounts that focus on the nature of the state apparatus that forms after colonialism ends.[3] Is it autonomous and accountable? Is it effective at pursuing collectively agreed-upon goals? Or is it captured, corrupt, and weak? In this section I will define and unpack the Philippine state as what the scholar Walden Bello calls an "anti-development state."[4] I enumerate three interrelated characteristics—each a dysfunction, really—and link them to the country's legacy as a colony of Western powers. First are *conservative social policies* that limit women's control over their reproductive health and fail to check population growth; second is a *captured political elite* more concerned with serving foreign interests than advancing the public welfare; and third is a *labor export economy* that funnels educated young people out of the country.

Spanish Colonialism and Seeds of Conservatism

Although Magellan met an untimely demise, the Philippines, named for King Philip II of Spain, would remain under Spanish rule for over three and a half centuries. In truth, for most of this time, "Spanish interest in the Philippines was perfunctory."[5] Spain, that is, made minimal attempts to systematically extract resources from the islands, to exploit its peoples, or to establish permanent settlements there. The Philippines was of strategic interest to Spain mainly because of its location as a key port for the galleon ships carrying silver home from its colonies in Latin America.[6]

Successive Spanish rulers were only too happy to "outsource" to the Catholic church the day-to-day work of managing the archipelago and molding the hearts and minds of its peoples. As Philippine historian Filomeno Aguilar writes, rather than establishing a comprehensive system of direct control via state administrators or permanent settlers, Spain relied on "Catholic priests and missionaries to the colony . . . to pursue the multiple tasks of winning souls, pacifying the *indio* spirit [, and] controlling the native clergy."[7]

An important result of this dynamic is that the Philippines was from the start more a papal colony than an Iberian one. Catholic ideology conquered the country to a much greater extent than Spanish force ever did.[8] This is seen clearly in the extent to which the Philippine populace to this day endorses views in line with those deemed proper by traditional Catholic doctrine. Whereas the Church has suffered a crisis of faith in Europe and North America, 85% of Filipinos identify as Catholics who attend mass regularly (the majority of the remaining 15% are Muslim Filipinos, based in the country's southern province of Mindanao). A reliable 2015 survey from the Pew Institute established that 93% of Filipinos believe abortion to be a mortal sin, while 67% believe divorce to be inherently immoral.[9] Such figures establish the people of the Philippines to be among the most socially conservative in the world.

This most devout of devotions to Catholicism has produced a policy regime disastrous for women and families in the Philippines. Here there is no "purdah," a private veiling by fathers and husbands, but, rather, a public regulation of women's reproductive health and personal well-being. From the decisions of *barangay* (neighborhood) councils to those of the Philippine Supreme Court, the Church has long had an outsized say in the drafting of social policy. Abortion is illegal in the country, as is filing for divorce. Schools both private and public provide little instruction on human anatomy, sexually transmitted diseases, or family planning.[10] Even married couples find it difficult to obtain basic contraception, insofar as the Philippine state has long "rejected all modern contraceptive methods as forms of abortion."[11]

As a result, the reproductive health revolution that swept much of the world in the latter half of the twentieth century largely passed by the Philippines. At the end of the twentieth century, the fertility rate (children born per woman) had dropped to 1.36 in Japan. 1.7 in Thailand, 2.0 in Vietnam, and 2.5 in Indonesia—to cite a few nearby examples. In the Philippines, it stood at four children per woman. As a result, the country's ratio of young to old persons is among the highest in Southeast Asia, at 2.7 to 1 (in nearby Vietnam, for instance, in stands at 1.2 to 1). As recently as 2017, 70% of Philippine households contained four or more people and 33% contained six or more, often extended families crammed into substandard living quarters. One out of five Philippine households is headed by a woman, and in 70% of these the woman is a lone parent with a child under the age of fifteen. In short, the ongoing influence of the Catholic church in the Philippines to this day hinders women's control over their reproductive decisions, their relationship choices, and their basic living arrangements.[12]

American Influence and the Illusion of Independence

Two years after MacArthur returned to the Philippines and drove out the Japanese military, the United States granted the country its independence. During its nearly fifty years of colonial rule prior, the United States, like Spain before it, perceived no real interest in establishing permanent settlements in the Philippines. The islands contain no significant deposits of gold, oil, or diamonds to be excavated and appropriated. Agricultural interests in the United States refused to allow American capital to build a plantation economy or even to modernize Philippine agriculture; as a result, the Philippine economy remained based on small-scale farming wholly dependent on exports to the U.S. market.

The United States' colonial administration of the Philippines was guided by President William McKinley's principle of "benevolent assimilation." Under it, the United States established political institutions such as a national legislature, and sent engineers, educators, and other experts to the Philippines to build schools, roads, and hospitals.[13] Ultimately, however, the islands were important to the United States, as they had been for Spain, because of their location. Both before World War II and especially during the Cold War that followed, the United States valued the Philippines as a military base and as a dependable ally in the Pacific theatre. Both goals depended upon pacifying the population and maintaining a state weak to the point of being captured.

The United States, during its colonial occupation of the Philippines, permitted a "powerful, regionally based landlord class" to monopolize power in the national legislature, in return for ensuring popular support for America's ongoing presence.[14] After independence, this landed elite essentially took over rule of the country. So, rather than an autonomous and competent bureaucracy accountable to the people, the Philippines inherited what Stanley Karnow labeled an "oligarchy of rich dynasties" that was all too happy to accommodate the needs of foreign interests and the U.S. government specifically.[15] Steven McKay elaborates its origins thus:

> The roots of the contemporary "weak" Philippine state and its capture by groups of powerful oligarchs can be traced to its colonial history. . . . [W]hen the United States wrestled colonial control, these landlords, or *caciques*, had become so powerful that the American colonizers struck a political bargain with them in order to win local support for the colonial regime. Buoyed by the support of the colonizers, these agro-exporters used their positions in the newly created national assembly to strengthen their political power, using their gatekeeper control over a weak central state as a key to accumulating rents, diversifying their businesses, and shutting out rivals.[16]

Sociologist Julian Go describes the relationship between the United States and the Philippine state following independence as one of "informal imperialism."[17] McKay's idea of an implicit "political bargain" captures well how such informal control worked. This bargain had multiple dimensions, some of which remain in place to this day. On one side, the United States provided financial support (in the form of post-World War II rehabilitation funds, grants from USAID, and direct foreign aid) to the Philippine government. It pledged to protect the Philippines from external threats (ranging from Japanese military aggression in the 1940s to recent Chinese attempts to claim islands in the South China Sea). And it propped up despots such as Ferdinand Marcos, who ruled the Philippines for twenty-one years via corrupt elections, martial law, and systematic murder of political opponents.[18] In return, the Philippine state actively served the interests of the U.S. government, most notably by allowing the American military to maintain military bases in the country and by adopting a hardline stance against communist movements both within the country and throughout Southeast Asia.

The fall of the Marcos regime in 1986 seemingly exposed the farce of democratic self-rule in the Philippines. Three years before, Marcos's main political rival, Benigno ("Ninoy") Aquino Jr., had been shot in the head and killed while walking off a plane at Manila International Airport. In February 1986, Marcos held a snap presidential election and defeated Corazon ("Cory") Aquino, Ninoy's widow, but only through widespread voter intimidation and fraud. Weeks later, hundreds of thousands of ordinary Filipinos packed the streets of Manila and gathered in front of Malacañang, the presidential palace. Key Catholic clergy and military leaders threw in their lot with the People Power Revolution of 1986. As American helicopters whisked Ferdinand Marcos and his wife Imelda away to Hawaii (along with their suitcases packed full of gold and jewels), it seemed that America's informal imperialism had come to an end. In 1992, during the last year of her presidency, Cory Aquino refused to renew the leases of American military bases in the Philippines.

The degree to which Marcos's ouster fundamentally transformed the nature of Philippine society remains a matter of debate. Visiting force agreements and a treaty of mutual defense allow American boots to remain on the ground throughout the Philippines.[19] In an attempt to attract foreign capital, the former military bases were transformed into "special economic zones" wherein tax rates are reduced and labor unions essentially prohibited.[20] Inequality remains high in the Philippines, while the landed families of "oligarchs" have remained in control of the state at national, regional, and local levels. This is what Bello refers to as the "great Philippine paradox: an extremely lively play of electoral politics unfolding above an immobile class structure."[21] During my fieldwork in the Philippines, Corazon and Benigno Aquino's son Benigno ("Noynoy") served as president, while even the populist firebrand Rodrigo Duterte, elected in 2016, hails from an established political family in the southern Philippines.

Migrant Labor as Development Strategy

During the decades following Marcos's ouster, many countries in East and Southeast Asia experienced economic booms. The Philippines did not. Consider table 4.1, which situates the Philippines in relation not to the famed Asian Tigers such as South Korea, Singapore, and Taiwan but, rather, to several peer nations within Southeast Asia (Vietnam, Thailand, and Indonesia). As of 2010, the Philippines remained an outlier in the region. Because of its

Table 4.1 Select Southeast Asian Countries Compared, 2010

	Philippines	Vietnam	Thailand	Indonesia
Annual population growth since 1980	1.62%	1.03%	0.49%	1.32%
Population below poverty line	24%	13%	7%	13%
Total FDI ($1Bn)	1.262	7.43	7.778	19.098
Tourist arrivals (Mn)	3.9	6	19.1	7.65

Source: Asean Secretariat, "ASEAN Statistical Leaflet: Selected Key Indicators 2010" (Jakarta: ASEAN, 2011).

retrograde reproductive health policies, it had been unable to lower fertility rates and thus achieve the demographic transition widely believed to be a necessary condition for sustained economic growth. A full quarter of its population subsisted below the poverty line. It had failed to attract foreign direct investment (FDI), especially in manufacturing. And tellingly, the Philippines has not developed an infrastructure to draw in foreign tourists relative to its neighbors in Southeast Asia.

Scholars use the term "development state" to describe how national governments in East and Southeast Asia nurtured domestic industries, especially in manufacturing for export, during the 1990s and 2000s.[22] Bello in turn labels the Philippine government an "anti-development state" that has repeatedly failed to foster growth and improve the well-being of the population as a whole.[23] The Philippine migrant labor system is typically held up as direct evidence of this failure. One of the few areas in which the Philippine state *has* proved to be effective is in its capacity to cultivate and manage a supply of trained, English-speaking workers who can be deployed abroad as contract workers for foreign capital.

The origins of this migrant labor system can be traced directly back to the era of American colonialism. While the U.S. government was mainly interested in using the Philippines as a strategic location in Asia, employers in America came to view the country as a source of cheap and accessible labor. During the early twentieth century, the U.S. Congress had passed a series of nativist immigration laws. Employers in turn took advantage of the fact that Filipinos had special status as U.S. nationals and so could legally be imported as workers. Farm owners in Hawaii and the western United States were among the first to do so in the 1930s, targeting rural men from the northern provinces of the Philippines. In the following decades, men and women from throughout the Philippines were recruited to perform a variety of skilled and unskilled jobs: as fish canners, soldiers, seamen, domestic servants, entertainers, construction workers, doctors, and nurses.[24]

Over time, the Philippine state came to embrace and perfect its role as a market intermediary between foreign capital and its own people. In 1974, two years after imposing martial law upon the country, President Marcos signed a Labor Code creating new government agencies to manage the out-migration of contract laborers not just to the United States but also to the rest of the world. This in essence "institutionalized labor export" as an economic strategy.[25] Government officials began to monitor global economic trends so as to project labor demand and then quickly coordinate training programs to have an appropriate supply of workers "ready to go."[26] This entailed teaching a range of specific skills in high schools, colleges, and state agencies, from nursing to singing, from accounting to housecleaning.

Integral to the overall strategy of orienting national pedagogy to the global labor market, however, was an emphasis on English-language instruction. To this day, regardless of their occupation or the region of the world they are deployed to, the assumption is that Filipino workers will be more marketable if they are "highly skilled, well-educated [, and] *English-speaking*."[27] Although over a hundred languages are spoken throughout the archipelago, only two—Filipino (essentially Tagalog, a regional language of the north) and English—are designated as official languages. All primary and secondary education includes English classes, while practically all postsecondary instruction is in English.

By the turn of the twenty-first century, four thousand Filipinos were leaving the country each day to work as contract laborers. At any given moment, 10 to 12 million were working abroad, and the remittances they sent home constituted the largest source of foreign exchange coming into the country and the largest contributor to the national GDP. It's thus not surprising that the Philippine state has long dubbed migrant workers *bagong bayani* (new heroes) as part of a larger project to instill in its people an "ethos of labor migration,"[28] to make "going out" to work a "secular form of religious duty."[29] But it is also not surprising that so many critical observers take the country's migrant labor system, which encourages its people to "imagine . . . their future and economic salvation to exist *outside* the Philippines," as an indictment of the Philippine state.[30] Whether weak, captured, or both, it has failed to lift its people out of poverty; it continues to fail to advance women's reproductive health; and its economy has for too long relied on educating its people and then shipping them abroad.

Anthropologist Benito Vergara speaks of a "long discontent" among Filipinos at being "impelled to seek their fortunes *elsewhere*."[31] I shall argue that this discontent, the product of decades of failed development policy, formed the basis for an initial attraction between young Filipino college graduates and international call centers. The two sides first met in Manila, the port city that by the late twentieth century had become a paradigmatic megacity of the Global South.

Metro Manila and the Philippine Dream

To say that the Philippines became the world's capital of voice is not fully correct. Manila did. By Manila, those from the Philippines refer to the metropolitan area surrounding the city of Manila itself, officially referred to as the NCR (National Capital Region) or "metro Manila." It occupies the strip of land between Manila Bay, providing direct access to the South China Sea, and Laguna de Bay, the largest freshwater lake in the country. As a hub in colonial Spain's galleon trade, Manila was designated the capital of the Philippines in the late sixteenth century and has long been the political, economic, and cultural center of the country.

Today it remains the center of gravity within the Philippines, pulling toward it people seeking escape from the long-impoverished provinces. Manila's airport handles the vast majority of international flights to and from the Philippines; the two trading floors of the Philippine Stock Exchange are based in Makati and Pasig City, key business districts within metro Manila; while rates of general literacy and English proficiency are higher in Manila than elsewhere in the country. Estimates of its population range from 12 to 24 million persons, meaning that somewhere between an eighth and a quarter of the country resides in the city.

Manila is a magnet not only for Filipinos but also for foreign voice capital. Little fanfare was made when the first call center opened in Makati in the mid-1990s. Twenty-plus years later, metro Manila is practically a call center archipelago. Radiating out from downtown are a series of business districts, each of which is anchored by a cluster of high-rises whose floors are essentially rows of call agents stacked atop rows of call agents. Bus- and trainloads of office workers stream each evening into (and each morning out of) Eastwood City, Ortigas, Fort Bonafacio, Cubao, UP-Diliman's Technology Park, and various other call center districts around the metro area. By 2012, after a decade in which the industry grew at a 23% annual clip, over 40% of all office space in metro Manila was occupied by call centers.[32]

Key to understanding how metro Manila became a call center hub is its recent transformation into a particular sort of *megacity*. Generally defined as conurbations with populations in excess of 10 million, megacities inherently face myriad problems in terms of providing transportation, sanitation, housing, and other basic services necessary for public health and a decent quality of life [33] Megacities of the Global North, such as New York, Tokyo, or London, are adequately resourced and governed so as to be able to provide these necessities for the bulk of their inhabitants. Many megacities of the Global South are not, and metro Manila is a perfect example.

At the beginning of the Second World War, Manila consisted of the old walled Spanish fortress of Intramuros and eleven surrounding municipalities administered by the Americans. Its population was well under a million. When Japanese forces arrived, they shelled the city heavily to wrest control of it, while MacArthur's subsequent campaign to push Japan out entailed extensive street warfare, 100,000 civilian deaths, and the obliteration of most of the city's physical infrastructure. After the war, America granted the Philippines independence and then withdrew not only its military forces but also its administrators, planners, and engineers. The subsequent history of Manila in the twentieth century was one of haphazard growth. Just as successive postindependence Philippine national governments failed to build an autonomous and competent bureaucracy, city and neighborhood officials throughout metro Manila knew or cared little about principles of urban planning. Too few resources were committed to building and maintaining basic infrastructure while street-level politics were dominated by corruption, graft, and infighting.[34]

During the postwar decades, the Philippine national government financed the construction of multiple concrete monoliths in Manila to serve as administrative buildings. A handful of colonial-era structures remained as points of interest for tourists. Office parks, shopping malls, and gated communities were built throughout the city. By the end of the twentieth century, however, the most striking visual aspect of Manila were the many "distinct slums . . . widely dispersed throughout the urban fabric" to the point that it "makes more sense to consider the nonslum areas as enclaves."[35] Just a few streets away from the skyscrapers of the Makati financial district one found neighborhood after neighborhood of ramshackle housing lacking basic amenities such as electricity and plumbing. The city's train and bus systems were (and remain) woefully inadequate to handle the flows of people moving daily throughout the city, resulting in perpetual gridlock and punishing commute times. Archaic sewage systems could not handle heavy rains, such that garbage-infested water regularly floods the streets and waterways (figure 4.2). If not quite the largest city on earth, Manila had become one of the densest and dirtiest.

Unable to care for its current inhabitants, Manila by the closing decades of the twentieth century was in no way prepared to deal with the demographic storm brewing in the rest of the Philippines. Although the country's fertility rate was slowly declining, the ongoing power of the Catholic church to limit women's access to contraception and other reproductive rights meant that the population continued to grow. Between 1960 and 2010, the population of the country more than tripled, from 26.3 million to 93.7 million (and this is not taking into account all those who permanently migrated out during these years). Meanwhile, the country's economy remained mired in a low productivity trap, unable to establish a manufacturing sector or to modernize agricultural production.

All of this fed directly into the growth of Manila itself. Migrants from the provinces flooded into the metro region in search of economic opportunities beyond agricultural work and subsistence farming.[36] Between 1980 and 2010, the size of the metro region at least doubled, from 6 million to 12 million

FIGURE 4.2 The Pasig River "flows" through downtown Manila.

persons (the latter figure being a conservative estimate, given the difficulty of accurately counting inhabitants of slum districts and urban encampments).

What most of these new arrivals to metro Manila found (and continue to find) is a hardscrabble existence. To support themselves and their families, they seek work in the low end of the formal economy, in occupations such as maids, cleaners, and security guards. If they are not so lucky as to find formal employment (or if they need to supplement the meager earnings that such work pays), they may participate in the informal economy—as street vendors, unlicensed drivers, garbage scavengers (figure 4.3), prostitutes, and so on. As in many poor megacities of the Global South, the informal economy constitutes a substantial portion of the real, as opposed to the official, economy in metro Manila.

As for internal migrants the world over, however, the move from country-side to city opens up *real* opportunities for intergenerational mobility. This is what I call the *Philippine Dream*: culling together sufficient resources to allow at least one child or dependent to obtain a postsecondary degree and thus a good job, ideally abroad. Because it is customary for adult children to share their earnings with both immediate and extended families, this has long been considered a sensible mobility strategy throughout Philippine society.

FIGURE 4.3 A hardscrabble existence for Manila's poor.
Source: Photograph by Florentino Floro.

The Philippine state directly nurtures the Philippine Dream with its television programs and presidential medals dedicated to *bagong bayani*, heroic migrants. It also does so indirectly, most notably through its support for a large, diverse, and flexible system of postsecondary education. At the time of my fieldwork, metro Manila was home to over 300 accredited tertiary education institutions enrolling around 700,000 students.

A handful of these schools are direct remnants of Spanish and U.S. colonialism. Clergy and colonial administrators established a number of elite universities modeled after the ideal liberal arts college. Their purpose was to Westernize the children of wealthy landowning families. To this day, established families from throughout the country send their children to schools such as Ateneo de Manila University (founded by Spanish Jesuits in 1859) or the University of the Philippines (established by American colonial administrators in 1908 to "give advanced instruction in literature, philosophy, the sciences and the arts"[37]). With the exception of Corazon Aquino, who was educated in the United States, every president of the Philippines since Ferdinand Marcos (including the populist Rodrigo Duterte) has graduated from an elite Manila university.

These elite schools have sizable faculties in the humanities, arts, and social sciences, and produce just about *all* of the country's PhDs and JDs. Admission standards are high, as are tuition fees, which can run up to 200,000 pesos (about $5000) per year, roughly equal to the median income for an entire household in Manila. Graduates of elite universities tend to take professional jobs in government or with foreign firms operating in the Philippines. If they do go abroad, it is for graduate education, tourism, or on a special work visa—and not as migrant workers.

In contrast to these elite schools, the vast majority of postsecondary schools in metro Manila cater to the aspiring offspring of the *masa*, the masses. These public and private colleges attempt to satisfy the longings of the Philippine Dream by producing bodies, hands, and minds ready for export. That is, they teach what are called "professions" in the Philippines but what those in the West would call vocational occupations or skilled trades. The important thing is that these courses of study are considered practical and marketable on the international labor market. In 2014, for instance, the most popular majors among the country's 2.6 million undergraduates were accounting, nursing, education, and seafaring. In contrast, enrollment in traditional liberal art majors was miniscule, with just 6% of the overall undergraduate population majoring in arts, humanities, or social sciences.[38]

Professional-qua-vocational degrees are much more affordable compared to a liberal arts education at an elite school. As of 2015, one could earn a Bachelor of Science in Industrial Education or Office Administration from the Guzman College of Science and Technology (fully accredited and located in the Quiapo district of Manila) for only 30,000 pesos ($750) per year, a sixth of the cost of attending Ateneo or the University of the Philippines (entrance to which is extremely competitive anyway).

In sum, as metro Manila's population mushroomed during the latter half of the twentieth century, so did its system of colleges and universities. Most of these schools catered to the *masa*, for whom educating children is an intergenerational mobility strategy. By the end of the millennium, Manila alone was producing around a quarter million new bachelor's degrees annually. *The resulting contradiction for the Philippine Dream is not hard to see.* The system of exporting labor via the Overseas Foreign Worker program could not quickly dispatch such a quantity of graduates, creating an oversupply of overqualified workers throughout the Philippines, and in metro Manila specifically. By the 1990s and early 2000s, furthermore, the majority of migrant workers were being sent not to traditional landing spots such as the United States but to countries in the Middle East, many of which were undergoing political and economic turmoil.[39] Poor families continued to send their children to college, in line with the widespread belief that a vocational education is a ticket out of poverty. But these tickets were increasingly an unsure bet. What were—and are—the implications of this crisis for the Philippine Dream? How do young college graduates in the Philippines today evaluate their options and prospects in the larger labor market?

Call Center as Middle Path

We have by now many excellent studies of the Philippine labor export system, the experiences of Filipino migrants, and the larger Filipino diaspora. One could easily conclude, upon reading this body of scholarship, that every able-bodied Filipino has left the country. Indeed, at any moment over 2 million Filipinos are working abroad.[40] But this means that for every person who "goes out," as it's called, many others stay behind—and not all of them are children and elderly *lolos*. Millions of Filipinos finish school and then attempt to find a good job at home. They decide to fight the odds to find a good job in their field of study.

The Philippine state ultimately mattered for the assembly of a global labor market in voice, I argue, because it concentrated a pool of educated young people in a chaotic megacity, then provided them two vastly different career—and life—pathways. This section considers how these young people evaluate this bifurcated labor market, this fork in the road that sorts the dutiful/adventurous migrant from the domestic/aspirant professional. It should become clear why call center work is so attractive to so many Filipinos: it represents a middle path between these two extremes.

Path A: The Migrant Worker

To go abroad as a migrant worker can be seen as the culminating step in a multigenerational Philippine dream.[41] One's grandparents (*lolo* and *lola*) toiled in the countryside, while one's parents (*tatay* and *nanay*) sacrificed by migrating to the metropolis of Manila and laboring long hours, often in the informal economy, to send one to college. Now one can complete the cycle, by using one's physical and human capital to go abroad and begin earning— and sending home—dollars or other foreign currencies. During the early 2000s, a Filipino contract worker with a postsecondary degree would expect to earn around US$1000 monthly—remuneration several factors larger than that earned by most "professionals" in the Philippines.[42] I found during my fieldwork that "going out" is something that just about everyone considers at some point, and especially upon finishing one's formal schooling.

Of course, there are other, more egocentric motivations for going out. Living outside the Philippines and earning foreign currency mean that, even after making the standard remittances back home, one can treat oneself to amenities not available to the Filipino *masa*, such as luxury goods and tourist trips. Nicole Constable, in her ethnography of Filipina domestic workers in Hong Kong, described how many use migration as a means to distance themselves from troublesome husbands, boyfriends, and in-laws.[43] And it is also the case that a temporary sojourn as a contract laborer can lead to opportunities for permanent migration. Connections with employers can be made, foreign language skills can be learned or improved, and romantic relationships can develop which might lead to marriage and thus, depending on the locale, a spousal visa or citizenship.[44]

Path A, the migration path, entails costs and risks as well. Both Anna Guevarra and Robyn Rodriguez, in their ethnographic studies, describe how aspiring migrant workers have to navigate a bewildering maze of state bureaucracies and private brokers before being cleared to leave.[45] The application process entails upfront expenses that can run into the thousands of dollars. Aspirant migrants routinely take out loans on bad terms from unscrupulous lenders. And as the supply of potential workers has come to outpace the state's ability to place them, waiting times (the dreaded period of *itamby* that Joy, the nurse deferred, found intolerable) increasingly stretch into months or even years.

Furthermore, while young graduates assume that they will work abroad in the field for which they trained, in reality the demands of the global labor market do not match the supply of expertise being generated by Manila's colleges and universities. As a result, many migrants give up their professional aspirations and accept work for which they are overqualified, such as the accounting grad who works on a construction crew in Dubai or the nurse who sings in a nightclub on a cruise ship.[46]

Then there is the lived experience of migration. The work that overseas Filipino workers do, it is widely recognized, can be fraught with danger. Pei-Chia Lan, an ethnographer, found that Filipina maids in Taiwan are often physically and emotionally abused by their employers; Rodriguez discovered Filipino contract workers laboring in sweatshop conditions in Brunei; while Parrenas witnessed Filipina entertainers in Japanese nightclubs being coerced into prostitution.[47] In recent years, Filipino migrant workers have had to be regularly evacuated from countries in the Middle East experiencing political unrest. And then there is the tragic case of Flor Contemplacion, a domestic worker who was executed by the Singaporean government on questionable charges of murder after an infant died in her care.

Perhaps the greatest cost associated with Path A, however, is the separation from one's kin that migration entails. This cost is especially pronounced for parents who must leave their children behind in order to work abroad.[48] While political leaders celebrate migrant workers as national heroes, while extended families pressure children to pursue the Philippine Dream, many young persons simply prefer not to go out. In fact, this has always been an option for them.

Path B: The Underpaid Professional

Relative to the literature documenting the experiences of Filipino migrants, much less has been written about those who stay and try to build a life in the Philippines. How does this pathway appear to them at this critical juncture in their lives?

I found that among those who have obtained a college degree, there is a baseline sense of security that staying at home will not condemn one to the poorest of the poor. It is widely taken for granted that a college education eliminates the risk that one ends up working permanently in the informal economy. College graduates do not imagine themselves selling fried bananas on the street, living as maids in wealthy families' houses, being pressured into prostitution, or scavenging along a riverbank.

Furthermore, there was the sense that a college diploma lifts one above the most onerous, dangerous, and low-status jobs in the formal economy. Ceejay, one of my case studies, explained her situation before college as such:

> After high school I was looking for a job. But unfortunately I was really having a hard time because the truth is that *companies* will only hire someone who at least has a college degree.

By "companies," Ceejay is referring to employers in the formal economy who offer jobs that require at least some technical or interactional skills. For young persons such as Ceejay, getting a college degree is a way to ensure that one doesn't spend one's life as a janitor, security guard, taxi driver, or parking lot attendant.

The main allure of pursuing a "company job" in the Philippines, what I call path B, is easy to discern. In contrast to the isolation of the migrant worker, path B allows one to stay at home and thus remain physically close to one's family and friends. Friendship networks (*mga barkada*) among one's schoolmates and neighbors can be maintained. One can indulge what the anthropologist Raul Pertierra describes as a "strong cultural orientation for constant and perpetual contact" with one's kin, both biological and imagined.[49] In addition, for those with a strong commitment to the profession or vocation for which one trained in college, working even an entry-level position in your field allows you to prolong the dream of eventually achieving true professional status.

Path B, the professional at home path, in no way guarantees prosperity. Unless one is a graduate of an elite school such as Ateneo or the University of the Philippines, the brutal reality of Manila's labor market quickly hits one full force. A bachelor's degree from a nonelite college typically leads to a generalist job that is at best tangentially related to one's field of study. My respondent Ian, for example, graduated with a degree in hospitality management but could only find work as a server in a TGIF franchise; Jian, with a degree in business administration, found himself working as an appraiser in a pawn shop; while Kai, despite having a degree in pharmacy, could only obtain work as a cashier in a drug store. When asked to name other typical jobs that a college graduate would likely land in metro Manila, my respondents readily reeled off a variety of occupations that they would be overqualified for: office secretaries, retail workers, Starbucks baristas, caterers, bank tellers, data encoders, and so on.

Just about all these jobs pay the minimum wage, which in Manila at the time of my study was about 300 pesos ($7.50) per day. A full-time worker will thus gross only about 80,000 pesos (just over $2000) annually, barely enough to support one person at a low quality of life (i.e., a life spent in a shared living arrangement, eating simple home-cooked meals or street food with white rice as the main calorie source, taking public rather than private transportation, and rarely "treating" oneself to luxuries of any sort).

To add insult to injury, local employers in the Philippines have been ruthless about taking advantage of the oversupply of overqualified workers.[50] Just about all require job applicants to be willing to do unpaid internships, colloquially referred to as On the Job Trainings (OJTs), which can last for months or even years. This of course makes the financial situation of new college graduates even tougher, as they must take out loans and/or continue to rely on their families for basic living expenses as they attempt to establish careers. Unsurprisingly, the OJT system is widely resented, with my respondents calling it "servitude," "unfair," and "volunteer work." Job hunters, however, have little bargaining power on the issue considering the vast number of applicants for each entry-level position. As my respondent Rodalyn recalled, "I really wanted a job related to my course, which is advertising. Companies told me that I can do for them some marketing plans, but it won't be a job. I saw that it's not that easy even to *find a paying job.*"

Other terms used to describe the jobs in Manila that a college graduate could realistically hope to obtain included "eight to five" jobs, "professional" jobs, and "minimum wage" jobs. In the context of a rich country such as the United States, these would be contradictory labels. But they capture quite well the reality of the labor market in a poor megacity such as Manila, with its large informal economy. Here, to say that one has an "eight to five" job is to establish that one is not mired in unemployment or the informal economy, with their irregular hours and activities. Rather, one raises at a regular time each day to commute (often lengthy distances) to a real workplace. One furthermore is a "professional" because one dresses in the attire required by most formal workplaces—such as black slacks and a white dress shirt—rather than the jeans, t-shirts, shorts, and flip-flops worn by cab drivers, street vendors, and other nonprofessionals. But workers aren't dupes, and they are as likely to describe the job of a bank-teller as a "minimum wage" one as they are a professional one. Such jobs provide far from a salary adequate to support their vision of a good life, and it's not at all clear that they provide pathways to better-paying jobs within a given company. Hence, the reality in which a job can be simultaneously a professional and a dead-end one.

A Middle Path

Go abroad or stay at home? For generations of Filipino college graduates, this was the fork in the road. And what divergent paths they are! Path A takes one abroad, to substantial earnings but also to potential isolation and danger. Path B keeps one home, near family and friends, but struggling to scrape by on the $150 or so monthly salary that a "professional" job in the Philippines provides. Call centers in metro Manila must be understood in this context. Given the starkly different paths long faced by graduates, *the call center industry represents a third path—a middle route—through the labor market.*

The "middleness" of this path is conveyed most vividly by the salary it offers. The sixty call agents in my study reported monthly salaries ranging from 12,000 to 30,000 pesos per month, with an average of just over 20,000 pesos (about $500) monthly. This is substantially distinct from the monthly salaries earned via the migration path ($1000) and the domestic professional work path ($150). As one call agent, Rachel, described her salary: "It's not much [laughter]. But when you compare it to other jobs, you'll prefer it." By "other jobs," Rachel was referring to the "eight to five" jobs that she would have been confined to had she elected to stay in the Philippines prior to the call center boom. Such jobs are now *not* the only option available to college graduates who prioritize remaining at home with family and friends.

Call centers also offer ease and speed in obtaining a job in the first place. New college graduates, almost all of whom live with their families, feel immediately motivated to begin earning money so as to become independent, secure, and responsible. Every day on *itambay* (standby) begins to feel like an eternity. To go abroad entails months and months of paperwork, fundraising, and waiting. To acquire the "professional" jobs provided by local industry entails submitting paper applications, waiting weeks for a call back, and often doing lengthy unpaid internships. The new call centers were—and are—a different story entirely, insofar as foreign firms look to set up operations quickly.

As I described in chapter 2, call center firms have perfected procedures and technologies for quickly evaluating job applicants. Speed and flexibility with managing labor markets is key to their survival. A potential call agent walks in and produces proof that she possesses the requisite educational credential (usually a college diploma or transcript); she waits for an hour or so to take a standardized verbal exam; the results are immediately tallied and, if a sufficient score is reached, she undergoes a short in-person interview with an HR specialist. Assuming that goes well, she is asked to report to work as soon as the next day. So here is a job that pays triple or quadruple that of a local professional job, and it can be acquired in hours versus weeks or months—for many it is too tempting to resist.

My respondent Manny, for instance, was finishing up a bachelor's degree in marketing and aspired to work in an advertising firm in metro Manila. He was well aware of what his friends called the "instant money" of call center work, and of the "fast track" along which such work could be obtained. But he had encountered several excellent teachers in college and felt committed to making a name for himself in the field of marketing. "Before I graduated college, I promised to myself not to enter the call center," he said. But after graduation, he struggled to get his foot in the door of any major marketing firms. As a graduate of a nonelite university, he saw that it was mostly students from Ateneo or UP-Diliman who had the connections and who were receiving calls back. And so he shifted his plans:

> When it comes to a call center, it's actually the easiest job to find. It's *instant money*, you don't have to wait. In other companies you will apply, you still have to wait for a month and they will call you for an interview and you have to wait. So I went to [his call center company]. You just walk in, tell them you want to apply, they will test you. Before the day ends, they will let you know, and the following day you have your [employment] contract.

As Manny's case illustrates, embarking upon the middle path of call center work entails a compromise. It allows one to stay at home, in the Philippines, but at the cost of not maximizing one's potential earnings. Even unskilled manual labor abroad pays more than a call agent position in Manila, meaning that call agents will continue to feel the pull of the migration path.

Furthermore, in exchange for "instant money," you put on hold personal aspirations to pursue a career in the profession for which you trained. Many of my respondents reported feeling uncertainty as to exactly what sort of profession a call center agent represented. An engineering grad who ended up working an entry-level "minimum wage" job in an engineering firm still thinks of himself and presents himself to the world as a member of a respectable profession. He can still aspire to further training in his field, and even to eventually rise within the ranks. In contrast, call center work did not fit into the existing cultural framework of professional work, and so it was not obvious what sort of career it offered.

This status uncertainty was spelled out to me by Jaja, one of my research assistants and a recent college graduate with a degree in education. Like just about all of her classmates, she had little hope of becoming a teacher right away but, rather, faced a long slog of networking, board exams, and unpaid internships. I often asked her why she did not just apply to a call center rather than work for me at her alma mater's minimum wage pay scale. She would frown at my question. "There is not a single course that you will take during your college that will suit you to work in a call center company. Like many, I am thinking it is not a real profession. What do you do? You just answer calls. And where do you go from there?"

She acknowledged that working in a call center would provide her more income in the short-term. But she worried about the impression it would make for potential employers in her field. Working as a research assistant for an American professor would look good on her vita, but call center work might be, in her words, "difficult to defend." Many Filipinos, and especially older elites who control entry to established professions, might "have the impression that you are not loyal" to your field of study.

This chapter has documented how a legacy of failed governance in the Philippines produces for young Filipinos a dismaying choice. They can pursue prosperity by migrating abroad, or they can stay at home as an underpaid professional. It is this sharply bifurcated labor market that explains the allure of call center employment in the Philippines today. Becoming a call agent represents a *middle path* between these extremes of migration and financial insecurity. But even this middle path has costs, such as suboptimal earnings and a questionable professional identity. Who precisely opts to take the middle path? And why do they find it sensible to then stay on this path? Workers, as much as firms and states, are active mediators whose decisions and strategies shape the larger labor market.

5

Labor

SEEKING THE PHILIPPINE DREAM

FEW VISITORS, ARRIVING for the first time at Manila's Ninoy Aquino International Airport, feel that they have alighted in some sort of nirvana. Upon hailing a taxi outside the international arrivals terminal, they soon find that, unless they speak a smidgen of Tagalog, their driver will conveniently forget to turn on his cab's meter and then demand an exorbitant fee upon arrival at their hotel. The ride itself will take what feels like an eternity, owing to perpetual traffic jams along the city's main arteries. While stuck in traffic, new arrivals cannot but become aware that this is not a typical city of the global north or even of a wealthy part of Asia. A fog of air thick with diesel fumes and other unhealthful particulates permanently cloaks the city. Overcrowded squatter settlements dot the banks of the city's main river, the Pasig, which is so polluted that *The Lonely Planet* guidebook warns tourists against attempting "to take a plunge into [it]; you might see some truly horrible things right before your body dissolves."[1] My respondent Josh, an avid reader of fantasy novels, describes Manila—his city—as "Mordor" (the nightmarish city of Tolkien's *Lord of the Rings* trilogy).

Beauty, however, is in the eye of the beholder. An American call center executive arrives in Manila today and sees, beyond the smog, congestion, and slums, that veritable nirvana. During the drive from the airport, she finds her (air-conditioned) company car surrounded by open-air buses carrying legions of smartly dressed men—and women—to their workplaces. The sidewalks and metro trains teem with young Filipinos wearing their colleges' distinctive uniforms. On the radio stations that blare from every bus, our executive hears a heavy rotation of American pop songs (during the time of my fieldwork, one could scarcely go ten minutes without encountering the latest by Katie

Perry or Bruno Mars) and DJs switching seamlessly back and forth between Tagalog and English (suggesting that listeners are adept at doing so as well). And when she returns to the airport for her flight back to the United States, she will find hundreds upon hundreds of Filipinos queueing up to be shipped abroad as OFWs—overseas foreign workers. Such migrants have long been ambivalent about leaving their families and friends behind, but they could imagine no way of making ends meet while staying at home.

Call center firms, in search of cheap yet skilled and loyal workers, initially traveled to India. By the early 2000s, they were relocating en masse to the Philippines. In this chapter, I describe what voice capital found in the Philippines, along with what young Filipinos find in the new call centers. I argue that what best explains the rapid growth of the voice industry in the country is those firms' discovery of a labor pool that is a seeming mirror image of India's. Existing ethnographies (summarized in chapter 3) depict India's call centers as stigmas and steppingstones; female workers find their reputations at risk while men from well-off families use call centers to launch IT careers and move abroad. In the Philippines, in contrast, vocationally trained students—including women—are drawn to call center work as a strategic *alternative* to migration. Drawing on case studies of sixty call agents in Manila, I show how this initial attraction turns into a form of attachment (symbolized by low attrition from the industry). I furthermore show how attachment is gendered, resulting in three distinct profiles of call center employees.

Neither Stigma nor Steppingstone

For new college graduates in Manila, call center employment represents a middle path through the city's bifurcated labor market. It is an alternative to either going abroad as a migrant worker or laboring at home as an underpaid professional. Joy, the nurse deferred whose life story I summarized in the opening chapter, is a good example of the type of person who pursues this middle path. So, too, is a worker I'll call Glynnis. Joy and Glynnis were two of the sixty call center employees whose lives I followed for at least two years between 2012 and 2015 (the methods appendix describes in detail how I assembled this sample).

Glynnis was twenty-four years old and working as a directory assistance operator for an American firm when I last interviewed her in 2014. She had grown up in a single-parent household in a slum district of Manila, having "not known [her] father at all." Her mother sold candy and cigarettes on the street, and received some financial assistance from Glynnis's grandparents, who lived with them in a small one-room apartment.

Upon finishing high school, Glynnis decided that it was her obligation to no longer be a burden on her family. "By the time I turned sixteen," she recalled, "everything was not going right in our house and especially in our finances. I need[ed] to find work." For the next three years, she worked the evening shift at a Jollibee fast-food franchise and borrowed money from relatives abroad to pay for her tuition at a local public teachers college. As soon as she graduated, however, she put teaching on hold and instead began applying for call center jobs. She had no problem passing the exams. Although no one in her family had spoken English consistently at home, Glynnis had been an avid reader of English-language books from a young age. In college, she and her schoolmates devoted countless hours to honing their fluency in anticipation of the teaching board exam.

Her initial attraction to the call center industry, Glynnis readily admitted, had been strong but instrumental in nature. "Here in the Philippines," she explained, "when you say call center, it is equivalent to compensation." Four years after finishing college, this remained a suitable arrangement for Glynnis; she had yet to follow up on taking the board exam and launching a career in teaching.

This brief sketch of Glynnis's life illustrates four general characteristics of the call center labor force in the Philippines. First, women face no special barriers to entering it. Second, the vast majority of workers hail from the *masa* and not from elite families. Third, speaking English is a point of pride among employees. And fourth, most workers find that they grow attached to the industry over time.

Women Unafraid

The female call agents depicted in *Working the Night Shift*, Reena Patel's heart-wrenching account of harassment and danger in Mumbai, had no parallels in Manila. Joy, Glynnis, and my other female case studies reported no reservations about working for foreign call centers, even when it entailed traveling late at night. At some point during my interviews with Filipina call agents, I would raise the question of whether they worried for their physical safety or social reputations by working as call center agents. My respondents were consistent and adamant in their denials that their work led to any such negative reprisals.

For instance, none of my female case studies reported being harassed during their commutes to or from work. We do not find in Manila the company-operated busses that are used in Indian cities to safely and discretely transport female employees to and from their offices. Filipina call agents use public transportation (or the occasional taxi) to commute, even late at night or early in the morning, and often unaccompanied. Consider Glynnis's own description:

JEFF: Do you commute by yourself?
GLYNNIS: Yes.
JEFF: Do you feel safe when you travel to work at night time?
GLYNNIS: It's all right. You know, I don't mind because I believe here in the Philippines we have peace and order. I know I will not have to [physically] defend myself and that's why I'm not afraid. I really do not hide where I'm working.

Another worker, Kai, scoffed in response to my questions: "No, I'm not scared in the dark of burglars or rapists! I'm not scared at all."

In the following chapter I will describe in greater detail how female call agents manage their reputations outside of work. Suffice it for now to say that working as a call agent generates none of the pushback from men or stigmatization within the larger community that is reported in India. Confining women to the home as a way to signify status is simply not a tradition in mainstream Philippine culture. Half of all OFWs leaving the country, for instance, are women, while the Philippines' female labor force participation rate, at 51%, is almost double that of India's, at 27%.[2]

From the Masa

A second unique characteristic of the Philippine call center industry is how the jobs that it provides are used as a classed mobility project. Whereas Indian call centers are the province of young adults from well-off families, all sixty of my case studies hailed from humble backgrounds. This reflects the fact that, compared to India, the Philippines is less of a status or caste-stratified society. A handful of elite families control the bulk of the country's real estate, arable land, and commercial enterprises; and they have long controlled the country's political system as well. Status distinctions among those who cannot claim direct lineage to one of these elite families are minimal. When asked to describe their own class backgrounds, the *masa*, or the regular working people, is how my case studies responded.

The mobility strategies deployed by the Philippine *masa* differ from those of India's call center workers and aspiring IT professionals. There is no equivalent in Manila of the "IT mania" described by Biao,[3] nor does the Philippines have a parallel set of institutions to the famed Indian Technical Institutes. As I documented in the previous chapter, however, the Philippines does have a large number of quality colleges teaching traditional vocations such as nursing, accounting, and seafaring. For Filipino families, sending at least one child to obtain such a vocational degree is the default mobility strategy—the Philippine dream—as there is the expectation that she or he will then become a migrant worker and remit material support home to the extended family. My interviewee Theo described the Philippine dream to me this way. His parents had demanded that he enroll in nursing school, he explained, because "if nursing is in demand, all Filipinos will go there. *They think that when your child is a nurse, you will be rich*. He or she can go abroad and give the family a better life."[4]

That such a mobility strategy was the default among my sample of workers is demonstrated in table 5.1. It shows the college majors of all sixty of my respondents. With the exception of seven students who majored in English literature, political science, or other liberal arts, all had followed vocational courses. Nearly half (27 of 60) were nursing or business majors.

Table 5.1 Majors of Filipino Call Center Workers

Field/Major	# of Workers
Nursing	15
Business/Accounting	12
Education	7
Liberal Arts	7
IT/Computer Science	6
Hospitality/Tourism	5
Pharmacy	3
Other	5
Total	60

A key characteristic of this vocational mobility strategy is that it is almost always parents or extended family members who select students' majors for them. As one worker recounted, "*Tita* [my aunt] sent me into pharmacy, so I was obliged to study it." There are several important implications for the subsequent structuring of the call center labor market. One is that graduating students often find that their skill sets do not match current demand in the labor market. The parents, aunts, uncles, and grandparents who pay tuition bills select vocational fields that they predict will offer the most secure and lucrative job prospects *based upon their own experience*. The danger is that *titas* and *lolas* are not necessarily the most well-informed about current and future labor market trends. Many graduates find that there is an oversupply of potential workers in their field of study.

Consider the case of nursing, the most common major field among my respondents. The longstanding and widespread belief among Filipinos, which Theo articulated, that a nursing degree is a ticket abroad and thus to prosperity, is increasingly untrue. By the time of my study, in the early 2010s, the country had a surplus of nursing graduates sitting around on "standby."[5] Both the hard and soft skills learned in nursing schools are in turn quite transposable to entry-level positions in the call center industry. These include becoming competent with basic office programs such as Microsoft Word, Excel, and Access; listening empathetically to clients; and reading technical manuals and course books written in English.

Another unintended consequence of the Philippine family-guided vocational strategy is a tenuous commitment to one's field of study. Quite simply, young people who are "obliged" to declare a given major are easily lured away from their supposed vocation. Consider the case of Christine, the youngest daughter in a family of four children. Her parents owned a small farm on the rural outskirts of Manila, and had sent her to college specifically to study agriculture and economics. Christina remembered feeling immense pressure, as the youngest sibling, to continue her family's agricultural endeavors. During college she took the bus home every weekend to walk the field with her father. As she described her dilemma at the time:

> My brother is a nurse in Canada. My sister works in the government. My other brother is a tennis coach in Australia. Like, oh my God! My father, every time he goes to the farm, there is no one to go with him. So, I thought I would have to be the one to go with him.

A call center job offered Christina a way out of this dilemma. It allowed her to stay in Manila and visit her parents regularly. She could also send home money each month for her father to hire adequate hands to keep up with the farm. Christina, who in her skinny jeans and designer shirts looks as far from a farmer as one could imagine, explained: "My major was not my choice. It's not my calling for my profession. It was my dad's choice." It's easy in this context to see how a young member of the *masa* would be attracted to call center employment.

And what about those who graduate not from vocational programs but from one of Manila's elite universities? All evidence suggests that the call center industry does not attract these elite graduates, nor does it desire them. I heard this repeatedly from students of these schools and from HR personnel in call center firms. One of the latter explained that she is wary to hire someone with what she calls "the Ateneo accent." This puzzled me because at the time I was teaching at Ateneo, perhaps the most elite university in the country, and knew that its students prided themselves on their ability to speak English with few grammatical errors and without a strong Philippine accent—seemingly the exact traits that a call center would be looking for!

When I asked her what she meant by "the Ateneo accent," the HR executive elaborated: "The wealthy accent. I hear it, then I know that they grew up in a wealthy family and dress with signature [branded, Western] clothes. They are really singled out from everyone else there." Only rarely do elite students apply at her call center, she went on to say, and even more rarely does she call them in for a final interview, regardless of how well they did on the standardized verbal exam. She reasons that they are planning to use call center work as a way to make a quick buck and will quit soon thereafter. She was even adamant that applications from elite students temporarily spike right after a new generation of iPhone or video gaming system is announced.

English Acceptable

Among Filipino call center workers there is very little pushback to speaking English and interacting with Americans. On the contrary, my respondents emphasized that blending in with other cultures and languages is for them a basic strategy of everyday life. Theo explained, "We Filipinos are very flexible when it comes to language; it's automatic for us," while Glynnis stated, "Whatever is the language of the environment, we can actually adapt to it right away. It's easy to adapt." Another agent, Rosario, explained, "I think many Filipinos . . . we easily adapt to any accent that we need to adapt. We have this thing like mimicry. We're good at it."

My respondents described multiple motivations and methods for becoming fluent in English. The majority (48 of 60) reported not speaking or learning English in their childhood home but, rather, Tagalog or some other Philippine language. All recounted, however, at least some degree of oral comprehension from an early age, mainly due to exposure to Western music and television.

Typically, the first systematic attempt to speak English occurred in the public school system. Melyn recalled that "even if we're in elementary [school], our teachers taught us how to speak simple English. Like 'Good Morning, Ma'am. How are you today? Have a nice day.'" Glen stated that in high school, he became involved with "oratorical competitions, extemporaneous speeches. . . . So I think that honed me to speak in English a little bit. Not fluent, I guess, but I can speak well." And Rodalyn described how in college, she and her classmates would monitor and even fine each other for speaking in Tagalog:

RODALYN: It started in first year college. I think that's the reason why it made me good in speaking English because we are trying to have this policy: English only policy, EOP. If we speak in Tagalog, we'll pay one peso.

JEFF: Why were you using this policy?

RODALYN: We thought to ourselves, English is our universal language and we really need that especially once we try to find a good job.

While all Philippine schools provide basic instruction in English, some students, as Rodalyn's story makes clear, are further motivated to master the language. They desire to read complex material, write with flawless grammar, and speak without a "Pinoy accent." For many respondents, this was part of a self-conscious strategy to distinguish themselves from their peers.

This was certainly true among my respondents who identified as gay. As the case of Belle, described in chapter 1, illustrates, speaking English well serves as a marker of status within the Philippine gay community. But there are other ways in which English fluency can serve to distinguish oneself. Joy's trajectory in learning English, summarized in the opening chapter, is a good example. After being placed in her aunt's household as a child, Joy's older female cousin began encouraging her to master English. As Joy recounted:

It was my cousin's influence actually. She was telling me, "We should not watch Filipino cartoons," and I would ask, "Why?" She's older than me and she said, "Because it's so yucky, it's for the poor kids." "Okay, we won't watch."

As the cousins grew up together, they began to label themselves *arte* (a play on the English word *artsy*). "We were the *arte* girls," Joy explained, "Dramatic, pretentious, and posh . . . we were so *arte*!" In addition to dressing fashionably, speaking English is a key aspect of being *arte*, and so Joy recalled that she would:

Read English pocketbooks and write the words I don't understand. Then I'm gonna look them up in the dictionary and write the meaning. Then I'm gonna try to use the new words that I've learned. I was very happy when others would notice it like, "Oh, the words you are using are not just simple words." A word is more posh if it's in English.

Yet another motivation for honing one's English was to pursue personal interests, hobbies, and passions. Dan, for example, described being a "nature fanatic" as a young boy and wanting to build a miniature zoo in his yard. At the local swap meet, however, the only nature books were in English, and so he would have his aunt, a teacher, tutor him how to read them. Another worker admitted to being "a nerd at heart" who had long been "addicted" to the Harry Potter series of books. Tagalog translations were not available, and so he worked his way through each book in the series using Google's translate function to search for and learn unfamiliar English words. Yet another felt that "the biggest factor that helped me become conversational in English is that we Catholics want to read the Bible in English." To feel adequate as a Christian, she studied extremely hard outside of school to master English grammar.

Finally, a handful of respondents credited the need to communicate with people living abroad as an incentive to learn English. Donessa, for example, remembered being embarrassed as a child by her poor English: "In elementary school, we need to speak English, but at that time I'm not that confident because most of the Filipinos are fault-finders. So when you pronounce one word not correctly they will laugh at you." However, when her sister married an American man, became pregnant, and relocated to the United States, Donessa overcame her fears. She knew that her future nephew would speak English and so she endeavored to master the language; the thought of being a *tita* who could not communicate with her *pamangkin lalaki* (nephew) was too much for her to bear. Gica, who worked in the same call center as Donessa, also mastered English to communicate with men abroad. In her case, she was actively seeking foreign friends (and possibly boyfriends) on various online dating sites and chat rooms. As she recounted "I practiced English because I have a lot of friends abroad, they are actually Americans. We chat about anything out of the blue, like the weather, families, government, politics. Sometimes I am on [the internet] like 24/7."

Sticking in Voice

Undoubtedly the most distinctive characteristic of the Philippine call center labor force is its low attrition from the industry. As I summarized in chapter 2, publicly available data suggest that employee turnover rates from Philippine call centers are extremely low by global standards. All the evidence I collected during my fieldwork supports this idea. Call center executives invariably downplayed accents and cultural affinities, pointing instead to the fact that Filipino employees are less prone to constantly resign and leave the industry. As one such executive explained, "In India, your staff is always looking to move up out of the call center or [out of] basic encoding because he's dreaming to be a programmer in Silicon Valley. That's his end game." She continued, "But here [in the Philippines], I'm under two percent [turnover] at some sites. You just don't have to deal with the hassle of hiring constantly."

Over the course of my four-year study period, only three of my sixty call agent case studies left the industry entirely. Eight were promoted from a call agent position to the level of supervisor or trainer. Six left the industry for a brief duration but returned. Twenty-two moved laterally within the industry, to another account or firm that offered a better salary or better hours. Certainly this attests to the fact that the initial allure of call center employment develops into a sustained attachment for just about all Filipinos who choose the middle path. But who takes this path in the first place?

The Middle Path

The labor pool that voice capital discovered in the Philippines differed from the labor pool in India. For college-educated Filipinos, call center work is neither a stigma nor a steppingstone. It is a sensible—and apparently sustainable—employment strategy given the other options available to them. In this section I will highlight two surprising findings about those Filipinos who take the middle path of call center work. First, the *actual* call center labor force differs from the *potential* labor force in terms of *gender* (the term denoting one's current gender identity rather than the sex one was assigned at birth). Cisgender women such as Joy (whose gender identities currently accord with the sex they were assigned at birth) and transgendered persons such as Belle (who were assigned the male sex at birth but who have since transitioned to a gender identity that, in line with their own usage, I label as gay) are overrepresented in Manila's call centers, while cisgender men are underrepresented. Second, there is significant variation among Manila's call center workers in terms of their financial resources and obligations, their experience of call center work, and their ultimate career aspirations. To account for this variation, I will map out three archetypes of call center workers in the Philippines—three pathways to attachment.

Gender on the Middle Path

The modal call center worker in metro Manila is young, ambitious, and college-educated. To see this one need only observe the crowds of smartly dressed twentysomethings file into and out of the city's call centers every evening and morning. Among the sixty workers in my sample, the average age was twenty-four, with a range from nineteen to forty-eight; only six were over thirty-five years of age. Women and openly gay persons, however, are much more likely to be call agents than would be expected, given the eligible population (i.e., all college graduates in Manila).

To estimate the extent of this imbalance, I asked all of my sixty respondents to name each member of their "batch," or cohort, of fellow call agents. As a new hire, one spends weeks in full-time training with one's "batch-mates," after which each batch then becomes a "team" on the call center floor. Batch-mates also typically spend a good deal of time socializing before and after work. Interviewees could thus easily recall by name all their batch-mates. In the event of a gender-ambiguous name, I would ask for clarification; I also asked each of my interviewees whether any of their batch-mates openly presented as gay. Two pairs of interviewees had been part of the same batch, and so I ended up with estimates of fifty-eight distinct call center cohorts.

The average size of a cohort was twenty-two (giving estimates of 1,276 call center agents total). In a typical cohort, seventeen workers were cisgender women ("female"), three were transgendered ("gay"), and two were cisgender men ("male"). As I discuss in chapter 7, mainstream Philippine society lacks a term, such as lesbian, to denote women who have relationships with other

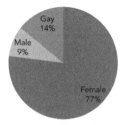

FIGURE 5.1 Percentages of the three categories of workers in Manila's call centers.

women; as of my fieldwork, gayness as a category referred exclusively to those assigned the male sex at birth but who subsequently transition to an alternate gender identity. Based on my interviewees' recollections of their batches, I illustrate in figure 5.1 my estimate of the overall gender composition of Manila's call center workforce.

These percentages diverge considerably from what we know about the potential labor pool. Filipina women constituted 52% of college graduates during the study period, yet they held approximately three-fourths of call center jobs.[6] Data are not available on the percentage of college graduates in metro Manila who identify as gay/transgendered, but it is unlikely to be as high as 14%. Straight men, who make up only a tenth of call center agents, are certainly underrepresented relative to their availability in the potential labor pool.[7]

Manila's call center labor market is largely homogenous in terms of age, class, and educational attainment, though unexpectedly heterogeneous in regard to gender. This led me to consider whether female, gay, and male call agents differ in terms of: (a) their larger strategies for navigating the labor market; (b) the uses to which they put their call center paychecks, given their resources and obligations; and (c) their overall experience of call center work. All three of these concepts were too complex to be reduced to a single piece of information or indicator. Yet I did seek some way to capture meaningful distinctions among my respondents. I thus coded each of their life history narratives, assembled across multiple interview sessions, so as to create eight key attributes, or binary variables (see table 5.2).

It is not my intention to reduce the lives of those whom I studied to a series of 0s and 1s. Throughout this book I present multiple case studies showing how call center work makes sense within the context of individuals' overall life situations. Across these stories a picture emerges of young Filipinos skillfully using call center jobs to resolve—or at least manage—dilemmas in their lives. The risk in looking at only these stories, however, is that we fail to

Table 5.2 Three Concepts for Classifying Call Agents

Concept	Attributes/ Variables
Labor market strategies	CC.CAREER PROF.ASPR ABROAD
Resources and obligations	BRDWNR SAVE COUPLE
Job quality	CALLER.NICE PAY.FAIR

see meaningful distinctions among workers in terms of the specific dilemmas they face and the strategies they use to deal with them. By coding for and then mapping the various attributes of individuals shown in table 5.2, I will demonstrate that there are three distinct pathways into call center work. In the three following chapters, I show how each of these pathways becomes a stable mode of attachment.

Labor Market Strategies

The concept that I call *labor market strategies* captures how workers navigate the three career possibilities that present themselves to college graduates in the Philippines: joining the call center industry, pursuing a "legitimate" profession in the Philippines, and migrating abroad. At the conclusion of each interview, and if it weren't already apparent, I would ask my subject where, in an ideal world, he or she imagined him- or herself in five years.

The responses I received to my "ideal future" question revealed uncertainty among Filipinos as to whether working in the call center industry can become a permanent and stable career. This was reflected in the variable CC.CAREER. Some of my respondents felt strongly that they could and would like to do so. A twenty-four-year-old female call agent, for instance, stated that "I like working at [her call center company], and if I will be given the chance to stay, I will stay." Exactly half (30 of 60) of my case studies did in fact hope to stay in the call center industry over the long term.[8]

Other respondents aspired to eventually move into a more traditional profession in the Philippines—a variable I labeled PROF.ASPR. I, for instance, coded a worker positively because she described her career aspirations as follows:

> It may sound dramatic or whatever, but I've always wanted to be a teacher as my career. Five years from now, I want to be a college professor, which means I will have done something with my college degree. So, in short, I have a career plan, but if I stay in a call center . . . I don't know.

Just under half of my case studies (27 of 60) continued to aspire to a professional career beyond call center work.

Yet others envisioned themselves outside of the country in five years. So, if a respondent articulated a desire to go abroad, and especially if he or she could describe concrete steps by which this would happen (such as paying fees to a specific agency or applying for a special visa), I coded the individual positively for the variable ABROAD. In contrast, a worker who made a statement such as, "when I was younger, I thought about it all the time. But as of now, I don't think about it. I'm focused on everyday living," was coded as a 0. On the whole, just over half (31 of 60) of my interviewees imagined themselves abroad in five years' time.

A basic count reveals more labor market strategies than respondents, which is to say that it was not uncommon for an individual to have multiple plans in play. Roel, for instance, was determined to turn his bachelor's degree into a teaching career. He spent his days interning as a math instructor at a public school and studying to take the board exam that qualifies one to be an elementary school teacher in the Philippines. At night he worked in a call center, where he prided himself on his perfect attendance record and top-notch "metrics." Roel didn't particularly like working as a call agent and, needless to say, was constantly exhausted owing to a lack of sleep. But he remained open to the idea of a career in the voice industry. Top-performing agents in his company, he explained, could apply for positions as trainers, which would be a great opportunity to do work related to his college training. In short, Roel was pursuing simultaneously two strategies (a call center career and a professional dream), though only with extreme effort. On the whole, twenty-nine of my sixty case studies were doing so—while one (extremely sleep deprived) worker was pursuing all three!

Resources and Obligations

Individuals' labor market strategies should be related to their current *resources and obligations*. In fact, as my study progressed, I found that my respondents were putting their salaries toward different purposes. All reported using their paychecks to provide for their own basic needs, such as food and household expenses. But there was variation in terms of where the remainder went and why—variation which I attempted to capture in three ways.

First, and most important, is the question of whether or not workers use their salaries to provide regular financial support for others. Filipinos who do so refer to themselves as "breadwinners," and I follow their terminology by labeling this variable BRDWNR. Having children made one highly likely to identify as a breadwinner. Just over a third of my sample had at least one child, and nearly all these individuals reported devoting a substantial portion of their pay to providing for their offspring. But there are, as I will describe in detail in the following chapter, a variety of other pathways to breadwinner status in Philippine society. For now, suffice it to say that it is quite common to find wage-earners supporting various others in their kin networks, such as parents, siblings, cousins, nieces, and nephews. On the whole, I classified just over half (32 of 60) of my respondents as breadwinners.

It made sense to assume that being a breadwinner would hinder one's ability to use surplus earnings to accumulate savings. All my respondents reported having bank accounts and ATM cards, as it is common for call center firms to issue paychecks via electronic direct deposit. And just about all desired to build savings—as security in the event of an emergency; to pay for quality-of-life improvements, such as better housing or transport options; to pursue other labor market pathways via postsecondary schooling, board exams, or agency fees to find work abroad; or to simply take a vacation. Yet only a minority (23 of 60) of my respondents reported being able to maintain any significant savings (a variable I labeled SAVE); the remainder described lives of subsisting paycheck to paycheck or of being in debt.

An important factor that seemed to help match one's income to one's obligations and aspirations was being coupled (typically in a romantic relationship) with another wage-earner. I called this variable COUPLE, and found substantial variation on it. Just about half of my interviewees were in a relationship, though only half of these (i.e., a quarter of my total interviewee pool) reported that their partners independently earned money and thus constituted a resource, rather than a responsibility, within the primary group.

The importance of being coupled with another wage-earner can be illustrated with two examples. On the one hand, is Benji, a twenty-six-year-old call center agent who was married with one child, a daughter. Benji's wife had an office job with a foreign NGO (nongovernmental organization) in Manila. Though it did not pay as well as Benji's call center job, the couple used all her salary and a portion of his to pay their rent and monthly food bill. This left them with a small but not insignificant surplus each month, which they put into a modest but growing savings account. The year before our interview, they had purchased a used car, which allowed them to escape the hassle of relying on Manila's inefficient and uncomfortable public transport system. Benji's wife was able to take an occasional yoga class, while their ongoing savings were being earmarked to ensure their daughter a "bright future."

The situation of Benji and his wife was quite different from that of Quiny, also a call agent in Manila. Quiny became pregnant at the age of twenty by her boyfriend, who was married but separated from his wife. Because of this, the two could not marry or live together. The boyfriend worked as a mechanic and told Quiny that he was devoting his (minimum wage) salary to saving up to pay the steep fee to have his marriage annulled (divorce, recall, is illegal in the Philippines). Quiny in turn lived with her son, her parents, and her four siblings in what she called "squatter conditions." Furthermore, as a daughter living at home, she was expected to turn her call center salary over to her parents, who use it to pay for her siblings' tuition and other expenses. Such obligations will continue to weigh her down until her boyfriend can pay for the annulment and the two of them can establish an independent household together.

The Experience of Call Center Work

I discovered variation among my respondents regarding not only their long-term labor market strategies, resources and obligations but also in terms of how they assessed the *overall experience* of working in a call center. Initially I would ask my respondents how stressful they found their jobs to be, but soon found that everyone reported finding the work to be at least somewhat stressful. In line with my own ethnographic experience as a call center agent, no one finds the work of answering calls in quick succession for hours on end and often all night long to be easy or stress-free.

By probing further, however, I discovered two sources of variation in how workers experienced and made judgments about their work. The first had to do with whether they felt that, on the whole, they were treated respectfully by callers (my variable CALLER.NICE). About half of my respondents (29 of 60) felt that even though their work was mentally and physically trying, they generally had courteous interactions on the phones.[9] Some examples of remarks which led me to code the CALLER.NICE variable positively were: "My callers are not abusive"; "Our callers where I work, they don't get angry"; and "For me, yes, callers are quite considerate. When they are irate or they are upset, they swear. But after they say that, they will apologize and they will acknowledge that it is not my fault . . . so it's understandable." In contrast, an interviewee received the code CALLER.RUDE if they characterized callers as, on the whole, disrespectful. One respondent's discussion of her ongoing experience on the phones is a good example: "They'll talk to you negative, like 'you're a bitch' . . . something like that. It's my first time to hear some Americans say something like that. So when I take calls, it is like a very, very hard time for me. I am often crying 'coz I can't take those words."

The other major difference in how my respondents judged the quality of their jobs was in their perception of the salary they earned. Here, the majority (49 of 60) reported feeling that their salary was fair (PAY.FAIR). This seemed to result from the fact that call center jobs were compared to minimum-wage office jobs, rather than to the salary that say a migrant worker might earn. "It's a good salary," Quiny thus reported. "BPO companies here in the Philippines, if you'll compare them to office jobs or fast-food [jobs], the salary is so different, like seventy percent more." Roel was similarly systematic in his accounting: "Yes, our salary is fair. When you compute it hourly, we actually earn more than one hundred pesos per hour. I am comparing that to simple jobs here, [which pay] three hundred pesos for the day." Respondents who were unsatisfied with their pay (PAY.UNFAIR) in turn tended to compare their specific call center company to other ones. Tina, for instance, worked for an American firm, and felt that "my company is too large to pay just 17,000 [per month]. There are other companies who will offer higher, up to 30,000."

The Labor Pool in a Picture

My case studies of sixty workers in metro Manila's call center industry revealed considerable heterogeneity. Women dominate the profession numerically, but there is variation in terms of career strategies, resources and obligations, and job satisfaction, as table 5.3 shows. To discern how these various characteristics of call center agents fit into larger patterns, I could have proceeded by comparing individual variable to individual variable. It can easily be seen in table 5.3, for instance, that the women in my study were more likely to be

Table 5.3 Descriptive Statistics for the Sample of Call Center Workers

	CC. CAREER	PROF-ASPIRE	ABROAD	BRDWNR	SAVE	COUPLE	CALLER. NICE	PAY. FAIR
Female ($n = 30$)	17	12	15	24	7	8	20	25
Gay ($n = 15$)	7	10	13	5	6	0	2	9
Male ($n = 15$)	6	5	2	3	10	6	7	14

breadwinners than were the men, and that gay workers were less likely than either women or men to be in a wage-earning couple relationship. Instead, I turned to a statistical technique—correspondence analysis—that allows me to illustrate in a single picture the relationships among all these variables simultaneously.

Correspondence analysis (CA) is a "method of data analysis for representing tabular data graphically," given that one has categorical data.[10] Basically, CA transforms a data matrix, or a contingency table such as table 5.3, into one or more two-dimensional graphs (often called maps). It does so by "analyz[ing] the association between two or more categorical variables, [then] representing the categories of the variables as points in a low-dimensional space. Categories with similar distributions will be represented as points that are close in space."[11] CA is at root an *exploratory or mapping technique* whose primary purpose is to discern patterns within a dataset that are otherwise hidden from the naked eye.

Correspondence analysis can be used to map the structure of large data sets, as the sociologist Pierre Bourdieu did in his landmark study *Distinction*.[12] In a series of two-dimensional graphs, Bourdieu depicted the results of a survey of the French citizenry, showing how certain attributes of individuals, such as their education, tastes in music, and culinary choices, tend to cluster. But there is no reason that CA cannot be used to make explicit patterns latent in smaller, qualitative datasets.[13] Bourdieu himself advocated using the technique to analyze statistically data sets generated via "in-depth interviews or ethnographic observations."[14] This is because CA does not claim to test hypotheses about statistically significant interactions among variables or to make inferences to a larger population, and so does not rely on a minimum sample size or random selection of respondents.

Figure 5.2 is the two-dimensional correspondence analysis map that captures the greatest amount of variation in my data.[15] It depicts in a single image every characteristic of all sixty of my case studies. For maximum exposition, I have disjunctively coded several of my variables. That is, every respondent was coded as either a breadwinner (BRDWNR) or not a breadwinner (NO.BRDWNR); currently saving (SAVE) or not currently saving (NOSAVE); coupled (COUPLE) or single (SINGLE); treated respectfully by callers (CLR. NICE) or not (CLR.RUDE), and satisfied with their pay (PAY.FAIR) or not (PAY.UNFAIR).

There are multiple ways to interpret a correspondence analysis map; here I will use a basic technique of discerning substantively meaningful "clusterings."[16] Figure 5.2, I argue, shows that the three main gender categories of Filipino call center agents—women, gays, and men—differ so dramatically in terms of their attributes as to constitute three distinct clusters, or archetypes, of call center employees.

Female workers, underlined at the middle bottom of the map, constitute a distinctive cluster defined by their status as breadwinners, their inability to save, their perception of respectful treatment at work, and their aspirations to make a career of working in the call center industry. Gay agents, underlined

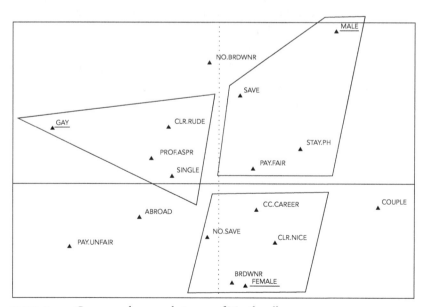

FIGURE 5.2 Correspondence analysis map of Manila call agents.

on the far left side of the map, constitute a second distinct subset of call center agents. They are defined by their single status, their aspirations to work as professionals, and their sense of being treated disrespectfully at work. Straight men define the upper right quadrant of the map. They occupy this space along with the variables for intending to stay in the Philippines, being satisfied with one's salary, and currently saving money. These groupings, I must point out, have a high degree of face validity. It instantly struck me upon generating the map that it captures the three main archetypes of call center agents I encountered in the Philippines, both as formal interviewees and during the course of my fieldwork generally.

This chapter has shown how workers, as much as firms or states, are active mediators in the construction of a global labor market for voice. The underlying bargain behind offshored call center jobs is clear: if you can speak English well enough, you can do stressful work for decent pay. Yet workers in different locales respond to this deal in different ways. All evidence suggests that in India, any initial attraction between call center firms and workers soon subsides. In the Philippines, in contrast, call center jobs become a "middle path" between migration abroad and poverty at home. Furthermore, my mapping of the Philippine labor force suggests that there are three distinct mechanisms through which the initial attraction of call center work stabilizes into an ongoing attachment between labor and voice capital. These, I argue, correspond to three archetypes of call center employees in the Philippines. The three chapters to follow elaborate these archetypes. Chapter 6 describes the female breadwinners whom I will refer to as *responsible* workers, while chapters 7 and 8 focus upon *restless* gay agents and *rooted* straight men. These three archetypes demonstrate that labor's attachment to capital derives from multiple sources; they constitute three distinct pathways to low attrition in the industry as a whole.

Three Archetypes

6

Responsible Women

DURING MY FIELDWORK I attended an "outsourcing summit" at a posh hotel located on Manila's waterfront. The point of this annual conference, sponsored by the Business Process Association of the Philippines (BPAP), is to bring together foreign firms, Philippine government officials, local business leaders, and other industry stakeholders. The keynote address was to be delivered by then-president Benigno Aquino III. Several hours late, the president arrived in the main exhibition hall and, reading from a teleprompter, delivered a short speech praising effusively the country's call center industry. It had created jobs, boosted the nation's GDP, and brought much needed foreign investment to the Philippines. When Aquino finished his speech, the crowd of conference attendees offered a prolonged if polite applause. Fred Ayala, scion of a large landholding family in the Philippines and then president of BPAP, stood off to the side of the stage during the president's speech and shook his hand vigorously as he left, both men flanked by security guards.

After a short interlude, the conference program resumed. The next speaker was a woman named Myrna, who headed a small company based in Davao, a city in the southern Philippines. By now, after the buzz of President Aquino's visit, most conference attendees had settled back at their tables and dived into their meals. Myrna began her talk, and it was as different as can be from the one that the president had delivered. It was personal. She projected onto an overhead screen photographs of herself as a child and her childhood home. We see a small girl in a bathing suit and homemade snorkel mask, standing in front of a simple hut made of thatched palm leaves. "To start with, I am a woman from the *masa*, from the poorest of the poor. I am the eldest of six children," Myrna narrated, "and I grew up in a very small undeveloped fishing village. Some of my earliest memories are the tears in my mother's eyes when we would go hungry. I would dive alone into the sea to gather seaweed and seashells to help feed my family."

By now, most conference participants, and especially those from the Philippines, had ceased their small talk and turned their attention toward the main stage. Myrna described how, as a teenager, she had strategized how best to help her family. "Like many other women born into poverty in the Philippines, my only chance to fulfill my dreams for my family was to go overseas to seek employment. I left my two children behind and spent twenty years working as a domestic helper [in Hong Kong] raising other people's children." One of the children in her care, Jonathon, taught her to type, use the internet, and even do some basic coding. At this point, she said, "I started dreaming. I dreamed of coming home and starting a business and of becoming a job creator. I did not want another mother or father to follow in my footsteps, to suffer the same pain and anguish of being separated from their families. I now know that I was envisioning business process outsourcing without knowing what BPO was." The crowd, previously sedate, was now animated. Some were standing up, and many shouted words of encouragement.

Myrna then described how in 2006 she had returned to the Philippines from Hong Kong and started a call center. Although it wasn't a large business, it provided her a steady income and allowed her to employ a dozen or so employees. Despite the moderate success of her venture, she had a powerful message for conference attendees:

> When I dove alone into the sea at the age of ten to gather seaweed to help feed my family, that was not heroic—that was survival. When I left my family to go overseas for twenty years, that was not heroic. That was a tragic necessity to help my family break the cycle of poverty. But when I returned to the Philippines and started a BPO that created jobs: that was heroic. What you are doing for our country is heroic, I applaud you.

At the end of her speech, the crowd stood and delivered an extended applause. It seemed there was hardly a dry eye in the place.

The model, indeed the archetypical, employee in Manila's call center industry is a female breadwinner. (As I established in the prior chapter, three-fourths of call center agents are female; as I will report in this chapter, the majority of these consider themselves to be breadwinners). The Philippine state, the many outsourcing firms operating in the country, and even BPAP all vigorously market call center work throughout the Philippines. In Manila, call center job advertisements literally wallpaper the train stations, bus stops, and alleyways. Not all potential workers heed the call, however. Women such as Myrna, obligated to "feed their families" but facing tangible obstacles to doing so, are especially motivated to pursue call center jobs—and tend to persist in them.

This chapter is divided into four sections. The first describes how call center work represents for women a positive stigma, a paradoxical concept that makes sense only once we grasp what it means to occupy the role of breadwinner in Philippine society. The next section offers a case study of one worker—*tita* Hannah—whose life illustrates how for breadwinners a call center job can serve as a *lifeline* out of poverty. The third section catalogues the various pathways through which a Filipina comes to find herself in the category of breadwinner. It emphasizes how gendered traditions, dispositions, and institutions channel one into a role the dominant logic of which is self-sacrifice. The final section links the various strands of the argument through the folk concept of *diskarte*, which denotes the way in which one strategically maneuvers to manage a difficult life situation.

Call Center as Positive Stigma

My review in chapter 3 of the ethnographic literature on India's call center industry highlighted a robust finding: women who endeavor to work in the industry are stigmatized. Longstanding patriarchal norms define working women as disrespectful and sources of shame for their families. The fact that call center jobs entail working the night shift only further raises a specter of impropriety. The women workers interviewed in these studies reported pushback from male family members, friends, and neighbors—to the point that many become fearful for their safety. This was not the case in the Philippines. The main worries for women workers and their families were health and appearance, not personal safety or public shame. Rodalyn, for instance, reported that her father frequently reminded her not to use her salary for unhealthy consumption: "He thinks that if you're in the call center, you're a smoker and a drinker, but I'm not." And Christina, whose family has a history of diabetes, described how her grandmother's pestering led her to start worrying that, "More money means more treating myself to food, and then getting fat."

Filipina call agents were quick with rationales as to why their jobs are actually beneficial for them. Several argued that working the night shift gives them time and flexibility to accomplish tasks that can only be done during the day, such as shopping or spending time with their families. As Christina explained:

> [The night shift]'s not giving me troubles. I think it works for me on my end because I can do some chores at home. I can do some other work at home. So I think it's good.

Gica described how, far from feeling self-conscious in public, she takes pride in her status as a call center worker:

> The thing is, when you work for [a call center], you are projecting yourself as a confident and money-earning person. So when you are on the street or on the train, the perception of those around you is positive when you work in a call center.

Gica's statement in fact suggests the true dilemma faced by Filipina call agents: managing *privately* the perception that one is a "money-earning person." In public, on the street or in the train, this can serve as a source of esteem. Within one's personal networks, however, being perceived as a high-earning individual can lead to constant requests for financial favors. These can range from cash loans, to the payment of bills, to the expectation that one will "treat" the table when eating out at a restaurant. The situation of call center workers parallels that of migrant workers, in that both groups are often inundated with requests for money from various friends and kin.[1] But call center agents earn less than migrant workers, and it is presumably easier to deny (or ignore) requests for assistance sent via email or Facebook as compared to requests made face-to-face. Quotes such as the following led me to conclude that call center work constitutes a *positive stigma* for my female respondents:

> [My relatives] only see the salary and *they think like I'm a millionaire.* They keep telling me to buy a house for my mom. (Christia)

> When you work in BPO, *your friends now view you as an ATM.* They think you are rich. (Queenie)

> Most of us, we are earning more than an ordinary employee. But then [friends and relatives] think you *can buy whatever you want, right*? (Tam)

> You asked before whether my family is OK with me working in BPO? Of course they are! *I support them.* (Glynnis)

Call center employment constitutes a positive stigma to the extent that the worker occupies the role of breadwinner. "Breadwinner" is a folk term in the Philippines, and it was widely used by my respondents to describes themselves and/or others. Their usage of the term differs from how it is generally defined in the West, however, in several important ways.

To start, standard thinking in the West situates "breadwinning" in the context of the *nuclear family*—that is, "parents with children."[2] A spouse who works in order to materially support children or a nonworking spouse is considered that family's breadwinner. But the family unit is not so bounded in the Philippines. A lack of sex education and difficulties with procuring contraception mean that average family sizes are larger here (at 4.4 persons per household) than in a country such as the United States (with 2.7 persons per household). As important, in the Philippines, one's primary kin group is not confined to one's nuclear family, and so neither are obligations to provide material assistance. For instance, siblings are considered "allies [who] are supposed to be mutually helpful" throughout the life course by providing financial support to one another and committing to care for one another's children.[3] The definition of "sibling," furthermore, is expansive, such that first and even second-generation cousins are often thought of as akin to brothers and sisters. Concretely, this means that "not just the children of one's siblings, but the children of one's . . . cousins become one's nephews and nieces."[4] Then there is a strong cultural norm that one should support one's parents in their old age. The end result is that the total number of persons whom a breadwinner feels obligated to support can be immense.

A further difference in how the breadwinner role is defined in the Philippines has to do with its gendering. In the West, it is usually assumed that a family's primary wage-earner is its breadwinner, and thus changes in gendered labor-force participation will change breadwinner expectations. For instance, the mid-twentieth century American model assumed that men would enter the labor force and women would stay at home to tend house and care for children. This "male breadwinner" model unraveled as female labor force participation increased, and today a "dual breadwinner" model prevails.[5]

In the Philippines, in contrast, a "female breadwinner" model has long prevailed. Unlike in other parts of East and Southeast Asia, where female offspring are considered a material burden on the family, "women [in the Philippines] are largely defined positively, as more reliable and responsible than men . . . as providers for the continuity and security of the family."[6] Studies have shown that up to 95% of low-income households in metro Manila rely on a woman's earnings as an income source; 80% of registered enterprises throughout the country are headed by women; and Filipino parents report a strong preference for daughters over sons.[7] Ultimately, it is women, and *ates* (eldest daughters) in particular, who are expected to "study conscientiously, keep stable jobs, and provide support" to kin.[8] One could easily interpret all this as evidence that Philippine society is gender egalitarian or even matriarchal. In a broad historical and anthropological perspective, this may be a defensible reading. But given contemporary economic and political realities, such a reading would be inappropriate.

The onus placed on Filipinas to serve as breadwinners for their extended kin too often constitutes a hardship. This is because there is no assumption in the Philippines of a secular welfare state whose mission is to provide its citizens with a baseline level of material security. In the West, and even in liberal market economies such as the United States, multiple social policies and programs mitigate risks for families. Universal health care, for instance, protects the domestic unit from financial ruin in the event of a medical emergency; programs such as social security and Medicare in the United States ensure that the elderly receive basic material support; while a panoply of benefits and subsidies protect children, the disabled, and the unemployed from immediate penury. I am not implying that poverty and inequality are absent from Western nations, or that such societies are homogenous in terms of their welfare regimes. But these are on the whole "rich democracies" and they differ profoundly from poor nations of the Global South.[9] In the Philippines, even the rudimentary components of a welfare state are absent, meaning that kin networks are the first and last resort for those in need.[10]

The absence of a welfare state, in conjunction with generalized poverty, makes it difficult for Filipinas to adequately prepare for being thrust into the breadwinner role. In the West, breadwinning corresponds to a predictable life stage, generally the two decades after one has had children. A Filipina does not have this luxury of predictability. A tragedy strikes and ripples through her social network, the shockwaves of which hit her hard and unexpectedly. Perhaps her elderly father becomes ill and loses his job; because there is no equivalent system to Medicaid, she is responsible for paying his medical bills and so she is now a breadwinner. Perhaps a younger sister elopes with a foreigner and leaves her children behind; these nieces and nephews are now her charges and she must find a way to provide for them. Perhaps her husband's alcoholism grows out of control and he begins to beat her; because divorce is illegal in the Philippines, she flees with her children and must find a way to make rent in a new housing unit.

Philippine culture glorifies breadwinners such as Myrna, who first dove into the sea and later crossed it as a migrant laborer, as *bagong bayani*—contemporary heroes who sacrifice for their families. But this obscures their quiet desperation. Earlier I labeled call center work a "middle path" between migration and poverty for educated urban Filipinos. For breadwinning women in particular, it can be a veritable lifeline.

Hannah, the Breadwinner

To be a breadwinner in the Philippines is make great sacrifices to help a range of kin besides one's own children.[11] Women, and eldest daughters especially, are obligated to fill this role, and many find that they do so because of some unforeseen calamity. Twenty-four of my thirty female respondents classified themselves as breadwinners, and over half of these women were *ates*. Nearly all could reference a particular trouble (usually involving men and poverty) that precipitated their entry into the industry. In order to understand why both *obtaining* call center work and *persisting* at it makes sense in the context of their lives, we can consider a case study of one such individual.

Hannah was forty-six years old when I first interviewed her, shortly after I had arrived in Manila to begin fieldwork (figure 6.1). She immediately took an interest in making sure that I learned the skills necessary to navigate the city's chaotic street life. Before long, *"tita* Hannah" and I were meeting for dinner or coffee several times a week before her shift began. Over such conversations I was able to piece together her comprehensive life history. Although she was somewhat older than the average worker, in just about every other respect Hannah was an exemplar of the female breadwinning call center agent.

Hannah's mother and father hailed from "the province"—specifically, a rural area of northern Luzon, hundreds of kilometers north of metro Manila. Seeking a better life than what subsistence farming could offer, they had migrated to the city in the late 1950s. Hannah was born in 1966. She was soon followed by two brothers, making her not simply an *anak na babae* (daughter) and *kapatid na babae* (sister), but an *ate* (and hence the one to be counted on to ultimately take care of the family). Hannah's *tatay* (father) and *nanay* (mother) earned money by working in the informal economy. *Tatay* Ray drove a Jeepney (private bus) as an informal contractor during the day, while *nanay* Dot sold snacks such as *lumpia* (fried rolls) from a pushcart. Following a periodic police crackdown on informal business enterprises in Manila, Hannah's parents decided to leave the informal sector. They consolidated the

FIGURE 6.1 Hannah, at work.

small capitals they had accumulated as a bus driver and street vendor to open a *sari-sari* store—basically a small (and officially registered) streetside stall selling a variety of perishable and nonperishable goods.

Hannah, as *ate*, was integrated into running the family business and monitoring the family finances from an early age. During adolescence and even before, she would spend her weekdays in a local Catholic school, but otherwise "grew up in the street." She today recalls "selling pineapples, slippers, eggs" alongside her mother; she also kept an eye on and supervised her two younger brothers. Rather than think of such times as hardship, she remembers feeling encouraged by her parents' commitment to the family and their pride in her success at school. "We were poor but happy," Hannah recounted with a grin, "We loved food and we believed in education."

With the help of her parents, Hannah enrolled at a low-fee, though respectable public college in central Manila. She was a serious and solid student, especially at mathematics (a fact which she attributes to her early bookkeeping experience), and so became an engineering major. She refused to dress in an overtly feminine way, describing herself as the academically high-performing, but socially "never-known type." Upon finishing her college studies, she was hired by PLDT, the country's public telephone service, as a technician. Although she was overqualified for the position, which paid only the minimum wage, she was happy to have her foot in the door of a large company. During her years in college and first few years on the job (from ages 16 to 22), Hannah lived with her parents and brothers in their small (two-bedroom) housing unit in central Manila (as would be normal for nonmarried women).

During her final years in college, Hannah was "courted" by a slightly older man who lived in her *barangay* (urban neighborhood). He eventually completed a vocational degree in accounting from a local college and found a stable job. When he proposed to her, Hannah accepted without hesitation and the two were married in 1986, shortly after her twenty-second birthday. With their joint incomes, they were able to afford their own apartment unit in the *barangay*, which pleased her parents immensely. At PLDT she was a good employee and, over the following five years, received a series of promotions, each of which entailed a modest pay increase. She gave birth to a daughter in 1987 and a second one in 1991. In short, by the early 1990s, Hannah seemingly embodied the Philippine dream. She was a humble child of hardworking migrants from the countryside; a good daughter who had earned a college degree, a profession, a husband, and a family.

This dream came crashing down in 1992, when Hannah made a shocking discovery. Her *asawa* (husband) had been coming home later and later each evening. She grew suspicious and began searching has pockets after he had fallen asleep. As she summarized what the letter she eventually found revealed, "My *asawa* was very *guapo* [handsome] and he had another family." That is, he had not only been keeping a mistress on the side but had also fathered a child with her and was now dedicating substantial time and resources to this "other family."

Hannah's initial impulse was to do everything possible to preserve her family. This led to a fateful decision. She quit her job at PLDT and used all her modest savings to open a cell phone repair stand directly in front of their apartment building. Her reasoning for doing so was twofold. It would encourage her husband to spend more of his time with her in the store, thereby strengthening their relationship and convincing him to abandon his other family. And it would allow her to mobilize her business acumen to generate income.

Hannah's plan failed. Her husband did not stop philandering and so she threw him out of their apartment. Because Hannah could not legally divorce him, her only option was to hire a lawyer and apply for an annulment of their marriage. Given his documented infidelity, this was not going to be a contentious case. The annulment processing fees, however, were in the range of a hundred thousand pesos (about US$2000). Hannah did not have the money, nor did she have any prospect of accumulating it any time soon. For while she had "hoped to be able to make good money with the [cell phone] store," she did not and it soon went under. In our conversations, she spoke with difficulty about this period:

> I thought that I would be able to keep my family if I will resign and then we will just settle for a business. It was a wrong choice. His actions did not stop. Resigning from PLDT was a wrong choice because I was giving away a decent job, a stable job, with good pay. Now suddenly I had nothing.

Lacking any income streams and unable to force her husband to remit any financial support, Hannah moved back into her parent's apartment with her two daughters. They hung a curtain across one of the apartment's two small rooms and settled into this 48 square foot space as their new home. (Her two brothers slept in the other half of the room). But the trouble did not end there. Soon after Hannah moved back in with her family, her father passed away and her mother began having kidney and heart problems. Hannah's *nanay* needed five thousand pesos ($125) each month to pay for doctor visits and medication. Neither of Hannah's brothers had followed in her footsteps by attending college and obtaining secure work. Both were unemployed. Here was a household of six, squeezed into a 200 square foot abode, and with no income.

It was at this point that Hannah acquired a new identity, that of a breadwinner—the self-sacrificing provider. Like many before her, Hannah's initial impulse for managing her predicament was to go abroad as an OFW. She had heard through her networks that those willing to go to Canada would have their temporary work visas expedited. On the day that she commuted to the Canadian embassy to follow up, however, she could not bring herself to leave her two young daughters behind. She made another fateful decision. In her words:

> At that time I was planning to apply to go to Canada to work. At the embassy, I was then thinking, what about my family? It was a choice between my daughters and the job. So obviously I chose my family because the kids were young but growing and they are ladies.

The only other option available to most college-educated Filipinos at this time (i.e., as of the early 1990s) was to find a minimum-wage office job and hope that it would lead to a stable profession. Hannah was not able to regain her position at PLDT, and so had to start this process all over again. She applied widely for all sorts of positions: "As long as it was legal and they were paying in pesos, I would show up and ask for a job." Over the following six years, she worked two and sometimes three jobs simultaneously—as a secretary, a researcher at a marketing firm, an insurance salesperson, a real estate agent, and so on. It was only by cobbling together such work and enduring grueling workweeks of eighty hours that she was able to keep her household afloat, and even then just barely. "My daughters were poor," she stated bluntly, "I was poor. We were a poor family."

It was in the early 2000s that Hannah first remembers noticing the call centers that were springing up in Manila's business districts. She applied for a job with a firm that was contracting with an American insurance company to handle their customer service inquiries, and was hired. The salary, equivalent to about US$350 per month, was more than the total income that she'd been earning by working two full-time jobs in the domestic labor market.

After three years, Hannah lost this job when the contract between the two firms was terminated. By this point, however, she had accumulated experience and a network of contacts in the industry. She was hired by Barclays, a large international bank which operates several of its own call centers in Manila. This job, which she was still working when I first interviewed her, entails handling incoming calls from bank customers who have queries about their credit cards. In addition to one of the top starting salaries in the industry, Barclays offers its agents the chance to earn various bonuses and incentives. Within months of beginning at the bank, Hannah was earning close to US$600 per month.

In short, Hannah had found her way onto the "middle path" represented by call center employment in metro Manila. Given her circumstances, this path was also a lifeline that pulled her (and her network of dependents) out of abject poverty, mitigated the physical toll of having to work multiple jobs, and allowed her to stay in the country with her two daughters.

Based upon everything that we know about working in offshored call centers, the two potential sources of discontent are the night shift and having to deal with difficult callers. When asked about these issues, Hannah acknowledged them but was adamant that that they did not trouble her. She claimed, for instance, to prefer the night shift over an "eight to five job":

> I no longer can imagine myself rushing, stuck in traffic for the eight to five job. I want to have the night shift because, like this, I can do my shopping. I can go anywhere. I'm able to meet or do some things that need to be done during daytime rather than be working in the morning.

And even when I probed about instances of callers treating her disrespectfully, she denied that such interactions negatively colored her experience of call center work:

> Yes it is true, there are difficult customers. But there are also many nice, a lot of nice customers. In the credit card department, they are more likely to be nice to you because maybe they think you're the boss in the credit card [department]. I like them and they are happy about me.

In addition to paying for her mother's ongoing medical care, Hannah's job allowed her to send both her daughters to private colleges in metro Manila. Her eldest daughter completed a nursing program, but decided after graduation not to begin the long process of board exams and unpaid internships. As an *ate* herself, this daughter felt obligated to help support her younger sister, who was just then finishing high school. So rather than continue on the professional track of nursing, she became a call agent herself and used a portion of *her* salary to pay for her younger sister's college tuition. Although Hannah was initially disappointed about this decision, she understood her eldest daughter's reasoning:

> Unfortunately, well actually I understand my daughter. She was young and she wanted to help our household. She got tired of the trainings and everything and so she gives up her nursing dream. She's very

hesitant because nursing here in the Philippines is no longer in demand. There's no job afterwards.

Three years later, when Hannah's youngest daughter finished college with a degree in information technology, she too forwent both an eight to five job and the opportunity to work abroad. She became a call center agent as well. Hannah admits to feeling saddened that neither of her daughters pursued the professions for which they'd trained. On the other hand, among the three of them, they today earn 75,000 pesos, or about US$2000, a month—a sum that has dramatically pulled them out of poverty and into prosperity. The three of them today constitute an independent, all–female household. They live in their own house, have purchased a car, and are engaged in a coordinated savings plan. Hannah still considers herself a breadwinner, in that she continues to support her mother and brothers. But poverty no longer lurks at the door:

> Now that my daughters are working, I'm harvesting the fruits of my labor. They often go out of town and can buy things for themselves. As for me, I will stay in the call center for as long as I am able to. I can hang out at the malls. I can buy my pair of jeans. I can even go out of town, maybe even out of country. Only on vacation I mean!

Becoming a Breadwinner

I discussed at length Hannah's life story because it is so typical of female call agents in Manila. Figure 6.2, which zooms in on the correspondence analysis map presented in chapter 5, conveys that female agents are distinguished by four characteristics in particular: their identity as breadwinners, their aspirations to make a career in the call center industry, their capacity to rationalize their interactions with callers as respectful, and yet their inability to accumulate savings. It was only on this final attribute that Hannah differed from other female agents, in that her two working daughters—the "fruits of her labor"—allowed her household to build a savings account. Note in particular how the points on the map for female and breadwinner practically overlap, suggesting that occupying the breadwinner role is central to the experience of female call agents generally. Such women, I argue, are drawn to call center work as a strategic and immediate solution to the dilemma of breadwinning. Over time, this initial lifeline turns into a durable attachment between these workers and foreign voice capital.

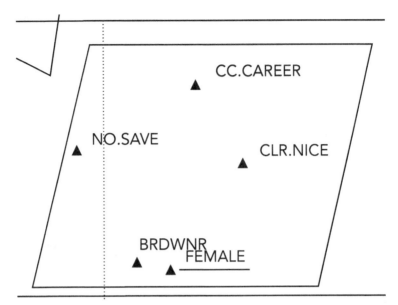

FIGURE 6.2 Correspondence analysis map of female call agents.

Many of my female respondents referred to call center work as the central element of a larger *diskarte*. The term, Spanish in origin but now distinctly Tagalog, refers to how creative and resourceful one is in the face of some challenge or difficulty. Becoming a breadwinner was certainly a dilemma that required immediate *diskarte*. There were two circumstances that could transform a Filipina woman into a breadwinner: being (or being perceived as) an *ate*, and encountering some sort of "man problem." Either alone was sufficient to accomplish the role transformation; when they coincided, as they did for Hannah, the weight of breadwinning was felt immensely and a *diskarte* was desperately needed.

The Diskarte of the Ate

Being an eldest daughter left one vulnerable to being rerouted from one's current life trajectory and into the breadwinner role. My respondents who experienced such a transformation described their responses to their new responsibilities and obligations with a matter of factness. They had read the situation then done what needed to be done.

Consider the case of Christia, who was twenty-one years old at the time of our final interview and who had been working in the call center industry for three years. Christia's father had abandoned the family when she was young;

her mother had left the country to work abroad when Christia was twelve years old. Christia and her three younger siblings were sent to live with their grandparents. *Nanay* remitted money home each month to pay for their basic needs, but as far back as Christia could remember, she had served as a maternal surrogate: "I was the one taking care of my three siblings," she explained, "I woke them each morning, fed and dressed them, made sure they did their homework, and disciplined them when they misbehaved."

Christia finished high school at the age of sixteen and immediately enrolled at a public college located in her neighborhood. She majored in Human Resources (HR) because it seemed an easy and practical course of study. During her sophomore year, however, Christia's mother informed her that she was going to remarry and quit her job, meaning that she could no longer send regular remittances home.

This was Christia's transformative moment. She found herself confronting the following dilemma: How could she justify spending their limited resources on her college tuition? "How," she despaired, "could I do this to my brothers and sister when they are hungry and need food today?" She quit college after her second year and began job hunting. As she recounted:

> I decided. I will just work instead of pursuing a college career and I will just end [my schooling] half-way through. My mom didn't say it directly, "Oh, you should stop, I can't afford it anymore." I really *volunteered*. I could see my mom can't afford it anymore. So, okay, I will just work. I *don't have any choice* but to do it.

This particular quote captures well how the process of becoming a breadwinner is experienced in a contradictory way. For Christia, giving up on college was both something she "volunteered" to do *and* something she didn't "have any choice but to do." In any case, this decision simultaneously elevated her status within her family and threw her prematurely into the labor market. She was seventeen at the time that she quit school to dedicate herself to breadwinning.

Hannah had become a breadwinner in the 1990s, just as the call center industry was being established in metro Manila. By the time Christia made the role transition in the late 2000s, however, offshored call centers dominated the city's labor market. She immediately set her sights on becoming a call center agent; here was a *diskarte*. "They offer competitive benefits and they give out really high salaries. They could solve my problems," she reasoned at the time.

One problem was that she did not have a college degree. By probing her school and neighborhood networks, however, she compiled a list of companies willing to hire agents with only two years of college. Another obstacle was that she could not apply until she turned eighteen, which was three months away. So in the meantime, she volunteered to work as an unpaid receptionist at a hostel in Manila that catered to British travelers. This allowed her to practice her English daily, so that by the time she turned eighteen she felt very confident in her language skills: "I knew I was talkative and *soshal* (sophisticated) and so would excel in that line [of work]." Indeed, by the time of our final interview, Christia had been promoted three times within her BPO firm—from an Australian to a British to an American account. In addition to earning 24,000 pesos (about $600) per month, she delighted in showing off her language skills by switching back and forth among these three accents.

As *ates*, Hannah and Christia came to find themselves in the breadwinner role. But the basic outlines of their stories I encountered again and again. Twenty-year-old Quiny questioned neither her obligation as *ate* to work for others nor the call center as the optimal solution to her dilemma: "I've got one dependent and I also provide for my parents. I'm the eldest, so I chose BPO as that gives me more salary, enough for me to sustain the needs of my family. If I did not have that salary I could not give anything to my parents." Twenty-three-year-old *ate* Queenie "chose to work in a call center because my brother and my sister were still studying and I need to support them," while twenty-four-year-old *ate* Melyn was a realist when it came to articulating her dilemma and the sacrifices it entails:

> I am the breadwinner of the family right now. I am earning for my son for all his needs, for my mother, and two brothers. I would love to focus on myself but I cannot because my mother doesn't have any work. Who will be able to support them? No one. It's up to me.

Studies of the Philippines have long documented women's high levels of labor-market participation (including as migrant workers) and the control that they exercise over household finances.[12] This stands in contrast to other South and Southeast Asian countries, where women are often excluded from the public sphere, sometimes entirely. The breadwinner stories told so far suggest though that the active participation of Filipinas in public life may belie a form of self-subjugation. For many, it may be the enactment of a strategy to save others via sacrifice. In a context of widespread poverty and hardship, feeling obligated to serve as the breadwinner of first and last resort for one's extended kin is an expression not of empowerment but of exploitation. It demonstrates how few resources are available to poor families in the Philippines, how the dominant institutions of Philippine society—the state and the church— have essentially outsourced caring for the needy to responsible women—to, that is, breadwinners.

Man Troubles

Among my respondents there was a second pathway to becoming a breadwinner—one encountered some sort of "man troubles." Most of these troubles derived from the inability of Filipina women to control their fertility, divorce their husbands, and/or claim material support from the men who fathered their children. In a society that guarantees women reproductive rights, formal legal equality, and even rudimentary forms of welfare, these troubles would not necessarily lead to immediate hardship. In the Philippines, unfortunately, they do. To illustrate how man troubles can transform a Filipina into a breadwinner—which in turn attaches her to the call center industry—I will sketch the lives of three workers: Emma, Queenie, and Maria.

Emma was in her third year of college, on a full-ride athletic scholarship, and studying to be a teacher when she became pregnant by her boyfriend. The two had not been practicing contraception of any sort. When asked why not, Emma shrugged. Abstinence until marriage is the official policy of the Catholic church and hence the default pedagogy of sex education throughout the country. Reproductive issues are a taboo subject in schools, and most parents do not discuss these issues with their children. Emma explained sheepishly that she had no idea how to obtain oral contraception, and at the time would have never thought to purchase or use condoms. Becoming pregnant, she believes, was her punishment for engaging in premarital sex—"I was a bad girl before"—while being a breadwinner was now her penance.

Emma's boyfriend, she found out shortly after she informed him of her pregnancy, was already married. He assured her that he was separated from his wife and would start supporting her as soon as he could have the marriage annulled. "He has proposed," Emma stated with a sigh, "but right now we can't get married 'cuz he's married before. He's saving for the annulment which here in the Philippines is so expensive." Having lost her scholarship, with a child on the way, and with no one to support her, Emma dropped out of college and applied for work at a call center. She was eighteen at the time.

Twenty-three-year-old Queenie had been working in a call center for two years when I first interviewed her. She had graduated from university at the age of twenty with a degree in hotel and restaurant management. Her ultimate dream was to apprentice as and then become a chef. Her schooling, along with that of her two younger siblings, had been financed by her father, who worked as a seafarer. He died of heart disease when Queenie was twenty, but this did not immediately put her family in bad financial straits. Queenie's mother took a job as a maid, but more important, her father had taken out a life insurance policy and had made regular contributions to his company's pension program. Both ensured them regular income (in dollars) for the foreseeable future.

The payments ceased, however, when it was discovered that Queenie's father was a polygamist. He had previously been married and had not had the marriage annulled before abandoning his first wife and their two children. Over the years, he had not communicated with his first family, but had surreptitiously sent them money on a periodic basis. When the envelopes stopped arriving, his first wife investigated and discovered that he had passed away. She then filed claim for his life insurance and pension payments. Queenie, her mother, and her siblings were shocked:

> When my dad died, we were depending on the benefits from his company. You know, his pension and the insurance money. But it was cut off over a year ago because everyone found out that that my dad had, like, a first marriage. It was so shocking because my dad was so not like that, you can't believe that he could do that.

With this one piece of unexpected bad news, Queenie found herself, as the *ate*, now a breadwinner. "We needed money like ASAP—as soon as possible!" she explained. So she set to the side her dream to work as a chef in an upscale restaurant and strategized a way to begin earning money immediately. She took a bus to nearby Eastwood City, a business district known for its skyscrapers full of call centers.

Maria was twenty-eight years old and working in a call center at the time of our first interview. Although she'd grown up in a poor family, her father was a pastor and so they were well-respected in their *barangay*. Maria always thought of herself as shy and conservative. "In high school," she explained, "I only wore a long skirt and baggy shirts, I was a Maria Clara type" (i.e., demure and studious). She was thrilled to receive a full-ride academic scholarship to study English at a private college in Manila.

While Maria was a junior in college and still living at home, a man in her *barangay* began to court her. Six years her elder and an OFW seafarer, he would wait for her each day after school and insist on taking her for snacks or a meal. She wasn't interested in him, or in dating at all. She began staying later and later at school in order to avoid him. But he was persistent and one day showed up outside her school on his scooter and insisted that she let him give her a ride home. Instead, he drove to a motel and ushered her into a room. "What is this place?" Maria said to him, "Let's go somewhere else." She tried to leave the room, but he blocked the door and forced her onto the bed. Describing to me this episode, which had taken place a decade before, Maria stated matter of factly: "I know now that he raped me, and did several times after."

Maria told no one about these sexual assaults until she learned that she was pregnant. She wanted nothing to do with the man nor did she want to have his child, but abortion is illegal in the Philippines and unthinkable for a devout Catholic such as Maria. She informed her parents, who were furious. Her father, the pastor, was adamant that she would bring great shame upon their family and upon his church were she to have a child out of wedlock. "In the Philippines we have a term for this," Maria said with a grimace, "he [her rapist] had me *cornered*."

So at the age of twenty, just days after her college graduation ceremony, Maria married the seafarer. Several months later she gave birth to a son. Her new husband moved the three of them into a clean and spacious two-bedroom apartment in her parent's *barangay*, which pleased Maria's *tatay* and *nanay* greatly. As a seafaring OFW, he was away for months at a time and earned dollars, which he dutifully remitted back to her. Soon Maria had a new car, a wardrobe full of branded clothing, a full-time nanny, and braces. To stay busy and mentally engaged, she work as an English tutor in a nearby school. Two years after her son was born, a daughter followed.

From afar, Maria had achieved the Philippine dream. But she harbored a dark secret. Her husband was insanely jealous and demanded that she be available to answer her phone or Skype at all times. When he came home on shore leave, a dismaying drama would play out. He would accuse her of infidelity, she would deny it, then he would beat, choke, and kick her. Maria came to keep a special wardrobe of scarves and long-sleeved blouses to wear during her husband's visits and for the weeks after that it took for her bruises to heal. It was, in her words, her "problem," her "shame."

It was only during a chance encounter with a former college professor that Maria broke down and for the first time told her story to someone else. Her teacher urged her to research domestic violence and recommended a book to read. "Instantly," Maria recalled, "I recognized my own story in it. I was abused physically. Mentally. Sexually. Emotionally."

Maria came to believe, after further research on the internet, that she would be successful at bringing abuse charges against her husband. By now she had an entire portfolio of "selfies" that she had taken of her bruised and battered body following his visits homes. But to pursue such charges would almost certainly mean that he would lose his license as a seafarer. This would in turn infuriate him and bring him back to the Philippines permanently, which was the ultimate nightmare scenario for Maria.

So far in this chapter I have used the metaphor of a "lifeline" to capture what call center employment means for many Filipinas. For none does it fit as well as it does for Maria, whose life was literally at risk. In 2012, she made a fateful decision: she would take her two children and flee their home. Doing so would entail losing access to her husband's remittances, it would alienate her from her immediate family, and it would mean living incognito in an entirely new section of the city. In short, it would transform Maria into a true breadwinner: a single parent responsible for providing for two young children without the help of a spouse, any kin, or the state.

But Maria had one trump card yet to play: her verbal English was flawless. A childhood of reading aloud Bible passages in front of her church, a four-year English degree, and years of tutoring aspirant English speakers had left her with a nearly impeccable grasp of the language. She had no problem passing the entrance exam at a call center operated by an American IT company. The salary allowed Maria to rent a small apartment for herself and her two children, and to put food on the table every day.

When I last interviewed Maria, in 2014, she reported having received a series of raises at her call center. She was now earning enough to pay tuition fees for her two children at private schools. However, she remained fearful that her husband would eventually track her down. For Maria, call center work was incomplete as a *diskarte*; her ultimate strategy was to send her children to live with her parents, then herself leave the country as an OFW. This would increase both her earnings and the physical distance between herself and her husband.

To accumulate sufficient savings to begin the process of obtaining a foreign work visa, she needed to supplement her call center salary. When last I interviewed her, she had just registered as a contractor on an online "e-lancing" site. She worked all day copyediting English-language texts and transcribing interviews into English, for a few dollars per hour. As one can imagine, this put immense time pressure upon Maria, who reported sleeping only a few hours each morning after her call center shift ended and her children left for school.

Diskarte and Attachment

Maria, like Hannah, Emma, and Queenie, was drawn to call center work as a strategic lifeline—a *diskarte*—upon finding herself thrust into the role of breadwinner. Maria was unusual, however, in that call center work was for her *not* a sustainable solution to her predicament. It was much more common to find breadwinners becoming effectively tied to the industry as time wore on. In this section I elaborate further the mechanisms behind this process of attachment. Given women's numerical majority in the workforce as a whole, this goes some way toward accounting for the Philippine call center industry's low overall attrition rate.

Just over half (17 of 30) of the female workers whom I studied articulated an express intent to make a career in the voice industry. This stands in stark contrast to how workers evaluate outsourced call center jobs in rich countries such as the United States (i.e., as bad jobs to be tolerated for a short while) and in India (where they are used as steppingstones toward better jobs). In both these other contexts, study after study has established, employees articulate a litany of complaints about various aspects of call center work. These include its deskilled and monotonous nature, the dearth of internal job ladders, and—most notoriously—callers who can become irate, abusive, or even racist. It is not that Filipina call center workers are immune or oblivious to these issues. But, rather, they appear to have developed a counter-discourse, one that minimizes these negative aspects of the work and essentially rationalizes them.

My respondent Rodalyn, for instance, who had put on hold her dream of working in the marketing field, remained upbeat about ongoing professional development in the call center: "We have constant trainings. That's one good thing in our company. They really offer useful trainings to improve the skills of us as employees." Rachel, working to provide for her son and extended family, remembered that "when I was in college, I thought of the call center as an easy job." However, she now considers it challenging and "loves the work," mainly because it helps her to hone her language skills. As she emphasized, "Communication-wise, you're being trained every day with different kinds of people, so you're forced to think and be confident. Before I was not too confident." Emma, who admitted to initially feeling "bitter" about giving up her teaching dream, spontaneously offered a prolonged defense of the call center industry and possibilities to advance within it:

> Actually, I'm aspiring to be a trainer, a process trainer or language trainer; that's why I'm working very hard. At [her call center], you can advance to the top easily because the accounts in BPO industries are always expanding. Once the client sees that the BPO companies are doing well or rendering good service they usually bring over more products and more processes that require more people. More people means they get to bring up more people from below the totem [pole], because they know the process. [It's better than] hiring people from the outside. Why not bring up the people from the inside?

Whereas the literature depicts widespread animosity between call agents and their callers, two-thirds of my female respondents characterized their phone interactions as, on the whole, respectful. Hannah's summation—"Yes it is true, there are difficult customers. But there are also many nice, a lot of nice customers. . . . I like them and they are happy about me"—is representative. She acknowledges that interactions can sometimes be "difficult," but ultimately concludes that these are exceptions. Tam, who works as a claims filing agent for an American auto insurance company, made a similar assessment: "There are times when they will not listen to reason, but mostly they are just asking for information and they are really nice."

Furthermore, a large majority (25 of 30) of female agents assessed their remuneration as fair. The general sentiment was that call center wages should be compared not to the earnings of a migrant worker but, rather, to salaries paid by local employers in the city's labor market.

Most (18 of 30) of my female respondents had given up any intent to return to the profession for which they had trained. In the call center, they had found a tolerable job that pays well enough to support the various others whom they feel obligated to provide for. A job, furthermore, that one can jump right into rather than endure the lengthy unpaid internships that local companies require of new workers. Twenty-four-year-old Jasmine, who had completed a degree in education, recounted her own shift of trajectory thus:

> I had always dreamed to be a teacher. It is a noble profession here in our country. In fact, I tried teaching. I had a job as a pre-school teacher but

the income is not that good. And since I'm the breadwinner I need to earn more money which is why I decided to apply for a call center job.

Or as Tina summarized: "The salary here is much higher than if I am working in a local company. So, why not work in a call center? I get all the benefits, medical and dental insurance. And all free coffees and chocolates."

There was greater ambivalence about the other path not taken: migration as an overseas worker. Half of Filipina call center workers continued to harbor aspirations to go abroad, mainly as a means to garner even more financial resources for their network of dependents. Queenie, the young women who unexpectedly became a breadwinner after her deceased father's previous marriage was discovered, is a case in point. Her call center job in Manila allowed her to support her mother and younger siblings. But she had her own plan in life: to "have a family—like a big family!" And so she planned to leave the call center eventually and work abroad for several years to build a nest egg. "I'm thinking practically," she reasoned, "I will someday need more income. I need to prepare coz I will have many children and they will be studying and I don't want to tell them that they cannot attend the best schools."

The intentions of Queenie and others like her were undoubtedly pure. However, one cannot help but wonder how such workers, as breadwinners, will be able to accumulate the resources and devote the time needed to exit the call center industry. Navigating the bureaucracy for gaining an OFW visa takes immense time and effort, while there are multitudes of others depending on their call center salaries in the here and now. Indeed, along with assuming the role of breadwinner, rationalizing callers as respectful, and aspiring to make a career in the industry, an *inability to save* defined female workers in the overall call center space. Only seven of my thirty respondents were able to set aside a portion of their paychecks in savings accounts or similar holding vehicles, in anticipation of future needs or plans.

Much more common were accounts such as Quiny's: "One of the things that I thought when I first started working for [her call center company] was, I thought I could save to finish my schooling and take the board exams. I would like to finish my studies and go out [i.e., migrate], but when I get my salary it's only enough for my son and also my mom and some family expenses." Melyn, who had trained as a nurse, described how challenging it is to leave the call center path once one has tapped into the income stream it provides:

Before, when I was looking at the future, I thought I would become a professional nurse and I was looking to go some place abroad. But now I don't have time, I'm already always busy working. And I need to support my family, I spend all my money for them. So now I don't think about it [i.e., going abroad to work]. I am focused on everyday living.

Ultimately, breadwinners, the backbone of the Philippine call center labor market, stay at their jobs because the industry provides them a solution to their dilemma. It is not that they have no other options. As college graduates with a solid command of the English language, they *could* eventually find their way abroad or into a domestic profession. But for them, offshored call centers are a middle path, a lifeline. The contrast with female Indian call center workers could not be starker. Patriarchal norms push the latter away from voice capital; whereas the expectation that Filipinas will materially support their kin attracts and attaches them to it.

Of course, not every female call center agent in the Philippines is a breadwinner. Some are not *ates* and so are not expected to be the main wage-earner in their households. Others have been able to avoid "man troubles" by establishing healthy relationships or avoiding men altogether. My respondent Blessed, for instance, insists that her boyfriend use contraception, reasoning that "it's not practical having children then struggling to survive," while Christine, who calls herself "extremely shy," feels that men have no interest in her and she, none in them.

Somewhat paradoxically, nonbreadwinners, because they have more disposable income, are more visible to the general public. It is they who congregate outside Starbucks and smoke cigarettes each evening before their shifts begin; and it is they who gather at the "resto-bars" to drink buckets of beer when their shifts end in the wee hours of the morning. It is they whom the occasional editorial in the *Manila Bulletin* singles out as evidence that call centers are encouraging the spread of smoking, drinking, and STDs. My research finds, in contrast, that these workers are not representative of call center employees. This is a fact not lost on breadwinners themselves. As Rodalyn put it, "Those partiers are not breadwinners like most of us; that's why they have lesser responsibilities. They have the money to spend on, like, drinks, the partying and all that it brings."

Even if they are not representative of all call agents, nonbreadwinners are important for this analysis.[13] They suggest that there are *other mechanisms* through which Filipinos become attached to the call center industry. In the following two chapters I will elaborate on two other categories of call center workers. On the one hand are gay agents who find callers disrespectful and aspire to go abroad, but who struggle to accumulate the savings needed to do so. They remain, though they are restless. On the other hand are straight men who feel ambivalent about working in the industry, but who use their salaries to build savings and enact Filipino masculinity. They remain because they put down roots.

7

Restless Gays

CONSIDER YOUR DAILY commute as a call center agent in metro Manila. You hail a taxi or jump onto a jeepney bus and head to one of the city's call center districts, such as Makati, Eastwood, or Ortigas. Your driver will undoubtedly be a man. "Magandang umaga kuya" (Good morning, brother), you may shout, to be heard above the thumping pop music that permeates the vehicle. But he'll most likely ignore you, intent as he is upon navigating the chaotic traffic that perpetually clogs the city. Upon arriving at your call center, you walk up to the main entrance and issue another "Good morning, *kuya*" to the security guard as he performs a perfunctory search of your purse or backpack. Once you are cleared, you smile and say a quick *kamusta ka* (How are you?) to the young woman staffing the reception desk, then swipe your ID card to access the production floor. There you join a mass of primarily Filipina women sitting in their cubicles, handling calls.

A single trip across metro Manila alerts one to a clear division of labor by gender (i.e., by one's projected identity as male, female, or transgender/gay) in Philippine society today. In the informal economy and at the low end of the formal labor market, this division of labor is quite extreme; one could spend a lifetime in the city and never encounter a female taxi driver, a male domestic worker, or an openly gay security guard (figure 7.1). Among occupations requiring a college degree, such segregation is less total but still present; women are overrepresented among nursing graduates, for instance, and underrepresented among new architects.[1]

Given this, it would have been surprising if the workforce in metro Manila's emergent call center industry did *not* exhibit a skewed gender ratio. The previous chapter explained why cisgender Filipina women are both drawn to call center employment and remain attached to it. For them it is a veritable lifeline, a solution to the dilemma of having to serve as a breadwinner.

FIGURE 7.1 Job segregation by gender in the Philippines.
Source: Photographs by Rudz Misa.

This chapter considers call center agents who identify as gay (as I will elaborate, the term "gay," while frequently used by my respondents, has a different meaning in the Philippines than in the West). As are women, gay persons are overrepresented among call center agents relative to their numbers in the country's potential labor pool. Proud and sometimes flamboyant, they have found in the new call center industry a safe and supportive employment niche. Nonetheless, my data suggest that gay call center agents are the most restless of the workers studied. They continue to aspire to professional careers and/or to work abroad, yet their inability to save, coupled with the discrimination they face in the broader labor market, precludes their pursuing these other paths. Gay workers, I argue, embody a second source of affinity between labor supply and voice capital in the Philippines.

Boi, the Restless

To convey why call center employment is so attractive to gay persons in the Philippines, I present the case of Boi, whom I first interviewed in 2011. Boi, like the majority of gay call center workers whom I interviewed, does not present as female by, for instance, crossdressing or wearing enhancements such as wigs. He is referred to by friends and family as *kuya* (brother), and can readily pass as a (stylish) straight male if the context demands it. Boi was referred to me by one of my research assistants, and he soon became a key informant for my study.

Boi was twenty years old at the time of our first interview. He had recently graduated from a public college in Manila with a degree in counseling, and he was now working the day shift at a call center located in a technology park near the university in Manila where I was teaching. We first met, shortly after his shift had ended, at a Starbucks across the road from the campus. Boi arrived wearing a black leather jacket and holding a motorbike helmet. Like the vast majority of Manila denizens, I dreaded my daily commute home via public transport and so my ears perked up when Boi mentioned that he drove right past my apartment complex on his way home from work every evening. I thus made no protest when he insisted on "treating me" to a ride home as we left the café. Weaving through traffic on the back of a motorbike, though disconcerting, is much faster than, and hence much more preferable to, being crammed like a sardine into a packed train or bus.

Boi's call center was a 24/7 operation, which meant that he worked a rotating schedule, switching between the night and day shifts on a regular basis. On the afternoons when he would finish around the time I was leaving the university, he would text me and offer me a lift. These offers I always accepted. Surely it buttressed his social status to be seen driving an American around on his motorbike, while it allowed me to cobble together, over the course of many months, Boi's full life history. These expeditions also allowed me to accompany Boi on his daily postwork routine, which consisted of shopping for essentials, window-shopping for luxuries, and trying to establish boundaries between the two.

Boi was born and raised not in Manila but in a small city on the northern part of the island of Mindoro. He was the eldest of three brothers (hence the *kuya* prefix commonly attached to his name) in a very poor family. His father was a mechanic and his mother stayed at home to tend the boys. Boi could not remember the family ever having access to income streams such as remittances from relatives abroad. Compounding their poverty was the fact that Boi's father drank heavily just about every day and late into the evening. Boi recalled that as a child he interacted with his father only rarely; he would be asleep long before his *tatay* returned home from playing cards and drinking rum with other men in their *barangay*.

As Boi entered his teen years, he came to discover that he was (and was being perceived as) different from the other young men in his neighborhood. In class, he was speaking English more often than were the other students, and with an accent different from that of his male classmates. This, he remembered, resulted in some teasing: "When I would recite [an assignment or required reading] in class, they would normally say, 'Oh, look at *kuya* Boi. He speaks English with a fancy accent.'"

Boi also felt increasingly uncomfortable wearing the baggy shorts and basketball jerseys that his brothers and male neighbors wore. He began lifting spare change and small notes from his father's pockets after *tatay* passed out on the floor following his drinking sprees. The next day, Boi would take the money and walk to the street markets downtown. There he would purchase t-shirts and short-sleeved polo shirts with imitation logos such as American Eagle or Abercrombie, along with form-fitting blue jeans. Such clothing, he recalled, made him feel "fancy" and "sophisticated." By using language and wearing clothing in a "sophisticated" way, Boi was learning to deploy bodily techniques that are central to the successful performance of a gay identity in the Philippines. At the time, he was only thirteen or fourteen years old and certainly did not understand his actions this way. He did not then identify as gay nor does he recall having had any desire to pursue intimate relationships with other men.

Unfortunately, Boi's evolving presentation of self coincided with a family crisis. At around this time, his father's drinking escalated out of control and he became physically abusive toward his family. "It was then, "Boi recalled, that "I understood truly that my father is a drunkard. He would drink so much and then after drinking he would be so mad. It became normal that he beat my mother, beat [my brothers and me]. Ever since then, I actually hate my father." To this day, Boi cannot say whether his own emerging identity had anything to do with his father's growing rage and abuse. Regardless, as soon as he graduated from high school, Boi manuevered to flee the situation.

Sixteen years old at the time, Boi contacted his mother's sister, who lived in Manila, and arranged to live with her family for the time being. Cramming his entire existence into a corner of an already crowded apartment, Boi resolved to become a guidance counselor for young people. "I really encouraged myself to work hard, to try always at my studies, to succeed at this profession," he stated, "so that I could someday help others because no one had been there to help me."

Boi so excelled during his first term at a local public college that he was awarded a scholarship. It paid for his tuition and provided a small stipend that covered school and transport expenses. His mother somehow managed to send him some pocket money each month, and Boi's *tita* was fine with letting him stay in her family's apartment. Nonetheless, Boi came to feel like a burden to both his mother and his aunt. He also hated not having any discretionary income. His scholarship paid for his school uniform, but otherwise he was wearing the same knock-off jeans and t-shirts that he'd bought in the provincial market years before.

As soon as he turned eighteen years old, Boi began applying to call centers. With no experience and not yet a college graduate, he was only eligible for the least desirable of jobs—namely, those that made outbound calls such as for sales or collections. He easily passed the language exam and so began a new routine: studying by day and working as a bill collector at night. Skimping on sleep and spending eight hours each night pestering Americans who had fallen delinquent on their accounts were physically and emotionally taxing. But the job paid a decent salary—triple that of the city's minimum wage—and Boi maintained this arrangement for two years. It allowed him to contribute some money to his *tita*'s household, to send some money home to his *nanay*, and to "treat himself" to some new clothing and the occasional meal out.

Shortly after turning twenty years old, Boi finished college. Like all new graduates, he faced a series of obstacles to starting the professional career to which he aspired. There was the time and money needed to study for and take the board exams required to license as a teacher or counselor. There were the resources needed to support oneself while doing the mandatory unpaid internships at a school. Boi thus continued working as a call center agent to support his dream of becoming a professional counselor. By now, however, as an official college graduate with two years of experience in the industry, he could apply to top-tier call centers. Within a week he received a job offer from an American e-commerce firm. Rather than pursuing delinquent payers, he was now handling service queries from corporate clients. This was a much higher-status position, one that paid approximately 30,000 pesos, or $750, per month.

It was a few months into his new job that I interviewed Boi at the coffee shop near our offices. He was at a turning point in his life. Over the next several years, I would witness firsthand his struggle to manage the tension between his developing commitment to successfully performing a gay identity and his long-standing dream to embark upon what he called a "noble profession." The high pay associated with call center work lay at the crux of this dilemma.

From the start, I noted how Boi's attire diverged from that of the vast majority of cisgender Filipino men whom I had encountered. Boi was in strict adherence with what one cultural participant calls the Philippine "gay 'uniform' of tight T-shirts and jeans"[2] (figure 7.2). His dark blue Levi's, Boi pointed out to me, were "skinny fit," "authentic," and cuffed twice to allow a full view of his black Tom's slip-ons. His polo shirt was bright yellow and bore the distinctive Abercrombie and Fitch logo on the chest. And he carried his smartphone and

FIGURE 7.2 Boi, relaxing.

other personal essentials in a brown distressed-leather shoulder bag. He later explained that he had "fallen in love at first sight with" the bag at a department store and had purchased it for the equivalent of just under $100. It did not take much calculation to value Boi's overall ensemble at well over $200, or a week's worth of pay. It was apparent that he invested heavily to embody the ideal of the urbane gay "socialite."

As time progressed, I came to discover just how wide was the gulf between Boi's sophisticated public personae and the austerity of his private life.

After college he had moved out of his aunt's apartment and into a small single room that he shared with two of his workmates, both also gay. A bunk on the wall slept two while Boi occupied a thin twin mattress on the floor. All three shared a single closet, dresser, and mirror. This was in a low-rent boarding house intended for students and young workers, such that it lacked a variety of basic amenities. The room had no bathroom; a single shower and sink in the hallway were shared by the entire floor. The building had no air-conditioning, just ceiling fans only about half of which appeared to be working at any given time. And Boi's room had no refrigerator, stove, or facilities for washing clothes.[3]

Even after minimizing has housing costs, Boi pared to the bone various other expenses. The monthly remittances to his mother in the province ceased (unlike the eldest daughters described in the chapter prior, Boi was not obligated to serve as a sacrificing breadwinner). For food preparation, he and his roommates purchased second-hand a rice cooker, hot water kettle, and some basic silverware and plates. On a typical day, he would eat his first meal at a food stall outside his boarding house, usually a scoop of rice and fried egg for 20 pesos (about 50 cents). Lunch, from his call center's canteen, was essentially the same: rice, some broth, and a chicken drumstick. Boi would prepare dinner himself. About twice each week, he would stop at a discount grocery store and spend about 200 pesos ($5) to purchase ingredients for several dinners. His lack of a refrigerator severely limited his cooking options. He would indulge in one or two pieces of fresh fruit, but these had to be consumed the same day; otherwise, groceries were small containers of tuna, cans of corned beef, instant noodles, a bag of potato chips, and an occasional bag of rice. After accompanying Boi on several such outings, it became clear that his slim physique was a result not of an intentional diet or exercise regime but of obvious nutrient deficiency.

Maintaining his wardrobe was another ongoing challenge for Boi. He would not dream of being seen in public without designer jeans, but he owned only two pairs: the Levi's that he was wearing on the day we met and a pair from an upscale Philippine brand, Penshoppe. Without a washing machine, his only options for keeping them clean and fresh (an ongoing challenge, given the heat and pollution of Manila) were to take them to a laundry or to launder them himself. Whereas the former could cost several hundred pesos per week, the latter cost only the price of a bar of laundry soap (six to eight pesos). Boi's routine was the latter, scrubbing by hand and line-drying his jeans nightly. The same held for his selection of tops, which consisted of three American-branded polo shirts. And it was no coincidence that most of his clothing items were dark colored and made of heavy fabric. Whites were not an option, he explained, as they were easily stained by spills or sweat, and hence had a short life span, while thin fabrics would not hold up to the wear and tear of daily hand-scrubbing. Boi's wardrobe, in short, was *soshal* but limited.

Despite this austere private life, Boi struggled to accumulate savings with which to pursue his dream of becoming a professional counselor. One major expense in his monthly budget was the motorbike (and fuel) with which he navigated the city. Another was what he called "impulse purchases," mostly beverages and snacks that he bought for himself and his work mates during their socializing times. Boi reported buying at least two Starbucks Frappuccinos per week (at 160 pesos per drink, this added up to $32 per month, or nearly 5% of his salary), and multiple beers and alcoholic drinks on a regular basis (at a sum he was unable to estimate, but likely in the $50– $60 per month range).

A third and quite significant expense was that of constantly gifting and treating a man named Carl. A slightly older Filipino man, Carl was responsible for driving and maintaining the shuttle van for Boi's company—a very "macho" job. Twice I was introduced to him, and Carl seemed to me to be the typical straight Filipino male. He spoke only Tagalog and dressed in loose-fitting khaki pants or cargo shorts along with shirts invariably adorned with NBA logos. Although I never witnessed Boi and Carl touch in public, Boi was adamant that "he is my boyfriend." Once, when Boi made such a statement in the presence of several female co-workers, they immediately began teasing him by pointing out that Carl was regularly dropped off and picked up at work by his girlfriend. Boi's parry, in which he attempted to clarify the nature of their relationship, illustrates his facility not just with English grammar but with wordplay (this, I would come to find, is central to a successful performance of gayness in the Philippines):

According to Carl, he is straight. Ha! So maybe my boyfriend has a girlfriend. Unfortunately, as they say, woe is me. According to him he is straight, but in this case the only thing straight is a ruler. [All laugh].

I never did discern the exact nature of the relationship between Boi and Carl. It may have been a "crush"—that is, an ongoing amorous pursuit—or it may have been a clandestine "boyfriend" relationship involving regular intimate contact. I can however report that a large part of Boi's afterwork routine consisted of walking through malls to decide upon purchases for Carl.

On several occasions I witnessed him purchase clothing items such as a U.S.-branded t-shirt worth 600 pesos ($15) and a Kobe Bryant NBA jersey costing 1800 pesos ($45). Assuming such gifts were provided on a somewhat regular basis, they equaled and perhaps even eclipsed Boi's expenditures on his own food, housing, and hygiene.

By late 2013, Boi was overloaded. He was working full time at his call center, studying for his board exams, spending several mornings a week interning at a local primary school, eating less than an adequate diet, and attempting to maintain an active social life. Here are examples of texts that an exhausted Boi was sending me at this time:

Jeff, I'm so haggard. Super STRESSED. As much as I would like to rest, I can't because of work and school ☹

It's so tiring. Actually, I didn't to go work tonight bc I'm not feeling well. So stressed. I have evry sat & sun days off. I'm still busy those days.

By early 2015, Boi *had* completed his internship and passed his board exam, at which point he quit his call center job and became a full-time primary school teacher. By this point I was back in the United States and followed Boi mainly via Facebook. His photos, status updates, and occasional messages certainly conveyed the impression of one who had happily settled into an "honorable" profession. Mentoring young children had long been a dream that Boi had seemingly achieved.

In early 2016, however, I logged onto his Facebook page and saw that his newest profile photo was of himself wearing the telltale ID badge of a call center agent. It hung from a lanyard around his neck (and over his yellow Abercrombie polo). He responded to my subsequent Facebook message by saying that, while he had loved teaching, it paid less than half of what he'd been earning as a call center agent at the e-commerce company. Several months earlier, he'd had to give up the motorbike he'd been leasing; then he had to cancel the internet service for his smartphone; and still he'd been unable to move out of the boarding house. The company had made it known that he was welcome to have his old job back—an offer which he finally decided to take. A professional salary in the Philippines had simply been incommensurable with his desired lifestyle, and so he'd returned—reluctantly—to the call center.

Being Gay in the Philippines

Openly gay individuals such as Boi were overrepresented as call center agents in Manila. In chapter 5 I used interviews with my case studies to estimate the presence of gay employees in the industry at about 15%. When I mentioned this number to call center managers and human resource staff, they agreed that it was a reasonable estimate. There are no reliable data on the gender orientation of college graduates in metro Manila, but it is highly unlikely that 15% of graduates—the *potential* labor pool for call centers—identify as gay. It is also the case that the *perceived* presence of gay workers in the call center industry outstrips their actual presence. In the general imagination, they are largely equated with the industry. Call centers in the Philippines are frequently referred to as a "gay paradise" or a "church of the gay religion."[4]

Multiple aspects of Boi's experience coming of age in Manila—his fluency in English, his need for spending money, his inability to save—suggest why there is such an affinity between gay persons and the city's call centers. Such an affinity seems to be unique to the Philippines. To fully explain it entails grasping the distinctive meaning of gayness in the Philippines: what the label signifies, how gayness is embodied and enacted, and how gay individuals are treated by society at large.

The meaning of gayness in the Philippines is not identical to its meaning in the United States and Europe. One major difference is that the concept applies exclusively to biologically sexed men who identify as nonheterosexual; throughout most of the country, there is no widely accepted term to describe women who identify as lesbians ("tomboy" is the closest approximation).[5] Exploring further what is unique about performing a gay identity in the Philippines illustrates why the country's call centers have earned the reputation of being a "gay paradise."

The longstanding Tagalog term for men who seek romantic and/or sexual relationships with other men is *bakla*. The term, gender scholar Susan Stryker points out, can serve as both an epithet and a badge of pride, much as does the word *queer* in the United States.[6] Increasingly, however, it is being supplanted by the English term *gay*, especially among young people in urban areas such as Manila. Most of my interviewees referred to themselves as "gay" more often than as *bakla*, even when speaking in Tagalog, and so I have and will continue to use the term "gay" in this discussion. But it is essential to keep in mind that, as sociologist Emmanuel David articulates, "while . . . Filipinos [usually] translate *bakla* with the word 'gay,' an exact English equivalent doesn't exist."[7]

In short, the Western term "gay", though regularly used in the Philippines today, belies "incommensurable cultural ideologies of gender and sexuality"[8]

Gayness in the Philippines emphasizes public performance over sexuality per se. To be gay is to be one who has "come out" (*paglaladlad ng kappa*, or having unveiled one's cape), regardless of whether or not one engages in sexual acts with other men. This public presentation may entail continuing to dress and present as male (though, as the case of Boi shows, in a stylized manner that differentiates one from the straight Filipino male); it may entail occasional cross-dressing; or it may (more rarely) involve cross-dressing exclusively.[9] Furthermore, those persons who present as gay have traditionally *not* pursued relationships with other gays. As anthropologist Martin F. Manalansan IV writes, "sexual relationships between *baklas* [have long been] seen as incestuous, unnatural and weird. Some *baklas* view the act in cannibalistic terms (*kumakain ng sariling laman*—"eating one's flesh")."[10] Rather, *baklas* (gays) pursue men who present as straight (such as Carl). The latter may be more or less open about their affairs with gay men without compromising their heterosexual identities, so long as they otherwise maintain a façade of masculinity.

The successful performance of gayness in the Philippines today is as much about class and national identity as it is about gender roles. Although both sex between men and cross-dressing (transvestitism) were documented in the Philippines prior to colonization, the current essence of a gay identity appears to have solidified in urban areas during the 1950s and 1960s.[11] The gay community in Manila (and to a lesser extent Cebu City, a provincial capital in the central Philippines) began adopting styles of dress and speech that marked both aspirations to a higher social class and a positive orientation to the West. This emergent ideal of "beauty [was] about appropriating American symbols of glamour"—in particular, those that suggested upper-class, urban femininity.[12] This ideal was alive and well among my respondents. Words that they commonly used to describe themselves or to complement others included *posh, diva, biyuti* (beauty), *soshal* (socialite), and cosmopolitan.

In everyday Philippine life, one performs a *posh* gay identity in two important ways: one's physical appearance and one's speech. As J. Neil Garcia, a gay poet, humorously describes: "In our country, gays . . . have a distinct quality about them. . . . They speak funnily, swish their hips, and wave their broken wrists as though they are already movie stars."[13] A thin yet curvy physique, stylishly cut hair, and stereotypically Western features (such as blue eyes) are idealized, and may be obtained via enhancements ranging from wigs, to colored contact lenses, to surgical augmentations of the breasts or buttocks (although gender reassignment surgeries are rare).[14] As for dress,

"Filipinos ... believe that the clothes that [a gay individual] wears are external signs of the inner core, of essential qualities of feminine sensibility and emotion."[15] Staying up on current fashions is a key component of this sensibility. Those who cross-dress wear closely cut dresses with short hemlines and heels. Those who, like Boi, maintain a male façade aspire to be seen in "branded" clothing and accessories. During my fieldwork, such a fashionable "socialite" would be adorned in skinny Levis, Tom's slippers, and a pastel Hollister t-shirt.

As much as clothing or cosmetics, having a particular way of *speaking* is key to performing gayness in everyday life. There is a longstanding linguistic style among gay Filipinos known as *swardspeak,* the term derived from a word meaning roughly "effeminate" or "sissy."[16] It constitutes "a particular argot . . . that encodes the speaker as [gay]."[17] Although few of my respondents referenced the term explicitly to describe how they learned and utilized language, it was clear that gay Filipinos continue to speak a distinctive linguistic style. This subcultural lingo entails being fluent in English, familiar with various "celebrities' names and trademark brands," and flexible with one's speech.[18] As an informant in a study by Bobby Benedicto explained, it is attractive to be "someone who speaks fluent English without trying"; "good English," stated another, "is a turn on."[19]

It follows that to successfully perform a gay identity entails being not at all reticent about speaking English in public, even to the point that one could be perceived as showing off. The English term "loud" (*malakas*) is often used to describe gay persons in the Philippines today. It refers less to the volume of a voice than to the speaker's general confidence and willingness to experiment with words and phrases. For "loud" speakers, every conversation is a game. It is an opportunity to demonstrate sophistication at moving back and forth between English and Tagalog, at making puns, and at taking advantage of phonetic ambiguities between the two languages. By "switching and shuttling between languages," Manalansan IV writes, a gay person "acquires a cosmopolitanism that is denied him elsewhere."[20]

Gayness as Accepted Spectacle

In both appearance and speech, gay Filipinos distinguish themselves from mainstream, or hegemonic, masculinity in the Philippines. The stereotype of the typical Filipino is that of a rotund man wearing baggy jeans or cargo shorts, flip-flops, and a basketball jersey; should he be at work or in a professional setting, his attire will be simple and traditionally cut. He will prefer to speak in Tagalog (or any regional language with which he is familiar), attempting English only when necessary. This difference between the gender performances of gay and straight men raises the question of how gay persons are treated in the Philippines generally. How does mainstream society interpret them, to what extent are they accepted, and what rights do they have?

The place of the gay community in the Philippines can be conceptualized as a reversal of the LGBT community's place in a wealthy country such as the United States. In what can be called the *political sphere*, the LGBT community in the United States has constituted itself as a visible and active movement. Over the past several decades, it has succeeded in securing various rights and protections for LGBT persons at the local, state, and federal levels.[21] These rights include the freedom to marry, protection from employment discrimination, and the passage of hate crime laws. In contrast, in what we can call the *public sphere*, the presence of the LGBT community remains largely out of view. Outside of neighborhoods in large cities such as San Francisco or New York—what sociologist Amin Ghaziani calls gay "cultural enclaves"—it is rare to see overt expressions of homosexuality in American life.[22] Even mainstream media such as television and film have historically avoided depicting LGBT individuals and dealing with issues of relevance to the LGBT community.[23]

The converse for the political sphere holds in the Philippines. Elected officials, judges, and other political actors have refused to extend rights and protections to gay persons in the country. In 2014, the UNDP (United Nations Development Program) and USAID (United States Agency for International Development) published a critical review of the Philippine government's handling of LGBT issues. They roundly condemned inconsistencies between the government's commitment to human rights generally and its extension of these rights to the LBGT community:

> As a member of the UN, the Philippines is signatory to various international covenants promoting human rights. However . . . the Permanent Representative of the Philippines to the UN did not support the June 2011 Joint Statement at the UN Human Rights Council urging States to end violence, criminal sanctions and related human rights violations based on [sexual orientation and gender identity]. . . . This is evidence that LGBT people are not always supported by the state.[24]

Policies and laws in the Philippines that do mention LGBT issues, the report continues, "portray LGBT people negatively because their sexual orientation and gender identity is associated as socially bad or psychologically detrimental, similar to how alcoholism and drug addiction are portrayed by the law."[25]

The powerful influence of the Catholic church in the Philippines explains to a large degree why "legal recognition and protection of LGBT people at the national level remains absent."[26] But so does what the Filipino literary scholar J. Neil Garcia laments as the "failure of a gay movement to take root in mainstream Philippine society during the late twentieth and early twenty-first centuries."[27] The UNDP and USAID report documented approximately one hundred organizations representing LGBT groups in the Philippines, but concluded that they were largely splintered and ineffective:

> There remains no umbrella LGBT organization in the Philippines. . . . [O]rganizations tend to work independently of one another. Due to these divisions, there remains no prioritization of efforts [and hence] . . . a lack of an agreed-upon national political agenda [and] no formal mechanisms available to allow them to participate in drafting public policies.[28]

Anthropologist Michael Tan attributes the tepid pace of mobilization for LGBT issues to the country's polarized class structure.[29] The majority of gay Filipinos, like the majority of Filipinos, are rural and poor; they live their lives as members of the *masa* tied closely to their families and their immediate neighborhoods. They confront a national state that follows the dictates of the Catholic church much more so than the emergent global norm of formal equality for LGBT persons.

As for the public sphere, gay persons in the Philippines, though disempowered in the political sphere, are highly visible in everyday life. In towns and villages, local gay communities form neighborhood groups known as *parloristas*.[30] These groups, while they are rarely political, organize shows and beauty pageants that are often well attended by the straight community. In both urban and rural settings, furthermore, it is not uncommon to see openly-gay individuals on the street and in other public places. Philippine television networks, meanwhile, carry a good many entertainment and variety programs featuring gay performers. As one group of scholars describe:

> [Gays] are a common sight in the Philippines. . . . In most towns and cities one can easily observe them going about their everyday life; shopping, meeting friends, going to the cinema, eating and drinking in cafes, using public transport, visiting their church. They appear on

television, are the subject of documentaries and magazine articles, and compete in beauty contests.[31]

Tolerance of gay persons in the public sphere suggests that ordinary Filipinos are much less under the sway of homophobic Catholic doctrines than are their politicians, judges, and legislators. A 2012 Pew Research Center survey found that three-fourths of Filipinos agreed that "homosexuality should be accepted by society."[32] This made the Philippines one of the most tolerant countries in Asia and significantly more so than in the United States, where only 60% of adults endorsed that statement. As the Pew report summarized, "Filipinos are considerably more tolerant of homosexuality than the country's relatively high levels of religiosity would suggest."[33]

It would be a mistake, however, to conflate public visibility—or even tolerance, as expressed in surveys—with true acceptance and equality. As Garcia writes:

> [W]hen visitors to the Philippines remark that Filipinos openly tolerate and/or accept homosexuality, they invariably have in mind effeminate, cross-dressing men . . . swishing down streets and squealing on television program[s] with flaming impunity. To equate Philippine society's tolerance for public displays of transvestism with wholesale approval of homosexual behavior is *naive, if not downright foolish*. . . . [T]he *bakla* as transvestic, effeminate, and *ludicrous . . .* elicits *benevolent disdain* [rather than] homophobic persecution.[34]

Gay Filipinos—even those who cross-dress—are tolerated in the public sphere only insofar as they conform to a specific stereotype and are willing to subject themselves to a certain amount of "benevolent disdain." As anthropologist Fenella Cannell summarizes it, gays (*bakla*) "are rarely the targets of hatred or prejudiced violence as . . . in the West; however, at the same time, *bakla* are not always treated as persons of equal dignity."[35] In a phrase, gay persons must accept that mainstream society is laughing at them, and not with them.

Neglected in the political sphere and tolerated as humorous "others" in public life, gay persons in the Philippines often encounter troubles within their kin groups.[36] Systematic evidence on how young Filipino men are received by their families as they transition to gay status is scarce. In a survey administered to a convenience sample of 147 gay Filipinos, Winter and colleagues found that the experience of coming out was more likely to encounter disapproval from the father of the household than from the mother.[37]

The UNDP/USAID report estimates that physical abuse of LGBT minors by older (especially) male kin is greatly underreported throughout the country.[38] My interviews with gay call center agents suggest that those who continue to live with their primary groups are more likely to superficially pass as straight men; workers who live alone or in boarding houses are more likely to adopt a female nickname (such as *tita*) and occasionally cross-dress.

This dilemma of passing versus presenting confronts gay persons in the labor market as well. Should they commit to a full female presentation, or even a highly effeminate one, they are usually consigned to narrow occupational niches. It is widely accepted that hairstylists, beauticians, fashion designers, entertainers, and wedding planners are among those few domestic occupations in which gay Filipinos can be fully "out."[39] For gay persons seeking employment abroad, the options are limited to positions such as performers on cruise ships and nightclub singers.[40] In short, there is widespread evidence that gay Filipinos face discrimination throughout the labor market and that the situation will not change anytime soon, insofar as "there are no intentions to pass national anti-discrimination laws that exclusively seek to protect LGBT people" in the country.[41] In Emmanuel David's words, gay persons in the Philippines have long been channeled into "purple collar ghettos."[42]

A Perfect Match?

The emergence of a call center industry represented a new field of possibilities for gay persons in the Philippines. From the start, there was a *mutual attraction* between foreign voice capital and the gay community. Consider the viewpoint of American (and to a lesser extent, British, Canadian, and Australian) call center firms as they began evaluating the Philippines as an investment site in the early 2000s. They must have been pleasantly surprised to find that the distinctive subcultural lingo of the Philippine gay community approximates nearly perfectly the form of human capital most desired by these Western call centers. In metro Manila today, the successful performance of a gay identity entails being fluent and confident in English, thinking on one's feet, being flexible with intonation and accent, and exhibiting a familiarity with various aspects of Western, and especially American, culture.

Call center managers in the Philippines repeatedly referenced these traits when discussing their gay employees. For instance, during a conversation with an HR officer whose duties entailed administering the English fluency exams, I asked whether he thought that gay applicants fared better in employment considerations. "Of course," he exclaimed without hesitation, "they are so *loud* [i.e., confident] in the interviews!" A similar sentiment was voiced to Emmanuel David during an interview with a call center manager in Manila: "they [gay agents] tend to be more *fearless* in their voice . . . than any ordinary men."[43]

Running alongside and in fact compatible with this supposed brashness is an assessment of gay lingo as softer and more adaptable. As one floor manager, himself gay, explained to me:

> We can really *adapt* well. Usually we can . . . how would you describe it . . . like *change* to sound more British or more *romantic* or whatever else. We are unlike [straight] men because they have, what would you call it, a *deep* tone, very *harsh* tone.

Or as an American executive with a Manila call center described it to me: "Gays are good *conversationalists*. They can speak *good English* and they are *sweet* with their voice."

Firms themselves do not systematically collect data on applicant and employee gender orientation, and so it is not possible to say with certainty that gay persons do better on the entrance exams or on the phones. But interviews with call center managers and HR personnel suggest a strong belief that such differences do exist. Insofar as voice capital desires workers who speak English confidently, competently, and flexibly, it desires gay Filipinos.

There are other sources of attraction between foreign voice capital and gay Filipinos. Because the gay personae is widely interpreted as "loud," "hilarious," and entertaining, gays often serve as a "social lubricant" inside the call center itself.[44] By joking with, teasing, and generally performing for their co-workers (the majority of whom are cisgender women), gay employees distract from the tedium and pressure of the work. There is a longstanding finding in industrial sociology, dating back to the work of Donald Roy and Michael Burawoy, that seemingly trite rituals such as joking can lessen the monotony of highly routinized jobs and thereby produce consent to the work.[45]

My data, and in particular my interviews with female workers, supported this idea. Multiple respondents mentioned, without prompting, how the presence of gays made their work tolerable and even enjoyable. As Rodalyn said, "At my work we have lots of gays, who are fun. Really, it's very fun to be with my gay friends." And in Hannah's words: "When we do team-building exercises, I like to partner with my homosexual friends because it's so easy to be with gays. They're happy and it's so nice to be with them."

The initial attraction between call centers and gay persons is mutual. As opposed to the female workers discussed in the previous chapter, gay persons rarely pursue call center work as a means of fulfilling the duty of breadwinner. Unlike *ates* (eldest sisters), the gay role in the Philippines does not require sacrifice to support extended kin networks. And because gays are unable to marry or adopt children, they are less likely to experience the equivalent effect of "man troubles" (such as annulment fees and children to feed). Rather, the middle path of call center employment is attractive to gay persons because it lacks the barriers they would encounter when pursuing mainstream professions and vocations. Gatekeepers in traditional fields such as teaching, nursing, and accounting discriminate against men who present as women or even display the styles and mannerisms associated with being gay in the Philippines. To be taken seriously as job applicants or visa candidates, the UNDP/USAID report found, gay persons have to pass—that is, to "present themselves as males by cutting their hair short, dressing in men's clothes, and acting in stereotypically masculine ways."[46]

The call center industry, in contrast, quickly developed a reputation for not only *not* discriminating against gay applicants but also for *accommodating* those who wish to express their gay identity. My gay interviewees were unanimous in reporting that, relative to other employers in metro Manila, call centers do not "give you that negative vibe" (as one respondent put it) when filling out an application or sitting down for an interview. Emmanuel David found that some call centers in Manila allow gay employees to cross-present on the phones (i.e., to adopt a female name and speak to callers in a female voice). Call centers also readily promote gay agents into managerial positions if they do well on the phones and they build a good rapport with their coworkers. As my respondent Roland explained:

> In the call center you're given equal opportunities no matter what you are. They don't look at your gender mainly. You know a lot of people, if they perform no matter what they are, they get the job. Most of the people in the supervisor position right now at my work, they're also mostly gays.

At CallCo, the firm where I performed fieldwork, the dress code was casual. Gay workers were free to wear stylish jeans, shirts, and sandals. Managers told me that they were not aware of whether workers were cross-presenting on the phones, but that they would not discipline such behavior unless callers complained about it—which they hadn't. Furthermore, transvestitism was fully integrated into the various extracurricular activities hosted by this call center. On Friday evenings, for instance, the call center's lobby was repurposed into a small event venue at which staff members could perform for their co-workers. Karaoke and quiz nights were in the rotation, but so were beauty contests and dance routines in which the performers would be gay employees fully cross-performing. The reaction to such performances was generally positive and boisterous, with lots of cheers, shouts of encouragement, and laughter that seemed more benevolent than disdainful.

Young and Restive

For young gay persons in Manila, call centers hold an obvious attraction. They provide high wages relative to other employers in the city, and they are spaces wherein expressions of gay identity are tolerated and even encouraged. It does not seem to be the case, however, that this initial attraction evolves into satisfaction or loyalty. Figure 7.3 shows that gay employees are distinctive within the larger space of call center workers for being single, but also for perceiving their interactions with callers as disrespectful and for continuing to aspire to professional work or a life abroad. In other words, they appear to be the

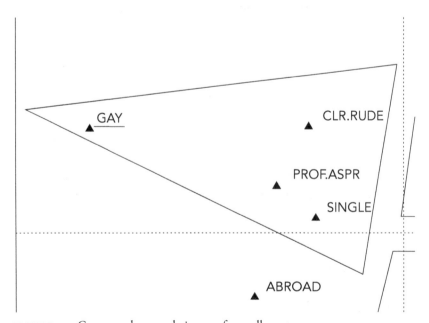

FIGURE 7.3 Correspondence analysis map of gay call agents.

least satisfied and most restless of agents. Considering each of these attributes suggests that gay employees remain attached to the call center industry both because it is a "gay paradise" and because they are unable to pursue larger dreams.

Going Solo

Gay employees had distinct sets of *social ties and obligations*. On the one hand, all fifteen gay call center agents in my sample were coded as "single," in that they were neither married nor cohabitating with a long-term partner. As established earlier, for Filipinos living on the edge of poverty, being single can put them at a disadvantage relative to others who are coupled, insofar as the latter arrangement allows the pooling of resources and consolidation of expenses. Many gay workers had romantic involvements and/or pursuits, some of which were long term. But because of prohibitions against gay marriage and difficulties with procuring a shared apartment (namely, discrimination from landlords, along with the general custom of romantic partners not cohabitating before marriage), none of these relationships produced stable, coupled households. Gay call center agents typically lived alone in boarding houses, or, like Boi, with roommates in a crowded flat.

On the other hand, gay call center agents were far less likely than female employees to occupy the role of breadwinner, with its attendant responsibilities and sacrifices. Whereas 80% of women reported using a substantial portion of their salary to materially support kin, only 33% of gay workers reported such obligations. The obligations of gay breadwinners, furthermore, did not seem to be as onerous as those of females.

A.J., for instance, is a twenty-eight-year-old agent who answers calls from American TracFone customers. He lives alone in a boarding house and reported supporting his parents on an infrequent basis. He explained to me that, "most of my earnings are my own personal money, but there are some cases that I give to my parents for their needs."

"Is it a regular thing?" I asked.

"I would say every three months," he replied, "They will contact me and say, 'We need money, we have to pay some bills for the electric, for the water bills.' And so then I give."

Although I classified A.J. as a breadwinner, it is clear that he provides for kin less regularly and less urgently than do women such as Hannah, who find themselves unexpectedly thrust into desperate circumstances.

"Words Affect Me"

Despite keeping the majority of their earnings for themselves, the gay workers whom I studied were the least satisfied with their employment in the call center industry. In particular, they were by far the most likely (at 87%) to perceive their interactions with callers as unpleasant and troubling. (Comparable figures for women and straight men were 33% and 53%, respectively). It does not appear to be the case that foreign callers were identifying them as gay and then making homophobic or hostile remarks. None of my respondents felt that callers were able to "read" their voices as those of gay persons.

While gay call center agents occasionally received the same sort of abusive treatment as did other workers, *they were less able to reframe or rationalize it.* Many respondents described themselves as unable to practice what in Tagalog is known as *pakikisama*, or suppressing one's emotions so as to ensure the harmony of a current interaction.

Breadwinner Hannah rationalized that, "When [callers] are irate or they are upset, they swear. But after they say that, they will apologize and . . . so it's understandable." In contrast, twenty-one-year-old Glenn, who fields directory assistance calls for a U.S. telecom, was greatly troubled when callers criticized his accent or expressed annoyance at speaking to a Filipino. "Here in Manila, if someone will speak bad words about me, it will not hurt that much. But on the international account, oh, my God! When they say those words, it really affects me." Francis, who services claims for an American insurance company, reported having one to two interactions each day that troubled and lingered with him. These were callers who perceived that Francis was not an American and demanded to be transferred to a U.S. representative. Francis understood that this was likely due to the caller's concern about transmitting sensitive information to an offshore locale. "They want to trust their own people with regards to their claim," he reasoned, "because there's money involved." Francis nonetheless experienced such requests as "offensive" and admitted lingering over them after his shift ended and feeling "bitter."

What accounts for gay workers' greater sensitivity to the irate and/or nativist callers that all offshored agents inevitably encounter? One explanation is that gay workers were less financially desperate than were the breadwinners, and so had less of an incentive to rationalize criticism. Another is that because being able to successfully pose as a native English speaker is an essential component of gay identity, negative appraisals from de facto experts on one's vocal performance—native English speakers—are particularly devastating. To be gay in the Philippines is to speak and mimic English well; failing to do so threatens one's larger identity and sense of self. The stakes in this language game were not nearly as high for cisgender women or men.

Dreaming of Elsewhere

Another indicator of gay respondents' restiveness at work is their ongoing aspirations to leave the call center. Of the three categories of employees in this study, it was gay persons who were most likely to continue to yearn both for work in a traditional profession (at 67%) and for a life abroad (at 87%). Josh, for instance, who had studied biology, continues to dream of becoming a scientist:

> For me, even before I embarked in a call center life, I already knew that it would be a temporary thing. It is not really a long-term career. You just need to have a good command of the English language, but I really would still like to pursue what I studied.

Roland, a twenty-four-year-old gay worker, was looking for a means to go abroad. At the time of our first interview in 2012, he was active on websites that connect Western (American or European) men with gay men in Southeast Asia. Recently he'd been chatting and Skyping with a significantly older man in California. Roland was trying to convince the man to come visit him in Manila or, better yet, buy him a plane ticket to Los Angeles. In the exchange that follows, Roland describes his plan to me in a stylized lingo exhibiting familiarity with American pop culture (or at least a greater familiarity than I possessed):

JEFF: Are you interested to go abroad someday, to live or work?
ROLAND: For me, yah. I will leave. I have plans.
JEFF: You have plans?
ROLAND: I have a king bed waiting for me in California. I found that there are a lot of California king beds.
JEFF: King bed?
ROLAND: It's a song [a 2010 song by Rihanna].
JEFF: Who is the king?
ROLAND: A guy, a cute guy. He's not just anyone, not just someone, he's the one.

As of 2014, when last I interviewed Roland, he had fallen out of contact with this particular "California king bed." He continued to work as a call center agent, however, and to peruse these dating sites in the hopes of finding "the one."

Francis, who left a nursing internship to work in the call center industry, also has a strong desire to leave the Philippines. As a teenager, he had traveled with his family to visit relatives in Germany. The trip had a profound effect on him: "After that, I'm planning to get away from the Philippines and stay away. I want to spend my life in Europe. I'm aspiring to work there." Europe seemed to represent to him the symbolic opposite of the Philippines:

> The lifestyle there is very easy. It's more like a bachelorette lifestyle. You know in Europe, they don't have traffic and the roads are so clean. All are taking the train. Yes. I see myself in Europe working and living an easy life.

Twenty-eight-year-old Bernard expressed a similar sentiment—and sentimentality—toward the West:

> I don't have plans of staying here [in the Philippines] for very long. I want to get out of the country. I'm getting older, and every time I think about New York, I want to be there. In *Cosmo* [*Cosmopolitan* magazine], it said that everyone there is so busy. I want to have that life. I want to be busy.

The dreams of Roland, Francis, and Bernard support Bobby Bendicto's argument that for gay Filipinos, "America [and other foreign locales] take on a key role as the site onto which dreams of mobility are projected."[47]

Not Saving and Therefore Staying

Manila's call center industry is widely known as a "gay paradise." The cultural competency most valued within the gay community—speaking English well—is also the key form of human capital desired by call center firms. Unlike in other fields of work, gay employees are not discriminated against and are free to express their gender identities. Nonetheless, gay call center agents are the least satisfied with the nature of the work and are the most likely to aspire to other careers or a life abroad. This restiveness does not, however, appear to manifest itself in terms of high turnover rates for gay workers. All fifteen of my gay respondents remained in the industry at the end of the study period (including Boi, after a failed attempt to enter the teaching profession). None of the dozens of managers and HR officials with whom I spoke felt that turnover among this subgroup was a problem. It certainly did not affect the industry's low attrition rate overall. If the women discussed in the prior chapter stayed at their jobs as an ongoing solution to the dilemma of breadwinning, what accounts for gay workers' attachment to the job?

As was established earlier, one reason why gay call agents are unable to move onto professional or migratory paths is that they would continue to encounter discrimination. The lack of legal protections for LGBT persons in the Philippines means that gatekeepers of these paths (such as employers and government agencies) can deny gay persons opportunities such as internships, jobs, and migration documents. Seriously pursuing these opportunities too often requires attempting to pass as straight. Boi, for instance, stated on several occasions that the main reason he has never considered presenting as female is that doing so would effectively end his dream of being a public school teacher.

Another obstacle is that embarking upon these other paths requires financial resources. One needs material support while seeking employment or performing a mandatory internship, application fees for an overseas placement must be paid in advance, and so on. It stands to reason that using one's call center earnings to save is a precondition for leaving the industry. This was one mechanism (among others) tying breadwinning women to the call center: their obligations to kin prevented them from accumulating savings. Three-fourths of the women reported living paycheck to paycheck. Despite having fewer financial obligations, gay call agents were almost as likely (at 60%) to lack any savings at all.

My gay respondents had a ready explanation for their low rates of saving: the successful staging of the gay identity is expensive. This explanation was typically embedded in some form of self-deprecating humor, typically about the inability to resist various temptations. Josh, for instance, joked that "Before we worked in the call center, we [could] only afford to buy the things that we need. But now we can also buy the things that we want."

When pressed to elaborate precisely the sorts of things that they now "wanted," my gay respondents mentioned various categories of goods. These included consumer durables that serve as markers of status and sophistication. Rather than shopping at bazaars for knockoffs of branded clothing and accessories, they could now purchase authentic goods from malls and department stores. To get an idea of how purchasing *authentic* goods cuts into one's ability to save, consider that at the time of my fieldwork a popular shoe such as Tom's sandals or low-cut Converse All-Stars sneakers could be bought as decent knockoffs for $3 to $10. Yet authentic versions cost the same as they would in the United States—between $30 and $50, or up to ten times as much. The same holds for electronics and especially cell phones. A simple flip phone or imitation smartphone could be purchased for the equivalent of $10 or $20, whereas a genuine smartphone (such as an iPhone) ran into the hundreds or even thousands. Nonetheless, according to Roland, "Because we are more *soshal*, like higher class, we are wanting to have the newest touch-screen [phone] to show off, or whatever."

Another common expenditure consists of gifts for ostensibly straight men. The high income associated with call center employment allows workers to enact what Martin Manalansan IV calls the "social script" of gayness in the Philippines, according to which the gay male "slaves away at work in order to . . . get what . . . he should desire—the 'straight' macho man."[48] My respondents spoke often and openly about their "crushes": straight men whom they were actively "courting" through extravagant gifting (especially of branded goods such as NBA jerseys or Ray-Ban sunglasses) and "treating" (that is, by paying for food, drinks, and transport). Several agents boasted of having acquired "boyfriends"—that is, straight men with whom they were having clandestine relationships. These relationships often involved regular physical contact, as well as a degree of emotional involvement (expressed usually through frequent texting via cell phone). The "social script" of gender behavior in the Philippines, it must be pointed out, allows the straight male to accept gifts and even money from his gay partner without thinking of himself as gay or transgender.[49]

Boi's constant expenditures on Carl, his "boyfriend with a girlfriend," described at the beginning of this chapter, were by no means idiosyncratic. Along with speaking English fluently and adorning oneself with authentic Western goods, maintaining one or more "macho men" is a key element of successfully performing a gay identity in the Philippines. And as Boi's experience of trying unsuccessfully to restart his teaching career illustrates, this performance effectively anchors gay workers to the call center industry. Taken as a whole, gay call agents embody a second source of affinity between local workers and foreign voice capital in the Philippines. Though restless, they have limited options beyond the call center and so they stay attached to the industry. This leaves just one further category of workers whose attraction and attachment to offshored call centers need to be understood: straight-identified men.

8

Rooted Men

STRAIGHT-IDENTIFIED MEN MAKE up only about 15% of the call center labor force in metro Manila. This puts their representation on a par with that of gay call center agents. But whereas gay employees are *overrepresented* in the industry relative to their numbers in the general population, straight men are *underrepresented*. Certainly, no one speaks of Philippine call centers as a "straight male paradise."

The first task of this chapter is to address the absence of men on the call center floor. Here are jobs that pay quite well relative to other opportunities in the Philippines. So, why do men, who are in so many ways advantaged in Philippine society, not monopolize them? Cultural conventions for performing masculinity, I will argue, lead men to self-exclude themselves from voice-work. Wages are only one of many factors that job seekers consider when ranking their employment opportunities. Job requirements such as speaking English, communicating well verbally, and being associated with a feminine or gay space effectively repel most Filipino men from the call center industry.

The second goal of this chapter is to speak about the lives and experiences of those men who *do* become call agents. Like all young and struggling Filipinos, they are drawn to the industry's high salaries. Unlike most men, however, they are able to adjust their gender identities so as to square call center work with the performance of masculinity in the Philippines. Once they do so, they appear to become contently "rooted" in the call center. They are not breadwinners, they do not aspire to go abroad, and they are able to use their call center jobs to accumulate savings. Select straight-identified men, I conclude, embody a third and final pathway to low attrition in the Philippine call center industry.

Absent Men

It is practically a truism among those who study work and inequality that men monopolize the high-paying occupations and professions.[1] This holds *across* industries (men predominant in high-paying corporate law, for instance, whereas women do in lower-paying elementary education), as well as *within* them (with men overrepresented among high-earning physicians and women among lower-paid nurses).[2] When women move into male-dominant occupations, the remuneration and status associated with those jobs drop accordingly.[3] Conversely, when there emerge new, high-paying industries—such as financial trading or information technology—men quickly rush into them and existing patterns of sex and gender inequality at work are reproduced.[4]

This latter pattern seems to fit the case of the Indian call center industry, as discussed in chapter 3. When Western voice capital first alighted in India, it discovered that the potential labor pool (the country's English-speaking college graduates) did not align with the actual labor pool. Young men from well-off families were attracted to the high wages offered by call centers and then used these jobs as springboards into better-paying and higher-status IT positions. Educated young women were similarly attracted, though the stigma associated with working outside the home—especially at night— made it difficult for them to obtain and persist in call center jobs. In the end, men monopolized call center jobs as a means to earn a quick buck and to accumulate relevant experience for subsequent mobility.

The history of the call center industry in India also illustrates that there is nothing inherent to talking on the phone that encodes voice work as masculine or feminine. Sociologist Arlie Hochschild made this point years ago, in her classic study of male bill collectors, as reported in the book *The Managed Heart*.[5] Why, then, are Filipino men so underrepresented in the call center industry? There is no disputing that these are good jobs relative to other opportunities available to college graduates in metro Manila.

Not Discrimination

It could be that Filipino men *do* seek call center jobs, but that firms and managers have a preference for female workers. This has been documented to be the case for offshored manufacturing facilities in the Philippines and elsewhere in the Global South. Foreign hiring managers seek, and countries themselves promote, female workers as ideal employees. Their "nimble" fingers and docile dispositions supposedly render them as perfect employees for doing monotonous work on assembly lines, while their lack of power makes them largely disposable in the eyes of foreign capital.[6]

I did not, however, find any evidence that call center managers in the Philippines used such stereotypes to give preferential treatment to female (or even gay) workers. On the contrary, when the topic was raised of how heavily skewed by sex and gender orientation were their workforces, they tended to express puzzlement. For instance, James, an HR manager at a Manila call center, agreed with my assessment that men are largely absent on the production floor. Yet he struggled to explain why: "We have these diversity policies in place and our HR staff is diverse. But eighty percent of our operators are women. It's all women. We're constantly looking for some guys to come work for us." While it's not clear whether James is including gay call center agents in his assessment of his firm's demographics, the larger point is that he does not appear to evince any bias against male workers.

Procedures for screening job applicants further suggest that the feminization of the Philippine call center labor force does not result from any sex or gender-orientation preference on capital's part. Across firms, the screening process is highly standardized. Applicants are directed to a facility's HR office, where they either submit a résumé or fill out a questionnaire concerning their work and schooling history. A point person will then quickly scan the document to verify that the applicant has met the minimum level of education required by the client on a particular account (typically a bachelor's degree).

There *were* two hints of bias at this stage about which I heard repeatedly. Many firms, it was widely believed, discriminated against nursing graduates, based on the belief that they were merely looking to accumulate enough earnings to pay for their board exams. Managers also supposedly tossed out applications from elite university graduates, who were viewed as only looking to make a quick buck with which to finance the purchase of a consumer good, such as a new smartphone. Even if such rumors were true, they would not explain the underrepresentation of male call center agents. Nursing graduates are more likely to be female, while it is doubtful that male graduates of elite universities are applying in large enough numbers to skew the overall composition of Manila's call center workforce.

Applicants with adequate education credentials then queue up to undergo a one-on-one verbal exam. The testers are typically former call center agents who have been trained and credentialized in one of several standardized English testing protocols. These testing systems are designed, according to one firm that markets them, to "identify agents with acceptable language levels quickly, *fairly*, and *objectively*."[7] In other words, just as the call center labor process is intensely standardized so as to leave the call center agents minimal discretion, the process of evaluating candidates is standardized so as to allow minimal discretion for evaluators.

These tests typically begin with the interviewer posing an open-ended query, such as "Tell me about yourself." After applicants finish their introductions, interviewers then pose a string of scripted questions and have the applicants read aloud written passages of text. As the interviewee speaks, the interviewer checks off a series of items on a standardized grading sheet. At CallCo-Manila, the facility where I performed fieldwork, this checklist required interviewers to assess both general grammatical proficiency and the degree to which the speaker's speech was accented. Examples of the former criteria, regarding basic grammar, included:

- Tense consistency (past, present, future)
- Word forms (singular/plural)
- Pronoun usage (he, she, it, etc.)

The following were, in turn, examples of checks for accented (and thus "incorrect") speech patterns common among Filipino speakers of English:

- Consonant *r* (no rolling of the tongue as in **thrrree for three**)
- Consonants *b* and *v*: (**ban**) and (**van**)
- Vowels *i* and *e*: (**sit**), (**seat**), (**set**)

Because interviewers are usually experienced call center agents who have been promoted from within, they are likely to be female or gay. And it is possible that they hold biases, implicit or otherwise, against straight men. However, with the system for recording errors and scoring an applicant's overall performance so standardized, it is unlikely that male applicants are being graded more harshly—and thus being prematurely rejected—than would be the case with female and gay applicants.

The Pipeline

This brings us to the supply side of the labor market. Are straight men applying for call center jobs in the first place? Are those who do able to pass the entrance exams at the same rate as do women and gay applicants? My research suggests that the answer to both questions is no. As a result, the potential pipeline is siphoned: men are underrepresented in the initial applicant pool, and they perform worse on the standardized verbal exams.

That men do not apply for call center jobs was taken as a truism among the HR personnel whom I spoke with and worked among. For instance, when I raised the topic with Ellen, the head of the HR department at CallCo-Manila, she told me: "Look outside our door. At that line." (As usual, the hallway was packed with job applicants, sitting on benches and standing against the wall.) "Now, how many of them are a regular [straight-identified] man?" she asked, only somewhat rhetorically. For as on most days, a quick head count suggested that women were easily the majority of job applicants, while quite a few of the men were presenting as gay.

There are no data on the gender orientation of call center applicants across the industry. Individual firms record the sex of applicants on application forms, but do not differentiate between straight-identified male and gay applicants, nor do they routinely collate the data they do collect. Ellen, in order to validate her hunch, granted me permission to analyze all of CallCo's call center applications for the previous calendar month (which had seemed to us to be a typical time period). All told, the facility had interviewed 898 applicants, or an average of about 45 per business day (at any time, two to three HR personnel were actively interviewing applicants, such that each accomplished between 15 and 22 interviews daily). Of these applicants, 73.5% (660) listed their sex as female and 27.5% (238) as male. If we assume that the pool of male applicants was evenly split between gay and straight men, these figures accord well with my independent assessment of the demographics of the call center workforce as a whole (reported in chapter 5 as approximately 70% female, 15% gay, and 15% straight-identified men).

HR managers such as Ellen, along with personnel who work as interviewers, were generally of the opinion that straight-identified men performed more poorly on the verbal exams than did other applicants. Here I was unable to empirically test their anecdotal assumption. Exam success rates were basically the same between the 660 women and 238 biological men in the applicant pool during CallCo's previous month. Because I could not differentiate between straight-identified men and gay applicants, however, it was not possible to infer how well straight men had performed. National data suggest that women have higher English literacy rates than men,[8] but these data are based on written rather than verbal tests. In short, whereas the evidence seems incontrovertible that men in general are applying to call centers at rates far lower than would be expected (given that they constitute half of all college graduates), it is only suggestive that they perform less well on the standard verbal exams.

Hegemonic Masculinity

The initial puzzle posed in this section—of why straight-identified men are underrepresented in Philippine call centers—can now be recast as such. Why do men simply not apply for such work? Why do they voluntarily exclude themselves from these relatively well-paying jobs? To answer such questions entails considering the dominant, or hegemonic, meaning of masculinity in the Philippines. Among the *masa* of poor and working-class Filipinos, to be "a man" entails a certain set of actions and performances. It is my contention that *English fluency* (the main requirement to obtain call center work), *continuous verbal dialogue* (the work task at the center of the call center labor process), and the industry's larger reputation as a *gay paradise* are, in combination, so disagreeable with hegemonic masculinity in the Philippines that even high wages cannot compensate. In short, just as cultural assumptions about "responsible" women and *soshal* gays explain the *attraction* of call center work for these groups, successful performance of Filipino masculinity generates a *repulsion* to this very same work.

The extensive literature on Filipino migrant workers is a good starting point for understanding this dynamic. Working as an OFW (overseas foreign worker) and working in an offshored call center share two things in common: one usually labors in a different time zone, and one is employed by foreign capital. Yet at the time of my research, the sex composition of OFWs was roughly equal—1.11 million of the 2.23 million Filipinos working abroad were male and 1.12 million were female. In other words, neither time-zone differences nor working for foreign firms is the reason men do not desire call center work. These two factors do not skew the overall sex composition of the OFW pool.

The literature on migrant workers *does* show that men and women aspire to and are channeled into different occupations and industries.[9] The underlying pattern of this sorting appears to be that of a *binary* separating tasks requiring *service interactions* from those requiring *manual labor* (and minimal interaction with others outside of the immediate workgroup).

The sociologist Robyn Rodriguez, for instance, in her study of the Philippine government's migration bureaucracy, found that the deployment of migrant workers "reflects gendered logics."[10] Women obtain visas for positions such as household service workers, professional nurses, and caretakers; while men predominate as plumbers, wiremen, welders, and general laborers. Steven McKay performed ethnographic fieldwork among Filipino OFWs who were employed as seamen. He argues that men are drawn to this work because it allows them to "fashion themselves an occupational identity as *masculine exemplars*."[11] Seamen look down upon men who "rely too much on books but [who] don't hold tools"; they take pride in their "ability to creatively repair machinery"; and they generally embody a "masculinity that celebrates manual dexterity and hands-on experience."[12] McKay's findings resonate with España-Maram's historical research on male Filipinos who migrated to the United States during the early twentieth century. For them, manual labor in dangerous occupations, gambling acumen, and pugilistic prowess served as strong status symbols.[13] In short, to the extent that hegemonic masculinity among Filipino men entails having independence to do manual labor, we would expect that call center work—scripted and sedentary as it is—would hold minimal attraction.

For Filipino men, speaking English fluently exposes one to a potential loss of status honor. This I gleaned from myriad interactions during my fieldwork, ranging from informal conversations between me and acquaintances to formal questioning of research respondents. The consensus was that, unless one is from an upper-class family or has graduated from an elite university, speaking English fluently does and has long marked one as feminine or even gay. For example, Glynnis, the female call center agent from a poor family in Manila, did not find the dearth of men in her call center at all puzzling. It reflected, she explained, a pattern she'd seen since childhood in her family, neighborhood, and schools:

It's always been my observation that it's not considered appropriate for [Filipino] men to speak in English. When they're with their friends they get teased if they are speaking in English. Don't speak in English their friends say, *you're a man*.

Hannah, the breadwinner discussed at length in chapter 6, expressed a similar observation:

Usually you don't hear boys speak English a lot here in the Philippines. It's kind of girly, it gives you an air of being educated and *kikay* [chic or sassy]. If you are a boy you would rather go to a cockfight, do something with your hands. *Be a macho man*.

And Ferdinand, a straight-identified man with whom I worked in CallCo's HR department, explained how in the Philippines, learning to speak any second or third language entails being unafraid to publicly make errors in grammar or pronunciation. Filipino men, he explained, are especially prideful and hence are shy about exposing themselves to potential snickering:

> Here's why [men] are shy to speak English. Because they are doubtful, they are shy to speak it wrongly and then somebody *might laugh at them.*

As a result, "real" Filipino men prefer manual labor over service tasks. They would rather not speak English lest they be perceived as feminine or gay. There is also a scholarly literature on the sexual division of household labor in the Philippines which contends that it is women who exclusively "deal with money and control family finances";[14] they are their family's "treasurers."[15] More generally, women are assumed to be "calculating, instrumental, and direct,"[16] to be "more reliable [and] more skilled in economic interactions."[17] Men in turn are presumed to possess the opposite set of characteristics. Rather than calculating, instrumental, and direct, they are supposed to be passive and nonconfrontational, "easy going, and fun-loving,"[18] and more reticent in interactions.

I heard some iteration of this binary—the calculating/direct women versus the passive/nonconfrontational male—repeatedly while doing my fieldwork. Many men described Filipino masculinity via flattering metaphors and stories. As Randy, a call center manager, put it: "We men are like the towel of Bruce Lee, we bend with the wind and go with the flow." Dixon, a young call center agent, liked to paraphrase an old folktale he'd heard as a child. Long ago, a Filipino boy came to understand that he lived in a verdant and fertile land. Why labor in the fields like children and womenfolk, he reasoned, when he could lie on his back with his mouth open and be adequately fed by the rain water and falling fruits? Flexibility and even passivity, in such tellings, are signs of strength and ingenuity.

Not surprisingly, women are less likely to describe stereotypical Filipino masculinity in such flattering terms. Ellen, the HR manager at CallCo, retold the same story of the boy who would lie beneath a tree with his mouth agape as a typical Juan *Tamad* (lazy Juan) folktale. In her opinion, it demonstrates how men are all too willing to let others—in particular, "responsible women"—work and provide for them. Another common trope among women concerned the husband who is content to let his wife work while he sleeps in each day and does but a few household chores. As Glynnis explained to me, "We call them the 'three o'clock bread men,' who drink all night and sleep all day and [who] can barely get on the motorbike to go fetch bread at three in the afternoon."

Talking with others in smooth, nonaccented English is a primary skill required to work in a call center. So, too, is engaging in interactions that are often conflictual and problematic. Because such tasks are constituted as feminine/gay/nonmasculine in the larger gendered cosmos of the Philippines, my respondents emphasized repeatedly, men will not apply for call center jobs regardless of how well they pay.

While these folk beliefs about men's dispositions are widespread in the Philippines, I sought some empirical indicators of their reality. It struck me that the internet cafés found throughout the malls and in the streets of Manila offered an opportunity to collect just such data. The majority of young Filipinos do not have computers with high-speed internet connections in their homes, so internet cafés are extremely popular among this demographic. But what sort of activities do café-goers voluntarily pay for? And do they differ by sex? To answer, I began regularly walking through the internet cafés in various settings (upscale malls, metro stations, congested urban neighborhoods) and discretely recording (in a small notebook) what patrons were doing on the computers. (For the sake of comparing women and straight-identified men, I did not record the activities of patrons who presented as gay.)

In total, I recorded the activities of 582 patrons at forty internet cafes. These activities I grouped into five categories, presented in table 8.1 in order of overall frequency. Social networking (mainly via Facebook) was the most common at 42%, followed by playing games (typically first-person "shooters" or fantasy strategy games) at 32%, watching media (such as YouTube videos)

Table 8.1 Activity in Internet Café, by Sex

	Men	Women	Overall
Social Network	103 (28%)	141 (67%)	244 (42%)
Game	180 (49%)	6 (3%)	186 (32%)
Media	31 (8%)	30 (14%)	62 (11%)
Surf	35 (9%)	11 (5%)	46 (8%)
Doc	22 (6%)	23 (11%)	45 (8%)
N	371	211	582

at 11%, generally surfing the net at 8%, and working on a document (such as a school assignment) at 8%.

Men and women differed considerably in their online activities. Gaming, an action-oriented activity that entails minimal verbal interaction with others, was an overwhelmingly male activity. Approximately half of all men online were gaming, while only 6 of 186 observed gamers were women. In contrast, women were significantly more likely to be engaged in social networking, which involves maintaining relationships with others via dialogue. Sixty-seven percent of women in internet cafés were networking, whereas only 28% of men were. In short, the activities voluntarily undertaken in internet cafés align with what we would expect, given folk understandings of Filipino masculinity.

Phil and Brody

Though underrepresented relative to their availability in the potential labor pool, men are not completely absent from Manila's call centers. According to my estimate, they constitute a small but significant minority (around 15%) of agents. Who are these men who do apply for call center work and are able to successfully pass the verbal entrance exam? How exactly do they differ from their female and gay workmates? And what is the basis of their ongoing attachment to the call center industry?

To address these questions, let's consider two agents whom I interviewed together in 2013 and again separately in 2015: Brody, aged twenty-four and single, and Phil, aged forty-two and married with two children. The two men were call agents on the technical support line for Intuit's QuickBooks program. Both had, for idiosyncratic reasons, mastered English early in life. Both admitted to occasionally struggling with the stigma of working in an industry associated with women and gays. Nonetheless, both men came to find themselves rooted in call center work, using it as a means to accumulate savings and achieve a relative degree of prosperity.

Brody, the twenty-four-year-old, describes himself as a "nerd at heart" and an avid "gamer." His standard attire matches this identity, with baggy straight-cut blue jeans and a black World of Warcraft t-shirt covering his wiry frame. He grew up as the younger of two children in a relatively stable family in the heart of Manila. His father was a human resource manager for a Filipino bank and his mother, who had a college degree in education, was primarily a housewife, though she worked as an English tutor several mornings each week. He remembers that his parents "were very particular about speaking

English in the house," and would only allow him to play his computer games if he performed well in his English class at school. "That" he explained," is how I got fluent at an early point" in life.

Brody did not have any serious professional aspirations or a dream career. He had majored in hospitality management at a private college, mainly because he liked the atmosphere in upscale restaurants and could picture himself managing one someday. To graduate, he'd been required to do on the job training (OJT), which he completed with the American restaurant chain TGI Fridays. It had sent him to do a month-long stint as a bartender in Saudi Arabia. Brody recalls feeling isolated and lonely during his brief time in the Middle East and was more than ready to return home when his OJT ended. He'd performed well enough abroad that the company hired him as a server in a TGI Fridays branch in a Manila mall. The pay was poor, however, and it was not at all clear how long he'd have to take orders and clear tables before being promoted to a front-line supervisory position. He lasted four months at the job before deciding that he "wasn't feeling the food service thing" and quitting.

At that time Brody was twenty-one years old and still living at home. Though his family was by no means wealthy, both his parents were wage-earners while his older sister worked abroad and remitted money back to the family. To this day, Brody does not think or worry much about money. He certainly, as the youngest son, is not expected to make regular contributions to family finances. In fact, he proudly refers to himself as a "spoiled mama's boy" whose mother cooks for him, does his laundry, and generally cleans up after him. It was only a desire for discretionary income—some "spending money," as he calls it—that enticed him to apply to call centers.

With minimal expenses and a call center salary, Brody is easily able to maintain his laid-back lifestyle. "I'm drunk every morning," he boasted to me when describing his routine of proceeding with several of his workmates after their graveyard shift to a nearby resto-bar. There they sit at outside tables and order buckets full of San Mig Light beer on ice. Soon they light cigarettes and order plates of french fries, crispy chicken, pork *sisig*, and other "drinking food." When he returns home in the late morning or early afternoon, he retires to his small room, falls onto his bed, and sleeps until his mother rouses him for dinner. After he eats, it's off to a nearby internet café for a few hours of gaming until his shift begins at 11 p.m. When I asked Brody where he sees himself in five or ten years, he replied, "dito lang" (just right here). His brief stint working overseas in food service had established in him no desire to leave the country for work or to pursue further the profession for which he'd trained. For the foreseeable future, at least, earning good money by working the phones fits his lifestyle perfectly. He is happily rooted at home.

Forty-two-year-old Phil often joins his co-worker Brody and their workmates at the resto-bar when the graveyard shift ends. He usually only stays for a beer or two, however. As a married man with two children, he prefers to head home to see his son and daughter off to school in the morning. Phil's pathway to the call center was a circuitous one. He grew up in Tondo, a notorious slum in central Manila where to survive one must have considerable street smarts. While many of his schoolmates and neighborhood buddies entrenched themselves in the informal sector, Phil decided to join the army upon finishing high school. While he confesses to having been an "average student" in school, one who blew off his English classes and did just enough to get by, he took immediately to the culture of the armed forces. Phil advanced rapidly up the ladder in his regimen and soon found himself working alongside American soldiers and commanders. Here, he says, he had no choice but to "really learn English on the fly."

After six years in the military, Phil was honorably discharged and returned to his old neighborhood in Tondo. By now his parents had relocated to California on a family-based immigration visa after his older sister had married an American man. Phil began working with some old neighborhood friends in an auto detailing shop and was soon courting a local woman several years his junior. They married, and over the next five years had two children. The problem was that Phil's earnings at the auto shop were intermittent; they scarcely covered his family's expenses. Several times he had to resort to asking his parents for financial help, which bothered him greatly. And so Phil, in his words, "opened up [his] eyes and took a good look at where [he] was." Just beyond the boundaries of Tondo lay Makati, metro Manila's financial district and home to hundreds of call centers. Why not put the English fluency that he'd honed in the military to use?

Phil, in our initial interview one weekday morning, arrived fresh from his shift wearing leather pants and holding his motorcycle helmet. He only half-jokingly referred to himself as a "call center warrior." With the earnings from his call center job, he explained, he and his wife had been able to rent a storefront on the bottom floor of their building and had opened an internet café there. She worked the counter and handled the daily running of the business. Phil in turn works all night at the call center in order to build their savings so they can expand the café—they'd started with four computers, expanded to twenty, and there was room for at least twenty more.

When, I asked Phil, does he find time to sleep? He chuckled. Staying up all night and day isn't a problem for him, he explained, because "when it comes to sleeping, I can adjust because I was in the military before. I can stay awake for thirty-six hours, forty-eight hours." Interpreting his call center job through his military experience was in fact a pattern with Phil. For instance, he described the work itself as follows: "When you're in technical support you have to think of a strategy [for] how to cope with this client or customer and how to get him back online. Like in the military, first plan how we will do it; after that, execute the plan. Bang, bang."

Both Brody the gamer and Phil the military man appeared quite satisfied working as call agents, despite being among the few straight men on the call floor (Figure 8.1). Brody expressed no desire to return to the world of food service while Phil was content to let his wife handle the daily running of their internet café. Neither anticipated going abroad for work. "It's good to be home [i.e., in the Philippines]," Brody stated, to which Phil concurred, "there's no place like home." When I inquired whether they were ever looked down upon or teased by male friends or relatives, they both laughed. "Yes they tease us," admitted Brody. "We're [known as] call boys," Phil said, "like we are prostitutes or something." But Phil continued on to describe how

FIGURE 8.1 Straight male workers, a numerical minority.

they eventually learned to counter such attacks upon their manhood: "The pay is good. That's what you have against them, the pay is so good." Brody concurred: "The same guy who will tease you one minute will be asking you for some money later. So, who is laughing then?"

Rooted at Home

The affinity that exists between straight-male call center agents and foreign voice capital is the inverse of that which exists between gay call center agents and the call center industry. The latter relationship was characterized by a strong initial attraction—call centers are a "gay paradise" where *soshal* English speakers can safely practice their gender identities. Yet the previous chapter shows that gay call center agents are restive in their jobs and continue to aspire for upward mobility and to move abroad; they remain attached only to the extent that other opportunities are foreclosed to them. For straight men, the configuration of attraction and attachment is the inverse. The call center industry's reputation as a gay and feminine space renders it unattractive to the vast majority of men; the figures reported earlier in this chapter on the small percentage of male college graduates who even apply for such work attests to this. Yet for those men such as Brody and Phil who do overcome this initial barrier to attraction, the subsequent attachment is solid. Call centers allow men to improve their existing lives in the Philippines; it allows them to remain rooted at home.

The category profile of straight-male call center agents, depicted in figure 8.2, supports this contention. It is unique vis-à-vis both breadwinning women and restive gay agents. Brody and Phil, we can see now, were representative cases insofar as they embody multiple attributes that distinguish straight-male call center agents. Neither were supporting a broad network of dependents, as were the female breadwinners. Both men were using call center work to accumulate savings. And like most of my other straight-male case studies, Brody and Phil were satisfied with their salaries and strongly preferred to stay in the Philippines rather than migrate abroad. They were rooted in their home country and in the call center industry as well.

Brody and Phil also exemplify the two most typical domestic arrangements among my straight-male respondents. Two-thirds of them were like Brody: unmarried and still living at home with their families. These young men reported that they were *not* expected to contribute money on a regular basis for household expenses—or even expected to help around the house with routine chores. Whereas Brody had described this lifestyle as that of a

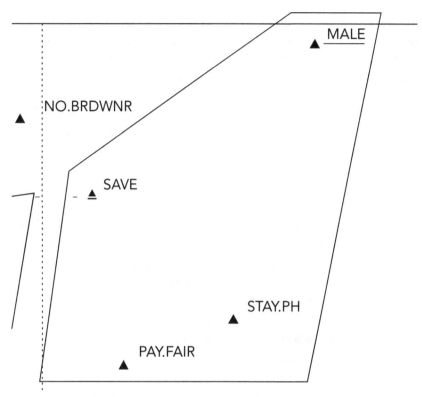

FIGURE 8.2 Correspondence analysis map of straight male call agents.

"spoiled mama's boy, Fermin was an unashamed "couch potato." A third of the straight men are, in turn, like Phil: married or cohabitating with a long-term partner. Benji, whom I introduced in chapter 5, is a good example. He works on an account for an American utility company that had opted to offshore its customer-service calls. He had met his wife in college, and she now works for an NGO based in Manila. Together, they'd been able to build a stable life in their chaotic city.

These straight men's ability to accumulate savings derived in large measure from the fact that they were not breadwinners. Only 20% of my straight-male respondents reported dedicating a substantial portion of their income to materially supporting multiple dependents (compared to 80% of female call agents). This did not necessarily reflect an absence of fertility. Just under half (7 of 15) of the men had fathered children. All five of the men who were in relationships had children, though only two considered themselves breadwinners. More common was an arrangement such as Benji's. His call center salary was deposited directly into the bank account that he shared with his wife. She was then responsible for paying the rent, bills, and expenses related to raising their two-year-old daughter. Benji himself rarely thought or worried about household finances, and knew not which part of his salary went to household budgeting versus saving. Clearly, his identity was not that of a breadwinner.

Two of the straight men in my study had fathered children out of wedlock. Their situations were basically the flip side of the many women discussed in chapter 6, whose partners had abandoned them and their children. Consider the case of Fermin. Thirty-four years old, he had married in his early twenties and fathered a daughter. When she was twelve years old, he separated from his wife and moved back home with his family. One of the main points of dispute in their marriage had been Fermin's lifestyle. Rather than come home when his shift at the call center ended to help his wife prepare their daughter for school, he would join his co-workers for a prolonged morning drinking session. Afterwards, he would "just go with the flow, roam around," not returning home until late in the afternoon. After leaving his wife, his partying only increased. This interfered with his ability to give money to his wife to pay for their daughter's school fees. As a result they argued regularly, a process he describes as being "nagged":

> At first I gave [my wife] a percentage of my earnings to cover the cost of living and education for my daughter. The thing was that mostly half of my income would go away each month, and it wasn't enough to sustain my lifestyle. So we're back to the nagging and I guess that's it.

Another of my case studies, Jian, was in a similar situation but reacted differently. He and his wife had separated, and their four-year-old daughter was now living with his wife's mother. He spoke harshly about not being able to obtain a divorce, complaining that his country was "stuck in the dark ages." He nonetheless visited his daughter several times a week and delivered to his mother-in-law 8000 pesos each month, or about a third of his salary. "I'm working now just for my daughter," he explained, "I'm the only one supporting her."

Because the Philippines neither permits divorce nor requires men to pay child support, Fermin's wife was reduced to pleading with him on an ad hoc basis for every instance of financial support, while Jian served as a breadwinner to his estranged family only out of a deep sense of devotion. In other words, being a breadwinner is for men *an option* in a way that it simply is not for women. As a result, the vast majority of male call center agents do not occupy the role of breadwinner.

This raises the question of what exactly men do with their call center salaries. Of all agents, straight men were the most likely to report being able to establish savings. Ten of fifteen had used their call center salaries to initially fund and grow a bank savings account. Not surprisingly, straight-male call center agents were by far the most likely to judge their salaries as fair. One hundred percent did so—compared to 83% of women and 60% of gay workers. Like the latter, straight men also described living lives with disposable income on hand. For instance, Ian, single and living at home, considers his salary "quite fair" and frequently "treats himself" to meals at chain restaurants in the mall next to his call center. Dan is a mixed martial arts devotee and has invested in a gym membership, along with an array of protein powders. By far the most common expenditure among straight-male call center agents, however, was the purchase of a video game system. Interviewees described the initial six or so months of call center employment as a period of self-disciplined saving, after which they would no longer be forced to wait in line at internet cafes for the chance to play their favorite game.

Further evidence of straight men's rootedness in Manila's call center industry is their lack of aspiration for other pathways. Among all agents, straight men were by far the least likely to express an interest in leaving the Philippines. Only two of my fifteen case studies did. Much more common were sentiments such as Theo's. When I asked him where he pictured himself in five years, he shrugged and said, "I don't know. I'll probably be here in the Philippines still." There was slightly more enthusiasm for eventually leaving the call center to pursue a more traditional profession. Ian, for instance, had graduated from law school several years ago but failed the bar exam. He took a job as a call center agent with the intent of saving enough to enroll in a review course and then retake the exam. As time went by, however, he felt less and less motivated to risk another "disaster," as he referred to his initial attempt to enter the legal profession. "Perhaps maybe I'll be a lawyer," he speculated. "For so long my plans were really molded on this endeavor. It's really getting hard for me since I feel this [call center] job is taking all of my time."

Straight-male call center agents were as likely to aspire to advance in the industry as they were to leave it for a traditional career. Ray, for instance, held a degree in business administration and spent six years working in a bank before losing his job in 2010. As he embarked upon a new employment search, he did some research:

When I was listening to the news and reading newspapers, I saw that BPO was the fastest growing industry in the Philippines. I was surprised to see that it was not affected by the [financial] crisis. So unlike banking it's very stable because every business needs communications and they are always trying to save costs.

After several years as an agent, Ray was confident that he could move up within the industry and acquire further skills:

I've very career oriented. I'm going for the manager position as soon as a position's open for it. If you're a manager, they design a special training for you. The training never stops. So it's a good setup.

A common criticism of the call center industry is that it offers minimal opportunities for advancement.[19] After one has mastered the initial challenges of learning to communicate with callers and operate the computer interface, the work becomes very routine. But straight-male call center agents in the Philippines—and women workers as well—do not interpret these jobs in this way. The rapid pace of industry expansion has introduced real opportunities for upward mobility into managerial positions such as supervisors, trainers, and technical personnel. Whereas women aspire to such advancement as a means to better fulfill their role as breadwinners, straight men do so in order to put down ever-firmer roots in the Philippines. In short, the rootedness of straight men represents a third source of affinity between foreign voice capital and Filipino workers.

PART IV

Conclusion

9

Gone, Baby, Gone

THIS STUDY COMMENCED from a curious observation: the Philippines, at some point in the mid-aughts, became the world's "voice capital." The country's capital, Manila, is today a veritable call center archipelago, with hundreds of BPO firms employing hundreds of thousands of young Filipinos throughout the city. To explain this development, it was necessary to look beyond single factors such as wages, policies, and accents. The booming call center industry in Manila, I discovered, signaled the unification of a truly global *labor market* in voice. Western (primarily American) firms came to the Philippines only after failed experiments in the United States and India. The result is a stable *assemblage*, at the core of which lies a unique affinity between Filipino employees and foreign firms. Low attrition rates from the industry are the most obvious indicator of this affinity; young Filipinos are both initially attracted to call center work and remain attached to it.

Assemblages are constituted by mediators: actors who produce, transform, or redirect flows of various sorts. The emergent call center industry consists of firms who were key mediators in the initial assemblage of a global labor market in voice. In chapter 2, I designated these firms "voice capital." From humble origins in supply rooms where stock boys would field catalogue orders, voice capital was transformed into a paragon of liquid capital. Modern telephonics such as fiber-optic voice lines, online work platforms, and undersea data cables allow customer contact centers to be located literally anywhere in the world.

As I showed in chapter 3, however, for voice capital, the world appears not flat but graded. A chief financial officer of an American bank decides to offshore the handling of routine phone queries; he reviews the directories, guides, and rankings issued by firms such as McKinsey and Tholons; he quickly discovers that his range of options for offshoring is narrowed to two large pools of labor, one in India and the other in the Philippines. Only these two countries can supply a sufficient number of college-educated and English-fluent workers at a fraction of the cost of even a minimum-wage worker in the United States.

Considering how these two pools of labor differ "on the ground" revealed how states matter as mediators. The Indian government has long supported IT training at the postsecondary level. As a result, the BPO industry in the country has been able to diversify beyond call centers into higher-value services such as programming. Young Indian men are attracted to call centers, but view them mainly as a steppingstone toward higher-status jobs in the "knowledge process outsourcing" field. The Indian state, in turn, has long neglected to support women's participation in the formal economy as workers. While many Indian women desire to work in call centers, doing so poses risks in terms of personal safety and social status; call center work is for them a stigma. In short, for both Indian men and women, any initial attraction to call center work fails to solidify into a lasting attachment. State policies—intentionally or not—preclude a full affinity between call center firms and Indian workers.

Successive Philippine governments also mattered for building a global labor market in voice. Legacies of colonization by Spain and the United States produced an "anti-development state" captured by the Catholic church and other foreign interests. This state apparatus cannot provide adequate welfare or opportunities for millions of educated and ambitious Filipinos struggling in overcrowded cities such as Manila. For most of the past half century, there have been two options available to them: stay in the country and work as an underpaid professional, or go abroad as a migrant laborer in search of the Philippine dream. What call centers represent to these people today is a third option, a *middle path*, that pays significantly more than local jobs but does not entail leaving behind one's family and friends.

This middle path is attractive to many, but not all, potential call center workers. To specify who is willing and able to take the work, it was necessary to unpack the biographies and life worlds of young Filipinos today. Workers, in other words, are themselves important mediators. A key finding here is that English fluency has a unique meaning in the Philippines, one that shapes the supply of eligible workers.

For the call center industry, English fluency is a form of *human capital*. It is an individual skill set that can be measured via a standardized verbal intake exam and subsequently deployed to generate value for firms. Throughout Philippine society, however, English fluency functions also as a form of *cultural capital*. It possesses value in contexts beyond the labor market, as a marker of particular social identities. Speaking English well in the Philippines is associated with intimate knowledge of certain cultural forms (such as Western popular music or Harry Potter novels), along with the ownership and display of particular cultural objects (such as "branded" T-shirts or Tom's slippers). It establishes one as urbane, cosmopolitan, sophisticated, and—as we saw in the previous three chapters—effeminate or gay.

Hence, there are three distinct archetypes of call center agents in the Philippines—three distinct sources of affinity between local labor and foreign voice capital. The backbone of the labor market consists of breadwinning women. They initially learned English in order to succeed on the lucrative migration track—for instance, as nurses overseas. They now repurpose their language skills for call center work, which allows them to fulfill the obligation of breadwinner without having to leave their families behind. Then there are gay Filipinos, who find in the call center industry a safe space to express their gender identities, but who nonetheless aspire to even more glamorous futures. And finally there are the straight Filipinos who become call center agent then must parry threats to their masculine identities in order to put down roots in the Philippines. Each of these three worker archetypes has its own reasons for being attracted to call center work and for remaining attached to it. For each, it is sensible, strategic even, to not only take call center jobs but also to *persist* at them. Relatively inexpensive, skilled, and "loyal," these workers are the reason the Philippines, and Manila in particular, has become the world's voice capital.

Implications for Two Debates

To conclude this work, I will consider the implications of my findings for two prominent debates among academics, policymakers, and the public. The first is what I call the *American jobs debate*. It is an ongoing attempt to make sense of the place that the United States holds in the new global economy, and by implication, to predict the jobs that current and future generations of Americans can expect to hold. The underlying premise of this debate is that the forms of employment that provided stability and even prosperity for so many working Americans during the past half-century or so are disappearing. Scholars of work generally agree that automation and new forms of information technology are playing a large role in this process by eliminating many occupations that require human hands and brains.[1] So, too, is the decline of labor unions in the United States, by eroding the quality and security of many traditional working-class jobs.[2]

In the public imagination, however, the main culprit for the disappearance of "good jobs" from the United States is offshoring.[3] It is thus not surprising that offshoring has been highly politicized in the United States—with important implications for how leaders are selected and how the economy is governed.

Politicians on both sides of the aisle, for instance, now try to win elections by denouncing companies that offshore and celebrating those that promise to "bring jobs home." Such posturing, and hence the politicization of offshoring, has reached a fevered pitch during recent presidential campaigns.[4] In 2012, Democrats derided presidential candidate Mitt Romney as a potential "outsourcer in chief," while in 2016, candidate Donald Trump pledged to stop China, Mexico, India, and other countries from "stealing" our jobs.[5] In these political dramas, it is typically blue-collar jobs in manufacturing that are romanticized as the "good jobs" to be repatriated. But increasingly, the offshoring of service and white-collar jobs to countries such as India and the Philippines is a source of alarm as well.[6] Given the findings reported in this book, what can we predict about the future of the call center industry in the United States? Is there any reason to think that such jobs might "come back"?

The second debate, which I will address in the following chapter, centers on the *race to the bottom* thesis. Many in the United States and other wealthy nations are rightly concerned about the lives and working conditions of those who do offshored labor in the Global South. Often such work is not only offshored but outsourced as well, as when U.S. or European companies contract with foreign manufacturers to oversee the nitty-gritty of production. The case of Foxconn, Apple's main contractor in China, exemplifies well the dangers that can result from offshore subcontracting. Critics contend that the Taiwanese company operates contemporary versions of nineteenth-century sweatshops, paying low wages, requiring long hours, and deskilling work relentlessly. Foxconn employs mainly migrants from the Chinese countryside, paradigms of precarious workers lacking both political rights and marketable skills. Should they voice complaints, they discover that manufacturing capital is mobile and can easily relocate to other low-wage regions of the world. Ongoing worker suicides at Foxconn's Chinese plants are often cited as evidence of how thoroughly these precarious workers are being exploited.[7]

Call centers, as service providers, differ from manufacturing plants, of course. Workers operate computers and speak English fluently; they work in air-conditioned offices and sit in ergonomically designed chairs. Nonetheless, as I described in chapter 2, scholars frequently use metaphors such as "digital assembly lines" and "electronic panopticons" to describe offshored call centers.[8] They argue that the call center labor process has been thoroughly routinized, agents are often forced to recite scripts or even change their accents, unions are largely absent from the industry, callers can be xenophobic and abusive, and the contracting arrangement means that workers can rarely count on employment security. But *are* offshored call center workers the service equivalent of vulnerable and precarious manufacturing workers? Should we view voice capital's move to the Philippines as just another piece of data supporting the race to the bottom thesis?

Throughout this book I have made extensive use of individual case studies. I retraced the journey of voice capital from the United States, to India, to the Philippines through the stories of workers such as Ashley, the young American who fled the call center as quickly as she could; and Mina, the young Indian women for whom call center work came to represent a stigma; and Joy, the Filipina who deferred a career in nursing to answer calls to Paypal. Drawing upon these case studies taken as a whole, I will make two closing contentions. First, barring an unprecedented shift in trade policy, offshored call centers are not "coming home" to the United States. There is here no basis for a stable labor market assemblage. Second, Philippine call centers are less sweatshops and more escape routes from poverty and patriarchy. The question is how long this particular assemblage can hold, given workers' current leverage and voice capital's never-ending quest for greater profitability.

They Shall Return?

> Over the last 10 years, about 2 1/2 million jobs in call centers, sales centers, financial firms, and factories were shipped overseas, and American taxpayers helped foot the bill. . . . The Bring Jobs Home Act will end these disgraceful subsidies for outsourcing and would give a 20-percent tax break to cover the cost of moving those jobs back to the United States. (Failed Senate Bill S5097, July 18 2012)

The evidence in this book does not bode well for the return of offshored business services to the United States. Populism and economic nationalism may someday push into law a bill such as S5097, which would have incentivized the repatriation of "jobs in call centers . . . back to the United States." Absent such a major shift in trade policy, however, it is hard to envision this happening on its own accord.

Chapter 3 documented how voice capital (the set of actors who control the telephonics necessary to run call centers) evaluates various pools of global labor today. It concluded that unless an American firm is required to keep its contact centers in the United States (for instance, because of government regulations such as health privacy laws), the value proposition is rarely in place. The labor pool in just about any medium-sized American city can supply plenty of workers with the necessary human capital for performing call center work (a high school degree and the ability to speak English well enough). But these workers are expensive, given readily available substitutes in the global labor market. A college-educated Indian worker can do the job with only a marginal diminution of quality and at a third or less of the cost. The Philippines, in turn, offers similar quality and upfront cost savings, *as well as a means to sidestep the high attrition rates that plague outsourced call centers in the United States, India, and elsewhere.*

American call center agents simply cannot compete with their offshore counterparts in terms of cost. The thorough standardization of call center work makes it difficult to compete on quality. The Philippines has become the go-to destination for voice capital because it offers what are by industry standards remarkably low attrition rates. Is there any chance that American workers can become more competitive on this front? Would voice capital be more attracted to American workers such as Ashley were they at least as "loyal" as their counterparts offshore? If they did not constantly express their discontent with call center work by voting with their feet?

No Grounds for Attachment

One could argue that the actual *doing* of call center work is so inherently unpleasant that no sane human being can or should put up with it for long. Certainly, Ashley and the other CallCo agents with whom I worked in the United States readily and repeatedly voiced a litany of complaints: about the pace and tedium of call center work, about having to absorb abusive statements from irate callers, and so on. The counterargument is that CallCo agents in the Philippines work within the exact same labor process and are *more* likely to encounter abusive (racist and xenophobic) callers. Yet the attrition rate in a typical Philippine call center is a fraction of what it is in the United States. This implies that the relationship between stimulus (call center working conditions) and response (the decision to leave versus to stay in the job) is not automatic. There is a process of interpretation that goes on, and like all interpretive acts, it is one with structural underpinnings. I will address three that I think best explain why American workers experience CallCo not as a "lifeline" but, rather, as a "hell" to be escaped from as soon as one can.

The first is that American workers do not perceive the material rewards of call center work to be commensurate with its experienced costs. Americans without qualifications such as a college degree have long labored in jobs that are physically and emotionally trying. Indeed, this was the essence of the Fordist compromise between American firms and workers during the bulk of the twentieth century. Automobile assemblers, steel workers, flight attendants, and even Las Vegas cocktail waitresses all put up with what can only be called tough working conditions. In return, they received living wages, regular raises, health benefits, retirement plans, and employment security. This was a labor market architecture stabilized by strong labor unions, the institutionalization of collective bargaining, and state policies promoting industrial harmony. American firms and workers were widely incentivized to remain with one another; here was an attachment via "golden chains."[9]

There is nothing golden about the relationship between CallCo and its American employees at the facility where I performed fieldwork. The attachment between the two sides was as thin as a wisp of hair. Unlike in a Fordist assemblage, the tangible rewards that CallCo offers for doing stressful and routinized labor are woefully inadequate. One American worker, who quit CallCo within three months of being hired, recalled having an epiphany that $11 an hour was not worth "getting yelled at for eight hours a day." Another called CallCo's policy of giving all workers an annual raise of 10 cents "downright insulting." CallCo advertises to potential American employees a "health insurance plan," but it turns out to be a largely worthless discount card for full-priced prescription drugs. More generally, a worker has no idea whether the current client is going to renew its contract with CallCo, and thus whether one will still have a job next year, or even next month. Without such stability and security, the daily indignities and stresses of the job loom large.

The second structural underpinning of the American worker's propensity to quickly quit call center work is the array of other job options available—even in a post-Fordist economy. For a young Filipino living in poverty, a call center job offers a wage 300 to 400% higher than a standard "local job." In a rich country such as the United States, in contrast, moving from an $8 minimum wage job to an $11 call center wage represents just a 37.5% total increase in income. This may represent a crucial difference in certain circumstances, as when Ashley desperately needed money following her father's abandonment of her and her ill mother. Most American CallCo workers, however, soon calculate that they would rather get by on a few dollars less in a job that is less taxing. In one worker's words, "I decided I'll tighten my belt and do without some things rather than being treated like shit." This person quit CallCo within three weeks and took a minimum-wage job working with disabled children. Other CallCo leavers move into retail, waitressing, bartending, and other jobs that offer less money but are free from scripts, irate callers, and constant supervision.

The third reason for high attrition at American call centers is that even workers in tough financial circumstances are eventually able to cobble together sufficient resources to escape the job. Consider the parallels between Ashley, the young American woman in distress, and Hannah, the Filipina breadwinner discussed in chapter 7. Ashley, suddenly and unexpectedly cast in the role of breadwinner, turned to the call center in a desperate bid to keep her family afloat. But she was eventually able to use the legal system and the government to locate non-wage sources of income. A lawyer assisted her in forcing her father to remit regular monetary support, while public assistance was available to them, given her mother's debilitating health condition.

The contrast with Hannah could not be starker. Hannah took *and stayed* in call center work to support her daughters after discovering her husband's infidelity. She was unable to divorce him, he was not legally required to support his family, and there was simply no government aid available to someone in her predicament. Even in America's "postwelfare" era, most individuals can locate and leverage some forms of financial assistance, even if it is only temporary; their counterparts in a poor and poorly governed country such as the Philippines all too often cannot.

Prognosis Unpromising

For American workers, the initial attraction of call center work is that it typically pays a modest premium (of a few dollars) above the minimum wage. This premium is insufficient, however, to establish a lasting attachment, given the stress and indignities of call center work. Can anything be done to change this equation?

One could imagine firms attempting to mitigate attrition by making marginal improvements to job quality. They could give agents a few extra seconds between calls, or update policies to allow them to "release" irate and abusive callers. Given the vitriol with which the vast majority of American CallCo workers described their employment, however, one must conclude that these measures would be inadequate. The necessary precondition for not only attracting but *also attaching* workers to firms would be a meaningful improvement in remuneration. The initial $11 hourly wage would have to be regularly increased to account for inflation and employee performance. Health insurance of some sort would have to be part of the employment package. Workers would need to have a sense that they possessed job security and that there were opportunities for mobility within the firm. In short, call centers in the United States would have to be transformed into a modern-day approximation of a Fordist workplace.

One pathway for this would be unionization of outsourced call center employees in the United States. By organizing, the employees would gain leverage—associational power, as sociologist Erik Olin Wright labelled it—with which to then bargain for contracts featuring improved wages and working conditions.[10] The Communication Workers of America (CWA) has long represented in-house call center agents at large telecom companies such as AT&T, and there is ample evidence that, net of skill level and service type, unionization improves remuneration and decreases attrition in these workplaces.[11]

Another path to a more stable assemblage would be the passage of industry-specific regulations—something like a "call center worker bill of rights." To affect attrition rates, any such policies would have to do more than punish companies for offshoring or reward them for reshoring. They would have to guarantee American call center employees better remuneration and some degree of employment security. These improvements, furthermore, would have to be industry-specific rather than part of a larger policy package to help all working Americans—such as an across-the-board hike in the minimum wage. Most call centers in the United States can generate even a faint initial attraction by offering a few dollars more than the minimum wage. Assuming that BPO firms are unwilling to then lift their starting wage even higher, any initial lure that call center work offers would dissipate.

It is difficult to imagine either scenario playing out. Private-sector unionization rates are at an all-time low in the United States, while the obstacles to unionizing subcontractor employees such as outsourced call center workers are particularly high.[12] Call center workers may carry a symbolic import in public debates about offshoring, but do they constitute a large or powerful enough constituency to push through an occupation-specific protection bill? It is doubtful. In any case, voice capital is a paragon of liquid capital, and customer service is that of a tradable, and thus offshorable, commodity. For firms, there is no reason to stay in the United States should such developments come to pass. The American workforce would become even less attractive to them, while workers in India, Philippines, and elsewhere would be more attractive. With the exception of idiosyncratic accounts that require calls to be answered in the United States, the call center industry looks largely to be gone for good.

10

The Relativity of Work

IF YOUNG AMERICANS experience call center work as precarious and un-pleasant (to put it mildly), workers in a poor country such as the Philippines should have it even worse. This is the reasoning behind the race-to-the-bottom thesis. To attract foreign investment, the Philippine government allows call center firms to operate in lightly regulated export processing zones. Firms, in turn, hire as call agents women and gay men, two groups long marginalized in Philippine society. The conditions for exploitation and abuse are seemingly ripe. Yet my case studies of sixty call center employees in the Philippines did not support the race-to-the-bottom thesis. While Ashley, the American call center agent, described her work as a "hell," the majority of Filipinos espoused positive sentiments about their jobs. Their actions spoke as loud as their words. As I reported in chapter 5, almost all of them remained in the industry over the course of the four-year study period.

Neither Sweatshop nor Savior

Were my respondents being deluded? Had they been brainwashed into seeing their jobs as something other than demeaning and precarious? Such an inter-pretation would not do justice to the life stories documented herein. It would fail to heed Steven McKay's admonition, quoted in chapter 2, to "go beyond the shop floor" when considering the bases of attachment between firms and a given labor pool. The workers in my study evaluated call centers not in a vacuum but, rather, in relation to other means of supporting themselves.

Within this larger field of opportunities, call centers possess positive value insofar as they offer formal employment. In a country lacking even the rudi-mentary infrastructure of a welfare state, obtaining formal employment of some sort is essential. Without work, one is forced to rely on the largess of others and/or try to cobble together an existence in the informal economy. Furthermore, for Filipinos with postsecondary degrees, call centers are an attractive option relative to existing forms of employment. These other options have long been bifurcated between poorly paid "professional" work at home and well-paid menial work abroad. Especially for those who are in some sort of trouble or predicament, a call center job is not a trap but, instead, a potential escape from one—a lifeline, a *diskarte*. For thousands and thousands of Filipinos, a good salary at a call center in one's own country is well worth the monotonous work and the occasional irate caller.

The analogy between the Chinese peasant laboring in a sweatshop and the Filipino plugged into a digital assembly line is thus not valid. The latter is not "disposable" in the way that the former is. On the contrary, given that English fluency is a scarce commodity throughout the Global South, and given the growing demand for such human capital from firms in the Global North, educated young Filipinos are far from powerless and precarious. Within the global market for outsourced business services, they hold a veritable monopsony over English fluency and a series of other traits desired by firms. They represent the only workers in the world who can speak English well, who will work for a fraction of the cost of American workers, *and* who find it sensible to stay in the industry over time.

Ultimately this distinguishes Filipino call agents from workers in the Global South who do basic manual labor and to whom the race-to-the-bottom hypothesis generally does apply. Manufacturing capital can abandon the American workforce and go to Mexico, it can leave Mexico and go to China, it can leave China for Vietnam, and on and on, so long as there is a cheaper pool of basic labor to exploit somewhere else. The world is not nearly as flat, however, for voice capital. Having nestled in the Philippines, where could it go next? There are pools of cheaper labor nearby, in countries like Cambodia or Laos, but not a sufficient number of college-educated English speakers. India perpetually beckons, but its intransigent cultural norms about women working and its booming IT sector suggest that its call center attrition problem will not dissipate any time soon.

A stable labor market assemblage in the Philippines, in short, can be said to derive from workers' *market power*. Because of their unique skill set and because of other options, such as migration, that are available to them, Filipino workers can command acceptable enough forms of remuneration. These include expedited hiring, wages significantly higher than those paid by local companies, benefits such as health insurance that are rarely offered by domestic employers, and an implicit guarantee of job security. This creates a stable arrangement in that neither side really has anywhere else to go. BPO firms currently need Filipinos as much as Filipinos need them.

Philippine call centers should not be thought of as sweatshops. At the same time, it would be an error to reach the opposite conclusion: that call centers are a panacea for the social and economic problems that have long plagued the country. It is true that the industry offers new economic opportunities to persons, such as breadwinning women and urban gays, who have long been disadvantaged in Philippine society. Yet it simultaneously solidifies longstanding inequalities between urban Filipinos—especially those living in metro Manila—and those from provincial areas. Young persons such as Daisy, whose failed quest to become a call center agent was described in the opening chapter, are less likely to speak English in their homes, to have fluent English teachers at their schools, to have access to English-language media (such as books, films, and music), and to interact on a regular basis with fluent English speakers.[1] The booming call center industry opens doors for some; for others, those doors are shut even more tightly.

There is also no guarantee that the Philippines will follow India in transitioning its offshored services industry from voice work to higher value-added fields such as programming and engineering. The country's education system continues to operate in line with a vocational logic, the assumption being that graduates will be readily employable—and deployable—in traditional occupations such as nursing and accounting. The skills needed to succeed in these vocations, I have shown, are often easily repurposed to call center work. To instead prepare entire cohorts of college graduates for work in IT and related technical fields would require a massive overhaul of the nation's education system. Such an undertaking, while not impossible, would take years (if not decades) in the best of circumstances; given the longstanding dysfunctions of the Philippine political system—resulting in the "anti-development state" described in chapter 4—it is hard to count on such an overhaul happening in the near future.

These caveats should not prevent us from recognizing that the voice industry in the Philippines currently provides decent work for over a million people. It provides Filipinos with an alternative to migrating abroad or living in poverty at home. The affinity that currently exists between foreign voice capital and Filipino labor has real and immediate benefits for workers and the myriad others whom they often support. Given this, it is imperative to think through the long-term prospects for this assemblage. What could undermine either side's commitment to it?

Hooked up for Good?

Call center firms invest in the Philippines not out of some sense of loyalty or philanthropy but, rather, because the country is the best value proposition in terms of cost, quality, and turnover. When one reads industry reports or talks to managers, it is clear that voice capital continues to have a wandering eye and a calculating mind. It looks longingly at nearby nations where labor costs are even lower than the Philippines—places like Vietnam, Sri Lanka, and Malaysia. Though there is little that firms themselves can do to improve English fluency in these countries, managers continuously monitor them by tracking statistics generated by governmental education commissions and consulting firms. The only real competitor to the Philippines in this regard is China, because of its sheer size and because of what Lin Pan describes as a "cult of English" sweeping the country.[2] The emergence of a large enough pool of low-cost English speakers in any major Chinese city, however, is likely some decades off.

A second development, over which firms do have some control, would be a major transition from communicating with English-speaking customers via voice to doing so via type in online chat programs. Both are forms of real-time communication. But, crucially, the latter requires a much lower threshold of English competency insofar as customer service representatives need only be able to write and read—not speak—fluent English. This would greatly expand the pool of workers available to what would now be "virtual contact capital." College graduates in the Philippine provinces, where living costs and thus salaries are lower, could replace highly paid call agents in Manila. So, too, could pools of qualified labor in some of the low-wage nations just mentioned. The main barrier to such a scenario playing out, given that online chat software is inexpensive and already widely available, is consumers' continued preference for voice-to-voice contact over keyboard-to-keyboard communication.

A third development—and really, this is voice capital's ultimate fantasy—would be the development of fully automated call-handling software. Given that consumers prefer not to speak to "robots," this software would have to be able to disguise its nonhuman nature to most human callers. Such technology would depend on top-tier voice recognition and artificial intelligence capabilities, both of which are currently available but likely to be prohibitively expensive (relative to the cost of English speakers in the Philippines) for the near future. Nonetheless, this technology is eagerly anticipated by voice capital as a way to free itself from having to commit to Filipino—or any other variety of human—labor. Voice capital would finally be beyond place entirely. It would be able to relocate itself, in the words of one industry prospectus, "from anywhere on earth to no location at all."[3]

If the three developments just outlined could undermine voice capital's commitment to Filipino workers, what could lead the latter to lose interest in the call center jobs that have thus far served as a lifeline for so many? This could certainly happen if the other two options for Filipino college graduates improved so as to become more alluring than working in a call center. Going abroad as a migrant laborer pays roughly double the net salary earned by staying at home and working as a call agent, although migration entails other costs such as fees paid to labor brokers and long wait times to secure the proper clearances. It stands to reason that should earnings for migrant workers increase substantially or should laws in wealthy countries change so as to make migration easier, more Filipinos would pursue the migration path. Writing this in the year 2019, as many rich countries are tightening their immigration policies and heightening border controls, it is difficult to imagine opportunities for migrant workers in the global labor market expanding in the near future.[4]

The other labor market path—that of staying in the Philippines and working in a profession that follows logically from one's college degree—continues to hold an allure for many of my respondents. It was mainly the lack of remuneration associated with these "local jobs" that makes this path nonviable. Accordingly, should salaries for nurses, accountants, teachers, and other professions in the Philippines rise *relative to call center salaries*, we would expect more college graduates to pursue these traditional professions. Furthermore, traditional professions would be more appealing if the Philippine government improved the social safety net for those, such as eldest daughters or separated mothers, who currently rely on wage income to support themselves and others. These improvements could include legalizing divorce, requiring fathers to pay palimony for their children, expanding access to birth control, and providing poor families with material benefits such as cash grants or equivalent services. These developments would themselves ultimately hinge on the national government's breaking with the Catholic church by passing legislation supporting women and the *masa* in general. Foreign firms surely have no interest in seeing such improvements come to pass.

The final possible development that could affect the stability of the Philippine call center industry would be for workers to transform their existing market power into associational power—that is, into true voice. In this scenario, call center employees would come to represent more than an occupational niche; they would become an emergent class of educated, urban Filipinos whose industry may now be the largest contributor to total national GDP. They would organize collectively into labor unions or worker associations, and they would pressure employers for further improvements, such as better wages, benefits, and guarantees of job security. The process of organizing workers in the Philippines is hampered by employer-friendly labor laws, especially in export zones, but there is an established union federation in the country that has achieved success at organizing not only manual trades in manufacturing and transport but also professionals in fields like medicine and the public sector[5]

It is taken as a truism that organizing outsourced and offshored workers is nearly impossible given that capital is so mobile, workers typically have little power, and there is so much churn in the labor force.[6] Once again, the Philippine call center industry appears to represent an exception. Should workers unionize and push for even marginal improvements in salaries and working conditions, it seems unlikely that voice capital would return en masse to India, let alone the United States or elsewhere. All my data support the conclusion that the majority of the million-plus Filipinos laboring in call centers would be content to turn these jobs into careers. Why not solidify further the existing labor market assemblage? Why shouldn't workers transform their literal voices into political voice at work? At what point does the risk become too great for those responsible, restive, and rooted workers whose lives are on the line?

Acknowledgments

AS I COMMENCED this project, I'd come to take for granted that voices don't matter. My household had cut its telephone landline years ago. Weekly phone calls to my mother had been replaced by daily text messages. And as for many of my generation, "the concept of leaving (and checking) voice mail" had come to feel "as obsolete as swing-dancing and playing NHL '94 on Sega Genesis."[1]

By the time I completed this project, five years later, I was convinced that voices still matter. They matter because they carry. They carry multinational companies around the world in search of ideal pools of cheap and loyal workers. They carry distinct meanings in India—where speaking English well can denigrate one as a "cyber coolie"—and in the Philippines—where it can distinguish one as a *soshal* (socially sophisticated) gay person. More generally, voices today carry the hopes and dreams of millions of young Filipinos in search of a decent life at home in their country.

Voices certainly carried me throughout this project; so many shared theirs with me. First and foremost were the sixty workers in Manila who took the time to talk with me in an open and candid way about their experiences, not just in the call center industry but in life generally. Despite their busy schedules, they accepted my Facebook friend requests, answered my emails, and logged on when I attempted to Skype. And as I have described, more than a few of these remarkable individuals took a real interest in me as a foreigner in their country. They drove me around on their motor scooters, insisted on treating me to San Miguel beers, and sat next to me on jeepneys in order to make sure that I got off at the right stops. I only hope that I did justice to their stories in the pages herein.

I'd also like to acknowledge a multitude of other voices that aided and assisted me while I was in the Philippines. Professor Emma Porio, director of the Department of Sociology and Anthropology (DSA) at Ateneo de Manila University, years ago took the time to respond to an email of mine and to write me a letter of invitation that proved essential for my Fulbright application. Professor Porio arranged for me to have a desk at Ateneo's DSA, but more important was a fount of information and connections to other academics in the Philippines. One of the persons to whom professor Porio introduced me was Raul Pertierra, an anthropologist at Ateneo. Professor Pertierra went out of his way to make me feel at home in Manila, inviting me to dinner parties, helping me buy groceries, and inviting me to weekends at his fieldwork site in a rural area south of metro Manila. In truth, all the faculty and staff at Ateneo's DSA were immensely kind and generous in offering their time to me as a visiting scholar.

Other folks in the Philippines without whom this project could not have come to fruition include Jaja Barriga, Christia Cruz, and Roel Rocero— research assistants who were invaluable for helping me to plan my project and conduct interviews. Raymond Lacdao (executive director of industry affairs at BPAP), Kate McGeown (BBC news correspondent for the Philippines), and Maria Rhodora G. Ancheta (professor at the University of the Philippines) all took the time to meet with me over *merienda* and share their thoughts on the call center industry. Esmeralda Cunanan, head of the Philippine-American Educational Foundation, steered me toward leads and made sure that I did not skip any sessions with my Tagalog tutor. Her assistant, Marge Tolentino, ushered me around Manila's hectic streets in search of suitable living quarters. And then there were the fellow members of my Fulbright "batch": Amber Ariate, Christina Nelson, Christina Butler, Laura Davis, Mokaram Rauf, and Andrew Plan. We seemed to single-handedly keep half of the fish markets and resto-bars in Manila afloat during our tenures as Fulbright scholars.

Back in the United States, this project benefited immensely from feed-back given at talks at the University of Arizona, the University of California, Berkeley, and Cornell University. My colleague at the University of Arizona, Ron Breiger, allowed me to take his graduate seminar on Formal Methods of Cultural Analysis, wherein I learned the basics of correspondence analysis. James Cook, my editor at Oxford University Press, and Javier Arroyo, the series editor, were incredibly helpful and patient with me as I developed this project into a book-length manuscript. Among those who offered helpful feedback on early drafts and ideas were Robyn Rodriguez, Steve McKay, Aya Fabros, Reena Patel, Nadina Anderson, Joe Galaskiewicz, and Eli Friedman. The usual caveat applies: all contributions and original ideas I share with those mentioned above; any errors or omissions are mine alone.

An Ethnographic Narrative

An American Nightmare

As one drives around the southwestern American city where I work and teach, one cannot help but notice numerous job advertisements on bus stops and billboards depicting young professionals dressed in business attire and sitting in comfortable office chairs. These adverts direct passersby to the website of a company that I have called "CallCo." It is a business process outsourcing (BPO) firm specializing in customer contact (call) centers. Catch phrases like "You Have Unlimited Potential," "Got Your GED? GET Paid," and "Find Your Dream Career Now" insinuate that CallCo offers denizens of this desert city a chance to snag one of the most endangered species in America today: a good job.

The academic literature on outsourced call centers disparages them as "digital assembly lines." I grew up in a depressed midwestern factory town, where acquiring an assembly-line job—digital or otherwise—was considered an immense stroke of good fortune. For my dissertation project, I had worked as a Las Vegas casino dealer. This is an emotionally exhausting job that nonetheless pays well and is considered one of the best jobs that someone without a college education can land these days. I was thus willing to suspend disbelief when it came to outsourced call center jobs. Perhaps working on a computer in an air-conditioned office while making a bit more than the minimum wage *is* today's version of a "good job."

Through chance I got the opportunity to test this hypothesis. At a social event one evening in 2011, I struck up a conversation with a friend of a friend who, it turned out, worked as an account manager at CallCo. As an avid poker player, his ears perked up when I told him about my participant observation study of casino dealers in Nevada. I asked him what he thought were the chances that I could gain access to *his* call center as a regular employee. He thought for a moment, then snapped his fingers. I should, he advised, go right away to the website advertised on all those bus stops and take the online verbal exam. CallCo was currently "ramping up" to hire a new batch of agents for an account with a national package-delivery firm, yet they were still a few successful applicants short. As long as I passed the exam, he would have no problem signing off on my research.

Thus, I became an outsourced call center agent. After five weeks of training, I and twenty-one other new hires took our seats on the production floor and began handling calls from customers of "ShipIt." We frantically tracked packages, fielded complaints, and rushed back and forth from the smoking patio during our short breaks. As a scholar of work, I knew that well-designed employment systems can keep workers relatively satisfied and engaged even when the work itself is routinized and demanding. The Fordist factories in and around which I'd grown up had done this; so, too, had the Las Vegas casinos I'd studied. CallCo was a different beast entirely. In an article entitled "Permanent Pedagogy," published in 2014, I described how new CallCo workers were rushed onto the production floor, where they had to play a discomfiting "learning game" in order feel competent on the phones.[1] Worse yet, once this game was mastered, work quickly became boring and seemingly pointless. The firm's initial promises of health benefits, career ladders, and technical training never materialized. Ultimately, I argued that given CallCo's position as a service subcontractor, this was all it could do to coordinate work: hand new hires headsets and then lean on their basic human desire to appear competent in their interactions with other human beings.

Evidence that employees did not like this employment system was not hard to find. Employee turnover was staggering. One of my batch-mates had a panic attack on the first day of training and never came back; two more quit before the training period was finished. Once we got on the phones, members of my batch continued dropping like flies. Six months into my fieldwork, most had quit or had been fired.

While attrition from this CallCo facility in the American southwest was high, there seemed to be a pattern to it. Every batch of optimistic new hires that marched in the door was diverse in terms of age, gender, and race or ethnicity. Yet, as these "newbies" came to be disabused of any hope that they had found a good job, most left—*but a few stayed*. In an article entitled "Exit Tales," published in 2016, I documented how men and young persons of both sexes were able to cultivate escape routes from the call center.[2] They used their youthful looks to acquire less stressful jobs in retail; they deployed their bodily capital in landscaping or construction jobs; or they simply moved back in with their parents. Even Ashley, the young American woman described at the beginning of this book, was eventually able to escape the "hell" of call center work.

There were two categories of American workers, however, who stuck it out in the call center. One group I called the "resigned." These were older persons, in their late fifties or early sixties, who had been laid off from their previous jobs or who had failed in their attempts to start small businesses. They perceived themselves to be too old for manual labor and for jobs, such as retail, that require "aesthetic labor." The call center was for them a means to tide themselves over until they became eligible for social security benefits.

Then there was a second group of stayers whom I labeled "breadwinners." These were young women, usually single mothers, who were left in the lurch and who desperately needed the few extra dollars per hour that the call center could pay. I wrote then about how both categories of stayers were able, as time passed, to temper their initial discomfort with call center work. At the time I did not realize that such breadwinners were, from the outsourced call center's point of view, a prototype of the ideal worker.

Over There

If I was going to continue my study of outsourced call centers, there was no question where to go next. I had to go global. CallCo's account with ShipIt, I had come to understand, was idiosyncratic in that it was spatially tethered to the United States. It required workers to have a detailed knowledge of American geography and climate, while we as call agents had to frequently liaison with American personnel in local distribution centers. In short, unlike the vast majority of CallCo's accounts, this one was not easily offshore-able. Whereas most of my co-workers were tied to this southwestern city by family and other obligations, CallCo was for the most part free to go wherever in the world it wanted to go.

This reality delighted managers. Whenever top CallCo executives would attend one of our team meetings, they would regale us with stories of recent trips overseas, where our brown-skinned counterparts showed up to work on time, respected their team-leads, and sang karaoke in the cafeteria. These tales didn't seem to be intended to frighten or intimidate us. Rather, the sparkle in managers' eyes suggested that they were genuinely enthralled with having discovered the ideal call agent: hard-working, cheap, and, in their eyes, "loyal." And where had these managers just returned from? The Philippines.

The first time I heard this, it surprised me a little, as I had assumed that offshored call centers were "an Indian thing." I went home one night after work and set up a Google news alert tagging the words *Philippines* and *Outsourcing*. Every few days an email would arrive with nine or ten stories from news services around the world. The Philippines, the *New York Times* reported in 2011, was now the world's new capital of call centers. The following year, CallCo, the firm that ran the depressing little call center in my struggling American city, became one of the largest private-sector employers in the Philippines.

With the help of a Fulbright fellowship and funding from the University of Arizona, I conducted two years of research in the Philippines over the course of four years. As I began this fieldwork, I literally lived atop a call center. My apartment in Manila was part of a larger complex that contained a mall, a food court, and a 200-person "customer contact center."

My initial entrée into the industry, however, came once again through a second-degree network tie. A friend's former classmate was now a manager at a CallCo facility in Makati, Manila's central business district. I met her one muggy August afternoon in the call center's lobby, and she gave me a quick tour. It struck me right away that the labor process here was very similar to the one I'd studied in the United States. The same computer hardware, the same software system, the same barrage of calls from Americans anxious to track their payments and accounts. And as in the United States, CallCo's training rooms were filled with new hires taking crash courses on customer service and database management. The chief difference was that these new employees were here *not* to replace departed ones but, rather, to fill new positions for existing accounts that were continuously being shifted to the Philippines.

I would spend the next two months working as an intern in CallCo-Manila's human resources (HR) department. The task that by far took up most of my time was that of administering the standardized verbal exam used to establish sufficient fluency for communicating with English-speaking callers. Given the deluge of applicants and surfeit of openings, this was practically an unending task (the details of which I described in chapter 8). In contrast, my other official duty—that of processing the paperwork for workers who quit or were terminated—was practically nonexistent. In two months I processed *exactly four cases* out of a workforce of nearly a thousand. All four were young women who had obtained a work or spousal visa with which to move abroad. Given that the labor process was pretty much "controlled for," what, I asked, explained the vastly different attrition rates between the United States and the Philippines? Why was it sensible for Filipino call agents to remain in their jobs?

From Labor Process to Labor Market

The answers to these questions were not be found in a single call center's HR department. As I had in the United States, I switched my focus—my empirical object, as I termed it in chapter 2—from the immediate labor process to the larger labor market. I wanted to understand what call center firms had found in the Philippines and what all of these (mostly) young Filipinos found in the call center industry.

To begin, I sought to understand how and why Filipinos initially decided to apply at call centers. I wanted to know how they evaluated this work relative to other options available to them. My experience in the United States had taught me that one's assessment of call center work can change from the pre-hire to the training to the post-hire stage, and so I wanted to follow people over a substantial period of time. Taking all this into consideration, I decided to perform a longitudinal interview study with a sizable yet manageable pool of Filipino call center workers from across a variety of firms. I ended up establishing a sample of sixty workers, with research conducted over a four-year span (2012–2015). At least two interviews were conducted with each worker during this time span, with a minimum of two years elapsed between the initial and final interview. I performed 150 interviews in total, while living in the Philippines for a total of twenty-four months.

I generated this sample of sixty call center employees using a method known as chain referral (or snowball) sampling. Basically I would, at the conclusion of an interview, ask the interviewee to provide me with the names of and contact information for two or three people in their social network who also worked in the call center industry. To make sure that not all my respondents were members of the same social network, I initiated recruitment from three unconnected "seeds." In early 2012, I hired undergraduate research assistants (RAs) from three different universities in metro Manila: Ateneo de Manila, the university with which I was affiliated as a Fulbright scholar; De La Salle University, a Catholic college in central Manila; and Philippine Normal University, a large public university.

I began by having each of my RAs refer me to friends, family members, and neighbors who worked in call centers. After an initial twenty interviews, however, I found that my sample consisted almost exclusively of heterosexual women. As I documented in chapter 5, the majority of call agents in Manila *are* such women. Yet I also by this point had learned that there are two other groups which, though numerical minorities, still constituted significant segments of the larger labor pool: gay and straight male call center agents.

To capture the attributes and experiences of these workers, I shifted my initial technique of snowball sampling to that of purposive sampling. I asked my research assistants to explore their networks so as to refer me specifically to these two other categories of workers. By the end of 2012, I had an initial sample of sixty call center agents: thirty female, fifteen gay-identified men, and fifteen straight-identified men.

A research assistant accompanied me to all initial interviews. It is customary in Philippine society to bring along a companion when first meeting someone, especially a member of the opposite sex. All these interviews took place in public spaces easily accessible to respondents, such as Starbuck cafes, mall food courts, and restaurant booths. Given these noisy environments (and with my interviewees' consent), I used a professional-grade Roland R-09HR recorder to record the interviews. Sessions lasted between 90 and 120 minutes, and were conducted in a mixture of Tagalog and English (Taglish). In my experience, two hours is the maximum that one can or should spend in a single interview session; any longer and the interviewee loses focus and becomes unlikely to agree to follow-up interviews. I committed to paying respondents 800 pesos (about $20) for two hours of their time, or about the equivalent of the U.S. minimum wage at the time of my research.

These initial interviews were attempts to establish the broad scaffolding of each worker's life story. Working from a single-page interview schedule, I would proceed through a series of prompts regarding:

* The person's family situation as a child
* The person's experience with formal education
* How the person had come to be comfortable speaking English
* The precise process through which the person had come to apply for a call center job

* The person's current relationship status
* Factors the person considered to be the best and worst aspects of call center work
* The person's future aspirations (i.e., where did the individual see him- or herself in five years?)

To translate and transcribe my interviews, I hired a local woman, Nena, who because of a physical disability was unable to work outside her home. I also paid her the U.S. minimum wage of $10 per hour for her work.

I collected additional data for all sixty respondents beyond the original life history interview. Over the following four years, I conducted at least one follow-up interview with each respondent. Most were in-person interviews conducted during return trips to the Philippines; twelve were conducted via Skype or Facetime.

I was also able to follow and stay in touch with most of my respondents when I was not in the Philippines. Filipinos, according to the anthropologist Raul Pertierra, are among the world's heaviest users of just about every social networking platform and mobile communication technology. My respondents were willing, if not eager, to communicate via Facebook, email, and free international messaging services when I was in the United States.[3]

During two years of fieldwork in the Philippines, six of my interviewees evolved into what are called key informants. These were research subjects with whom I interacted on a regular basis, whose lives I got to know in a detailed fashion, and who were "highly articulate, and for whatever reason of their own, ready and willing to walk [me] through their culture."[4] In the local terminology, we became *kasama*—someone you count on to accompany you on your daily commute via jeepney, on your shopping expeditions, or for conversation over a meal at a Jollibee fast-food outlet. Joy, the nurse deferred whose story I told in chapter 1, was one such informant. So, too, were Hannah, the breadwinner, discussed in chapter 6, and Boi, the ambitious young gay man discussed in chapter 7.

As I read through the interview transcripts and field notes that I'd compiled for each of my sixty case studies, I sensed certain patterns. For starters, it was remarkable that, in contrast to the call center workers I'd studied in the United States, very few Filipino call center agents voiced complaints about their jobs. Nor were they "voting with their feet" by quitting the industry. Another emergent pattern was that there seemed to be variation among my respondents in terms of why staying in call center work made sense for them. In chapter 5, I described how I coded my qualitative data so as to capture this variation through a series of binary variables. In this same chapter, I explained how correspondence analysis (CA) captures—in a succinct and compelling manner—variation among my respondents.

The CA map depicted as figure 5.2 validated my initial hunch. Interviewees' attributes clustered so as to reveal three basic archetypes of Philippine call center agents, each with its own constellation of resources, obligations, and aspirations. Although I grounded my analyses in chapters 6 through 8 in terms of these clusters, another common way to interpret such a CA map is by identifying which points are contributing to the inertia, or variance, of each dimension. Nearly half (47.3%) of the variance along the first dimension (that is, the horizontal axis) derived from the points GAY (19.3%), COUPLED (16.5%) and PAY.UNFAIR (11.3%). In turn, the points FEMALE (15.3%), BRDWNR (15.3%), MALE (16.7%), and NO.BRDWNR (18.9%) contributed to well over half (66.2%) of the variation in the second dimension (the vertical axis). Interpreting these two dimensions provides further evidence that the call center labor pool in metro Manila is internally heterogeneous. It is divided, on the one hand, between dissatisfied gay men and those who are able to establish financial stability (especially by coupling with another wage-earner); and on the other hand, between women who work to support kin and straight men who work to save and spend.

From Labor Market to Assemblage

While interviewing and conducting fieldwork among call center workers in the Philippines, I was working to develop a conceptual framework with which to make sense of their experiences. I had come to understand that just about all young persons in the Philippines confront a sharply bifurcated decision tree as they approach adulthood: go abroad as a migrant worker in search of the Philippine dream, or remain at home with family and friends. Given this, it was perfectly sensible for them to interpret the call centers that have sprung up around Manila as sources of good—or good enough—jobs.

But why were the call centers there in the first place? And why had so many generations of young Filipinos been confronted with the excruciating choice of migration versus poverty? To confront such questions, it was necessary to expand my focus beyond the workers themselves. They were important actors, to be sure. But so were the firms that sought them out, and so was the Philippine state, whose policies structured the entire field of possibilities available to them. Figure 2.2 represents my attempt to model the relationship among workers, firms, and the state as a market assemblage. Here I will summarize the data that I used to understand the latter entities as active mediators within this assemblage.

Shortly after beginning fieldwork at CallCo's Manila facility, I found myself in the office of its HR manager. She asked if I would look over a PowerPoint presentation that she was preparing for an upcoming meeting with corporate personnel. As I flipped through the slides on her laptop, one image in particular jumped out at me. It was a graph in which twenty or so countries were ranked as viable investment locales according to labor costs and labor quality. At the top were two countries highlighted in green: India and the Philippines. What struck me as remarkable about this graph was the way in which it transformed countless factors—wage rates, costs of living, education systems, colonial legacies—into a single, simple image. This was, I recall realizing, how CallCo executives, perched in their office suites, saw the world. And I suspected other firms saw the world this way, as well.

Google searches for the terms "voice," "outsourc*," "offshor*," "rank*," "evaluation," and "call center," in various combinations, turned up a number of reports—labeled "location indices," "sourcing snapshots," and so on—authored by business consulting firms. They were available to download for not more than a few hundred dollars apiece. In chapter 3, I describe how I used this management literature to reconstruct the manner in which call center firms see and evaluate different regions of the world as investment locales. India, for various reasons, became the taken-for-granted sourcing locale for voice in the late 1990s and early 2000s. Fortunately, we by now have a sizable ethnographic literature on firms' experiences there. In chapter 3, I draw upon this literature—and especially upon excellent studies conducted by Reena Patel, Xiang Biao, Kiran Mirchandani, Shehzad Nadeem, and A. Aneesh—to recount how this "experiment" was a mixed bag. Firms found cheaper workers, but ultimately there was and is no mutual affinity between Indian workers and Western call centers.

Documenting how the Philippine state functions as an active market mediator was also a process of discovery. I had initially assumed that its main role was that of promoting the country to foreign investors. But this wasn't the case. Early in my fieldwork, I interviewed the director of the Business Processing Association of the Philippines (BPAP). He laughed when I asked him how his organization was marketing the country to potential investors. "We don't have to sell our country," he said, "Just listen." In the background, I could hear multiple phones ringing. "Those are companies calling us!" he continued. "On our end, it's not a demand thing but a supply thing." He would go on to rephrase the issue as that of a "talent problem," one of making sure that the country had enough workers with college degrees who were eager to apply to call centers.

Hence an epiphany, which appeared in figure 2.2 as a weak line connecting the Philippine state with foreign capital, yet a strong line connecting the state with Filipino workers. Said state matters because it structures the abilities, aspirations, and opportunities available to young Filipinos. It makes call center work sensible and sustainable for literally millions of them. Chapter 4 drew upon a variety of source materials to describe how and why this happens. Groundbreaking ethnographic work by scholars such as Robin Rodriguez, Anna Guevarra, Steven McKay, and Rhacel Parreñas dissected the workings of the Philippine migration system. Reports produced by Philippine government agencies and international organizations provided data on poverty rates, foreign direct investment, education levels, and other subjects. Historical and anthropological studies in turn illustrated how colonial occupation by Spain and the United States essentially sabotaged development in the Philippines during the latter half of the twentieth century.

Around ethnography—that craft of writing down lived experience—there swirl endless debates about its *status as a method*.[5] On one side are those who argue that ethnographic methods should be held to the standards of the natural sciences. Ethnographic findings should be *replicable*, many hold, such that subsequent researchers should be able to perform the same study as did the original researcher and generate the same findings. My experience has taught me the opposite—that a rich qualitative study "is not a laboratory experiment that can be replicated again and again under the same conditions."[6] This does not, however, excuse ethnographers from producing clear, concise, and transparent accounts of what they did in the field and how they arrived at their conclusions. Such is what I have attempted to do in this brief research narrative. I find it hard to imagine that anyone would replicate my study—by first working as a call center agent in the United States, then working as a human resource officer in a Philippine call center, and then tracking a sample of Philippine call center workers over multiple years. Should one ever "revisit" my field site, I'd be curious to know whether an affinity between call center firms and Philippine workers still remains. If not, I'd really like to know why. More generally, I hope that others may find my methodological strategy— of supplementing interviews and fieldwork with empirical "extensions" out to relevant mediators —productive for documenting assemblages of various sorts.

Notes

CHAPTER 1

1. Customer contact jobs are usually classified as front-line service work requiring soft skills, in contrast to back-office tasks requiring some technical expertise such as programming, database management, or accounting. In other words, the BPO sector as a whole is usually divided into "voice" and "knowledge" sides, although the usefulness of this distinction is, in my opinion, questionable.

2. The methodological appendix describes in detail this and all the fieldwork I performed for this research project.

3. The interested reader should refer to my argument in Jeffrey J. Sallaz, "Permanent Pedagogy: How Post-Fordist Firms Generate Effort but Not Consent," *Work and Occupations* 42, no. 1 (October 20, 2014): 3–34.

4. During one call I handled in January, while a snowstorm was hammering the American Northeast, a woman asked me if the bottle she was shipping to a medical clinic as part of her job's mandatory "piss testing" would freeze if she left it on the side patio of her mobile home for a delivery driver to pick up and, if so, if such freezing would affect the accuracy of the testing. Snowstorms, piss testing, and mobile homes are partially unique to the United States; without some rudimentary understanding of them, such an issue would be near impossible to deal with satisfactorily and in a timely manner.

5. Reena Patel, *Working the Night Shift: Women in India's Call Center Industry* (Stanford, CA: Stanford University Press, 2010).

6. The term "outsourcing" is too often conflated with "offshoring." Outsourcing entails an organization's contracting out some non-core business activity to a third party, regardless of where said third party is located. Offshoring, in contrast, designates any relocation of productive or service work to a different country. "Captive offshoring," for instance, refers to a process whereby a firm operates its own facility in a different country. Many would mistakenly label this as outsourcing.

7. Ibid., 87.

8. Ibid., 53.

9. This is an issue that I address at length in chapter 3, this volume.

10. In the Philippines, the Cebuano language is often referred to as Bisaya.

11. Tagalog and other languages spoken in the Philippines do not feature gendered pronouns. For example, the Tagalog word *siya* means both "he" and "she." When using pronouns to describe those individuals in my study who identify as nonheterosexual, I have tried to follow their preferred identification. Belle, for instance, referred to herself in relation to Daisy as a *tita* (aunt) rather than a *tito* (uncle).

12. As I elaborate in chapter 7, the English word "gay" does not capture the range of meanings associated with transgender identities in the Philippines today. The label was, however, widely used by my respondents to describe themselves, and so I adopt their terminology throughout this work.

13. My field notes indicate that of the eight applicants I screened that day, four failed, three were classified as near-hires, and one passed.

14. As I was preparing to leave Manila in 2015, Daisy and I arranged one last coffee. She brought with her an older Dutch man whom she had met online and who had made the trip to the Philippines to meet her. He seemed pleasant, and we all chatted about Philippine popular music. While he was in the restroom, I teased Daisy about making sure that he wasn't another "Creepy Thomas," as we had been calling her former long-distance affair. She assured me that he wasn't, and several days later posted on Facebook a photograph of a plane ticket from Manila to Amsterdam in her name.

15. At the time of my research, approximately half of all Filipino children had at least one parent living abroad. See Emma Porio, "Global Householding, Gender, and Filipino Migration: A Preliminary Review," *Philippine Studies* 55, no. 2 (2007): 211–242; Maria Joy B. Arguillas and Lindy B. Williams, "The Impact of Parents' Overseas Employment on Educational Outcomes of Filipino Children," *International Migration Review* 44, no. 2 (2010): 300–319; Patricia Cortes, "The Feminization of International Migration and Its Effects on the Children Left Behind: Evidence from the Philippines," *World Development* 65 (2015): 62–78.

16. Kate McGeown, "Nursing Dream Turns Sour in the Philippines," *BBC News*, July 5, 2012, http://www.bbc.co.uk/news/world-asia-18575810.

CHAPTER 2

1. "A New Capital of Call Centers," *New York Times*, November 26, 2011, https://www.nytimes.com/2011/11/26/business/philippines-overtakes-india-as-hub-of-call-centers.html.

2. Christine Counsell and Chris Steer, *Industrial Britain: The Workshop of the World* (New York: Cambridge University Press, 1993).

3. Figures in this paragraph were compiled from: Devjyot Ghoshal, "How Manila Trumped the Teacher," *Business Standard India*, July 3, 2012, http://www.business-standard.com/article/technology/how-manila-trumped-the-teacher-112070300021_1.html; Don Lee, "The Philippines Has Become the Call-Center Capital of the World," *Los Angeles Times*, February 1, 2015, http://www.latimes.com/business/la-fi-philippines-economy-20150202-story.html; "The End of the Line," *The Economist*, February 6, 2016, https://www.economist.com/news/international/21690041-call-centres-have-created-millions-good-jobs-emerging-world-technology-threatens; Business Process Association of the Philippines, "Information Technology and Business Process Management and Global In-House Center Industry Roadmap 2016" (Manila: Business Process Association of the Philippines, 2016).

4. Chris Tilly, "Rev. of Disintegrating Democracy at Work," *Contemporary Sociology* 43, no. 1 (2014): 78.

5. See Arlie Russell Hochschild, *The Managed Heart: Commercialization of Human Feeling* (Berkeley: University of California Press, 1983); Amy S. Wharton, Sarah Chivers, and Mary Blair-Loy, "Use of Formal and Informal Work–Family Policies on the Digital Assembly Line," *Work and Occupations* 35, no. 3 (2008): 327–350; Peter Bain and Phil Taylor, "Entrapped by the 'Electronic Panopticon'? Worker Resistance in the Call Centre," *New Technology, Work and Employment* 15, no. 1 (2000): 2–18; Premilla D'Cruz and Ernesto Noronha, "Technical Call Centres: Beyond 'Electronic Sweatshops' and 'Assembly Lines in the Head,'" *Global Business Review* 8, no. 1 (February 1, 2007): 53–67.

6. Richard Susskind and Daniel Susskind, *The Future of the Professions: How Technology Will Transform the Work of Human Experts*, repr. ed. (Oxford: Oxford University Press, 2017).

7. An eloquent and sensible summary of this debate appeared in: "Defending the PHL Outsourcing Industry," *Business Mirror*, August 2, 2017, http://businessmirror.com.ph/defending-the-phl-outsourcing-industry/.

8. Karen Lema, "Philippines Has Enough Buffers to Withstand Capital Outflows," *Nasdaq*, February 8, 2018, https://www.nasdaq.com/article/philippines-has-enough-buffers-to-withstand-capital-outflows--cbank-gov-20180208-00036.

9. Winifred R. Poster, "Racialism, Sexuality, and Masculinity: Gendering 'Global Ethnography' of the Workplace," *Social Politics* 9, no. 1 (2002): 151.

10. Rosemary Batt, David Holman, and Ursula Holtgrewe, "The Globalization of Service Work: Comparative Institutional Perspectives on Call Centers," *Industrial and Labor Relations Review* 62, no. 4 (2009): 454; see as well the assessment provided by: Lloyd Anthony, "Understanding the Post-Industrial Assembly Line: A Critical Appraisal of the Call Centre," *Sociology Compass* 10, no. 4 (April 4, 2016): 284–293.

11. Balaji Parthasarathy, "The Changing Character of Indian Offshore ICT Services Provision, 1985–2010," in *The Oxford Handbook of Offshoring and Global Employment* (New York: Oxford University Press, 2013), 380–404.

12. Christine Avendano, "Arroyo Lauds PLDT Investment in Cyber Infrastructure," *Philippine Daily Inquirer*, May 28, 2008, http://technology.inquirer.net/infotech/infotech/view/20080528-139260/Arroyo-lauds-PLDT-investment-in-cyber-infrastructure.

13. "Philippines: The New Outsourcing Hub" (Manila: KPMG International, 2010).

14. Marites Vitug, "Lost in Translation," *Newsweek*, May 28, 2006, http://www.newsweek.com/lost-translation-110311.

15. Business Process Association of the Philippines, "Breakthroughs! The Philippines Business Process Outsourcing Newsletter" (Manila: Business Process Association of the Philippines, January 2009).

16. Karen Lema, "More than Just Talk: Philippines Eyes Broader Outsourcing Role," *Reuters*, March 8, 2012, http://www.reuters.com/article/2012/03/08/us-outsourcing-philippines-idUSBRE8271C420120308.

17. Lee, "Philippines Has Become the Call-Center Capital of the World."

18. Roel Landingin, "The MTV School of English: How Philippines Overtook India in Call Centres," *Financial Times*, December 9, 2010, http://blogs.ft.com/beyond-brics/2010/12/09/the-mtv-school-of-english-how-philippines-overtook-india-in-call-centres/.

19. Timothy McDonald, "Philippines Outsourcing: 'Customers Want People, Not Robots,'" *BBC News*, June 21, 2017, http://www.bbc.com/news/business-40337360.

20. On the intense standardization of call center work, see: Sallaz, "Permanent Pedagogy"; A. Aneesh, *Neutral Accent: How Language, Labor, and Life Become Global* (Durham, NC: Duke University Press, 2015), 54.

21. See: Lawrence Casiraya, "Solon Wants English Exams for Teachers to Help BPO Industry," *Inquirer.Net*, July 24, 2008, sec. Education, http://www.inquirer.net/specialfeatures/education/view.php?db=1&article=20080724-150382; Pawan S. Budhwar et al., "Insights into the Indian Call Centre Industry: Can Internal Marketing Help Tackle High Employee Turnover?," *Journal of Services Marketing* 23, no. 5 (July 31, 2009): 351–362; Tino Pamintuan, "Supply of Qualified Talents Can't Keep Pace with Demand of BPOs," *GMA News*, September 20, 2011, online edition, sec. Business, http://www.gmanews.tv/story/232898/business/supply-of-qualified-talents-cant-keep-pace-with-demand-of-bpos; Lema, "More than Just Talk."

22. Outsource2Philippines, "Periodic Survey #2: Constraints to Growth" (Manila: Business Process Association of the Philippines, 2006); Penny Bongato, "Talent Development Initiatives for Globally Competitive Professionals," *Breakthroughs! The Philippines Business Process Outsourcing Newsletter*, September 2011.

23. Kate Mulholland, "Workplace Resistance in an Irish Call Centre: Slammin', Scammin' Smokin' an' Leavin'," *Work, Employment & Society* 18, no. 4 (2004): 709–724.

24. David Owen, "The Happiness Button: Customer Satisfaction in the Emoji Era," *The New Yorker*, February 5, 2018.

25. Outsource2Philippines, "Periodic Survey #2: Constraints to Growth," Niels Beerepoot and Mitch Hendriks, "Employability of Offshore Service Sector Workers in the Philippines: Opportunities for Upward Labour Mobility or Dead-End Jobs?," *Work, Employment & Society* 27, no. 5 (October 1, 2013): 823–841.

26. Julka Harsimran, "Philippines to Turn Call Centre Capital of World," *Economic Times*, November 4, 2010, https://economictimes.indiatimes.com/tech/ites/philippines-to-turn-call-centre-capital-of-world/articleshow/6868468.cms.

27. Vance Cariaga, "US Call Centers Dial Up Profits," *Investors Business Daily*, September 27, 2006; Rosemary Batt and Alexander J. S. Colvin, "An Employment Systems Approach to Turnover: Human Resources Practices, Quits, Dismissals, and Performance," *Academy of Management Journal* 54, no. 4 (2011): 695–717; Jeffrey J. Sallaz, "Exit Tales: How Precarious Workers Navigate Bad Jobs," *Journal of Contemporary Ethnography* 46, no. 5 (2017): 573–599.

28. Jon C. Messenger and Naj Ghosheh, *Offshoring and Working Conditions in Remote Work* (London: Palgrave Macmillan, 2010), 126.

29. Darcy Lalonde, "Large Potential for BPO Sector Remains in Philippines," *Business Mirror*, March 13, 2014, http://businessmirror.com.ph/index.php/en/business/companies/28894-large-potential-for-bpo-sector-remains-in-phl.

30. Steven C. McKay, *Satanic Mills or Silicon Islands?: The Politics of High-Tech Production in the Philippines* (Ithaca, NY: Cornell University Press, 2006).

31. Pei-Chia Lan, "Legal Servitude and Free Illegality: Migrant 'Guest' Workers in Taiwan," in *Asian Diasporas*, ed. Rhacel Parreñas and Lok C. D. Siu (Stanford, CA: Stanford University Press, 2007), 253–278.

32. See Matthew O'Connell and Mei-Chuan Kung, "The Cost of Employee Turnover," *Industrial Management* 49, no. 1 (2007): 14–19.

33. Robin Leidner, *Fast Food, Fast Talk: Service Work and the Routinization of Everyday Life* (Berkeley: University of California Press, 1993).

34. Catriona M. Wallace, Geoff Eagleson, and Robert Waldersee, "The Sacrificial HR Strategy in Call Centers," *International Journal of Service Industry Management* 11, no. 2 (2000): 174–184.

35. Albert O. Hirschman, *Exit, Voice, and Loyalty: Responses to Decline in Firms, Organizations, and States* (Cambridge, MA: Harvard University Press, 1970); Erik Berntson, Katharina Näswall, and Magnus Sverke, "The Moderating Role of Employability in the Association between Job Insecurity and Exit, Voice, Loyalty and Neglect," *Economic and Industrial Democracy* 31, no. 2 (May 1, 2010): 215–230.

36. Critical labor process scholars would more likely explain such commitment as deriving from the strategic organization of the labor process, internal labor market, and external labor market so as to produce ideological consent.

37. Steven C. McKay, "Securing Commitment in an Insecure World: Workers in Multinational High-Tech Subsidiaries," *Economic and Industrial Democracy* 25, no. 3 (2004): 375–410.

38. Berntson et al., "The Moderating Role of Employability in the Association between Job Insecurity and Exit, Voice, Loyalty and Neglect"; Kamel Mellahi, Pawan S. Budhwar, and Baibing Li, "A Study of the Relationship Between Exit, Voice, Loyalty and Neglect and Commitment in India," *Human Relations* 63, no. 3 (2010): 349–369; Steven Si and Yi Li, "Human Resource Management Practices on Exit, Voice, Loyalty, and Neglect: Organizational Commitment as a Mediator," *International Journal of Human Resource Management* 23, no. 8 (2012): 1705–1716.

39. Pierre Bourdieu, *Language and Symbolic Power* (Cambridge, MA: Harvard University Press, 1999).

40. McKay, "Securing Commitment in an Insecure World," 405; emphasis mine.

41. Matthew Desmond, "Relational Ethnography," *Theory and Society* 43, no. 5 (September 2014): 547–579, 548.

42. https://www.merriam-webster.com/dictionary/affinity.

43. Matthew Watson, *The Market* (Newcastle: Agenda, 2018).

44. Neil Fligstein, *The Architecture of Markets: An Economic Sociology of Twenty-First Century Capitalist Societies* (Princeton, NJ: Princeton University Press, 2001), 30.

45. An excellent summary of the origins and ascendency of economics as a field is provided by Marion Fourcade, *Economists and Societies: Discipline and Profession in the United States, Britain, and France, 1890s to 1990s* (Princeton, NJ: Princeton University Press, 2009).

46. Adam Smith, *An Inquiry into the Nature and Causes of the Wealth of Nations* (London: W. Strahan and T. Cadell, 1776), 14.

47. B. De Martino, "Frames, Biases, and Rational Decision-Making in the Human Brain," *Science* 313, no. 5787 (August 4, 2006): 684–687; Daniel Kahneman, *Thinking, Fast and Slow* (New York: Farrar, Straus and Giroux, 2011); Richard H. Thaler, *Misbehaving: The Making of Behavioural Economics* (New York: Penguin, 2016).

48. William A. McEachern, *Microeconomics: A Contemporary Introduction* (Boston, MA: Cengage Learning, 2016), 65.

49. Karl Polanyi, *The Great Transformation: The Political and Economic Origins of Our Time* (New York: Farrar and Rinehart, 1944).

50. Vivian Zelizer argues that even in our most personal lives, "[p]eople constantly mingle their most intimate relations with economic activities . . . instead of alien intrusions, economic transactions serve to create, define, sustain, and challenge intimate relations." See: Viviana A. Zelizer, *Economic Lives: How Culture Shapes the Economy* (Princeton, NJ: Princeton University Press, 2013), 167.

51. Marion Fourcade and Kieran Healy, "Moral Views of Market Society," *Annual Review of Sociology* 33 (2007): 285–311.

52. Ibid.; Zelizer, *Economic Lives*.

53. Jamie Peck, *Work-Place: The Social Regulation of Labor Markets* (New York: Guilford, 1996).

54. Polanyi, *Great Transformation*, 75.

55. Jeffrey J. Sallaz, *Labor, Economy, and Society* (Malden, MA: Polity, 2013), 98.

56. Mitchell L. Stevens, Elizabeth A. Armstrong, and Richard Arum, "Sieve, Incubator, Temple, Hub: Empirical and Theoretical Advances in the Sociology of Higher Education," *Annual Review of Sociology* 34, no. 1 (2008): 127–151, 128.

57. Greta R. Krippner, "The Elusive Market: Embeddedness and the Paradigm of Economic Sociology," *Theory and Society* 30, no. 6 (2001): 775–810.

58. https://www.merriam-webster.com/dictionary/embed.

59. Polanyi, *Great Transformation*; Mark Granovetter, *Getting a Job: A Study of Contacts and Careers* (Chicago: University of Chicago Press, 1974); Mark Granovetter, "Economic Action and Social Structure: The Problem of Embeddedness," *American Journal of Sociology* 91, no. 3 (1985): 481–510. The 1985 article was included as an appendix in the 1994 reprint of *Getting a Job*.

60. Granovetter, *Getting a Job*, 95.

61. See, for instance: Paul DiMaggio and Hugh Louch, "Socially Embedded Consumer Transactions: For What Kinds of Purchases Do People Most Often Use Networks?," *American Sociological Review* 63, no. 5 (October 1998): 619–637; Alya Guseva and Akos Rona-Tas, *Plastic Money: Constructing Markets for Credit Cards in Eight Postcommunist Countries* (Stanford, CA: Stanford University Press, 2014); Brian Uzzi, "Social Structure and Competition in Interfirm Networks: The Paradox of Embeddedness," *Administrative Science Quarterly* 42, no. 1 (1997): 35–67. Given the imagery of markets embedding themselves within existing interpersonal networks, the methodology of social network analysis is a common tool in this research tradition's toolkit.

62. Pierre Bourdieu, *The Social Structures of the Economy* (Malden, MA: Polity, 2005); Jeffrey J. Sallaz, "The Making of the Global Gambling Industry: An Application and Extension of Field Theory," *Theory and Society* 35, no. 3 (October 3, 2006): 265–297; Neil Fligstein and Doug McAdam, *A Theory of Fields* (New York: Oxford University Press, 2015).

63. Viviana A. Zelizer, *The Social Meaning of Money: Pin Money, Paychecks, Poor Relief, and Other Currencies* (Princeton, NJ: Princeton University Press, 1997); Bruce G. Carruthers and Laura Ariovich, *Money and Credit: A Sociological Approach* (Malden, MA: Polity, 2010).

64. Donald MacKenzie and Yuval Millo, "Constructing a Market, Performing Theory: The Historical Sociology of a Financial Derivatives Exchange," *American Journal of Sociology* 109, no. 1 (2003): 107–145; Marion Fourcade, "Price and Prejudice: On Economics and the Enchantment (or Disenchantment) of Nature," in *The Worth of Goods: Valuation and Pricing in the Economy*, ed. Jens Beckert and Patrik Aspers (New York: Oxford University Press, 2011), 41–62.

65. Paula Jarzabkowski, Rebecca Bednarek, and Paul Spee, *Making a Market for Acts of God: The Practice of Risk Trading in the Global Reinsurance Industry* (New York: Oxford University Press, 2015); Rene Almeling, *Sex Cells: The Medical Market for Sperm and Eggs* (Berkeley: University of California Press, 2011); Lori Qingyuan Yue, Jue Wang, and Botao Yang, "Contesting Commercialization: Political Influence, Responsive Authoritarianism, and Cultural Resistance," *Administrative Science Quarterly*, April 5, 2018; Kieran Healy, *Last, Best Gifts: Altruism and the Market for Human Blood and Organs* (Chicago: University of Chicago Press, 2006).

66. Carla Freeman, *High Tech and High Heels in the Global Economy: Women, Work, and Pink-Collar Identities in the Caribbean* (Durham, NC: Duke University Press, 2000); Barbara Ehrenreich and Arlie Russell Hochschild, eds., *Global Woman: Nannies, Maids, and Sex Workers in the New Economy* (New York: Holt Paperbacks, 2004); Aihwa Ong and Carla Freeman, *Spirits of Resistance and Capitalist Discipline: Factory Women in Malaysia*, 2nd ed. (Albany: State University of New York Press, 2010).

67. Ofer Sharone, *Flawed System/Flawed Self* (Chicago: University of Chicago Press, 2013); S. Michael Gaddis, "Discrimination in the Credential Society: An Audit Study of Race and College Selectivity in the Labor Market," *Social Forces* 93, no. 4 (June 1, 2015): 1451–1479; Lauren A. Rivera, *Pedigree: How Elite Students Get Elite Jobs* (Princeton, NJ: Princeton University Press, 2016).

68. Fligstein, *Architecture of Markets*; Karin Knorr Cetina, "How Are Global Markets Global? The Architecture of a World Flow," in *The Sociology of Financial Markets*, ed. Karin Knorr Cetina and Alex Preda (New York: Oxford University Press, 2004), 38–61; Jens Beckert and Matias Dewey, eds., *The Architecture of Illegal Markets: Towards an Economic Sociology of Illegality in the Economy* (New York: Oxford University Press, 2017).

69. Fligstein, *Architecture of Markets*, 53.

70. A useful summary of actor network theory appears in: Bruno Latour, *Reassembling the Social: An Introduction to Actor-Network-Theory* (New York: Oxford University Press, 2005).

71. Michael Burawoy, *Manufacturing Consent* (Chicago: University of Chicago Press, 1979); Leslie Salzinger, "Manufacturing the Ungendered Subject," *Contemporary Sociology* 30, no. 5 (2001): 451–453; Ofer Sharone, "Constructing Unemployed Job Seekers as Professional Workers: The Depoliticizing Work-Game of Job Searching," *Qualitative Sociology* 30 (2007): 403–416.

72. Michael Burawoy, "The Extended Case Method," *Sociological Theory* 16, no. 1 (March 1998): 4–33.

73. Sallaz, *Labor, Economy, and Society*, 9.

74. Peter L. Berger and Thomas Luckmann, *The Social Construction of Reality: A Treatise in the Sociology of Knowledge* (New York: Anchor, 1967).

75. Thomas S. Kuhn, *The Structure of Scientific Revolutions*, 2nd ed. (Chicago: University of Chicago Press, 1970).

76. Writing of the importance of generating then solving empirical puzzles, Burawoy says: "The vitality of a theoretical tradition depends upon continually being put to the test and then meeting it with ingenious strategies of survival." Michael Burawoy, *The Extended Case Method* (Berkeley: University of California Press, 2009), 9.

77. Rosemary Batt, "Explaining Intra-Occupational Wage Inequality in Telecommunications Services," *Industrial and Labor Relations* 54, no. 2 (2001): 425–449.

78. Latour, *Reassembling the Social*, 174; emphasis mine.

79. Pierre Bourdieu, *The Field of Cultural Production* (New York: Columbia University Press, 1993), 188.

80. "Patriarchy" in Oxford English Dictionary, https://en.oxforddictionaries.com/definition/patriarchy.

81. Latour, *Reassembling the Social*, 132.

82. Michael Burawoy et al., *Global Ethnography: Forces, Connections, and Imaginations in a Postmodern World* (Berkeley: University of California Press, 2000), 140.

83. Ibid., 29.

84. Neil Fligstein, "Social Skill and the Theory of Fields," *Sociological Theory* 19, no. 2 (2001): 105–125.

85. Latour, *Reassembling the Social*, 39.

86. Pierre Bourdieu, Jean-Claude Chamboredon, and Jean-Claude Passeron, *The Craft of Sociology: Epistemological Preliminaries* (New York: Walter de Gruyter, 1991), 13.

87. Gregory Jackson, "Socio-Economics in 2018: More Global, More Ethnographic and Less Comfortable, Please," *Socio-Economic Review* 16, no. 1 (January 1, 2018): 1–3.

88. Paul J. Gollan, "All Talk but No Voice: Non-Union Employee Representation in Call Centre Work," in *Call Centres and Human Resource Management: A Cross-National Perspective*, ed. Stephen Deery and Nicholas Kinnie (New York: Palgrave Macmillan, 2004), 245–266; Brandon Vaidyanathan, "Professionalism 'from below': Mobilization Potential in Indian Call Centres," *Work, Employment and Society* 26, no. 2 (April 1, 2012): 211–227.

89. Jeffrey J. Sallaz, *The Labor of Luck: Casino Capitalism in the United States and South Africa* (Berkeley: University of California Press, 2009); Rivera, *Pedigree*; Burawoy, *Manufacturing Consent*.

90. Ernesto Noronha and Premilla D'Cruz, *Employee Identity in Indian Call Centres: The Notion of Professionalism* (Thousand Oaks, CA: Sage, 2009).

91. A. Aneesh, *Virtual Migration: The Programming of Globalization* (Durham, NC: Duke University Press, 2006).

CHAPTER 3

1. Thomas L. Friedman, *The World Is Flat 3.0: A Brief History of the Twenty-First Century* (London: Picador, 2007), 5. A first version of the book was published in 2005.

2. Ibid., 234.

3. Francis Fukuyama, *The End of History and the Last Man* (New York: Free Press, 1992).

4. Richard Florida, "The World Is Spiky," *The Atlantic*, October 2005, https://www.theatlantic.com/past/docs/images/issues/200510/world-is-spiky.pdf.

5. James Ferguson, *Global Shadows: Africa in the Neoliberal World Order* (Durham, NC: Duke University Press, 2006).

6. Alan Tonelson, *The Race to the Bottom: Why a Worldwide Worker Surplus and Uncontrolled Free Trade Are Sinking American Living Standards* (Boulder, CO: Westview Press, 2002).

7. See Joel S. Fetzer, "Economic Self-Interest or Cultural Marginality? Anti-Immigration Sentiment and Nativist Political Movements in France, Germany and the USA," *Journal of Ethnic and Migration Studies* 26, no. 1 (January 2000): 5–23; Robin Dale Jacobson, *The New Nativism: Proposition 187 and the Debate over Immigration* (Minneapolis: University of Minnesota Press, 2008); Harel Shapira, *Waiting for José: The Minutemen's Pursuit of America* (Princeton, NJ: Princeton University Press, 2017).

8. Tamara Kay, *NAFTA and the Politics of Labor Transnationalism* (New York: Cambridge University Press, 2011).

9. Friedman, *World Is Flat 3.0*, 9; italics mine.

10. Ibid., 10; emphasis mine.

11. Ibid., 10; italics in original.

12. This is *not* to say that the outsourcing industry as a whole has failed in India. In fact, the success of the more knowledge-based "non-voice" side in large measure accounts for the failure of the voice side.

13. Claude S. Fischer, "'Touch Someone': The Telephone Industry Discovers Sociability," *Technology and Culture* 29, no. 1 (January 1988): 32.

14. As quoted in Patrice Flichy, *Dynamics of Modern Communication: The Shaping and Impact of New Communication Technologies* (Thousand Oaks, CA: Sage, 1995), 89.

15. Bureau of the Census, "Historical Census of the United States, Colonial Times to 1970, Part II" (Washington, DC: Bureau of the Census, 1975), 783, http://www.census.gov/library/publications/1975/compendia/hist_stats_colonial-1970.html.

16. Claude S. Fischer, *America Calling: A Social History of the Telephone to 1940* (Berkeley: University of California Press, 1992), 3.

17. Sidney H. Aronson, "The Sociology of the Telephone," *International Journal of Comparative Sociology* 12 (1971): 153–167; John Brooks, *Telephone: The First Hundred Years* (New York: Harper & Row, 1976); Flichy, *Dynamics of Modern Communication*.

18. Edwin A. Asmann, *The Telegraph and the Telephone: Their Development and Role in the Economic History of the United States: The First Century, 1844–1944* (Lake Forest, IL: Lake Forest College, 1980).

19. Ithiel de Sola Pool, ed., *The Social Impact of the Telephone* (Boston: MIT Press, 1977); Ruth Buchanan, "Lives on the Line: Low-Wage Work in the Teleservice Economy," in *Laboring Below the Line*, ed. Frank Munger (New York: Russell Sage Foundation, 2002), 45–72.

20. De Sola Pool, *Social Impact of the Telephone*; John V. Langdale, "The Growth of Long-Distance Telephony in the Bell System: 1875–1907," *Journal of Historical Geography* 4, no. 2 (April 1978): 145–159; Sarah E. Igo, *The Averaged American: Surveys, Citizens, and the Making of a Mass Public* (Cambridge, MA: Harvard University Press, 2007).

21. Buchanan, "Lives on the Line," 47.

22. Federal Communications Commission, "Trends in Telephone Service" (Washington, DC: Federal Communications Commission, 2001), 3, https://transition.fcc.gov/Bureaus/Common_Carrier/Reports/FCC-State_Link/IAD/trend801.pdf.

23. Andrew J. R. Stevens, *Call Centers and the Global Division of Labor: A Political Economy of Post-Industrial Employment and Union Organizing* (New York: Routledge, 2014), 6.

24. Harsimran, "Philippines to Turn Call Centre Capital of World"; Katherine Visconti, "Philippine BPOs Court Democrats', Republicans' Goodwill," *Rappler*, October 8, 2012, http://www.rappler.com/business/13823-philippine-outsourcing-firms-courting-democrats-and-republicans-good-will - disqus_thread; Miriam Altman, "Industrial Strategy, Offshoring, and Employment Promotion in South Africa," in *The Oxford Handbook of Offshoring and Global Employment* (New York: Oxford University Press, 2013).

25. James Ferguson and Akhil Gupta, "Spatializing States: Toward an Ethnography of Neoliberal Governmentality," *American Ethnologist* 29, no. 4 (November 2002): 981–1002; Nitsan Chorev and Sarah Babb, "The Crisis of Neoliberalism and the Future of International Institutions: The IMF and the WTO in Comparative Perspective," *Theory and Society* 38 (2009): 459–485; David Harvey, *A Brief History of Neoliberalism* (New York: Oxford University Press, 2007).

26. For an introduction to Bauman's argument, refer to Zygmunt Bauman, *Liquid Modernity* (Cambridge, UK, and Malden, MA: Polity, 2000).

27. Karl Marx and Friedrich Engels, "Manifest of the Communist Party," in *The Marx-Engels Reader*, ed. Robert C. Tucker, 2nd ed. (New York: W. W. Norton, 1978), 476.

28. Bauman, *Liquid Modernity*, 149.

29. Neil Fligstein, *The Transformation of Corporate Control* (Cambridge, MA: Harvard University Press, 1993); Paul DiMaggio, ed., *The Twenty-First-Century Firm: Changing Economic Organization in International Perspective* (Princeton, NJ: Princeton University Press, 2003); William Lazonick, "Innovative Business

Models and Varieties of Capitalism: Financialization of the U.S. Corporation," *Business History Review* 84, no. 4 (2010): 675–702.

30. Karl Marx, "Wage Labor and Capital," in *The Marx-Engels Reader*, ed. Robert C. Tucker (New York: W. W. Norton, 1978).

31. Jamie Woodcock, *Working the Phones: Control and Resistance in Call Centres* (London: Pluto, 2017), 13.

32. Sallaz, "Permanent Pedagogy," 3–34.

33. Wallace et al., "Sacrificial HR Strategy in Call Centers," 174–184.

34. David Harvey, *The Enigma of Capital: And the Crises of Capitalism* (New York: Oxford University Press, 2011).

35. Phil Taylor and Peter Bain, "'India Calling to the Far Away Towns': The Call Centre Labour Process and Globalization," *Work, Employment and Society* 19, no. 2 (2005): 261–282.

36. Buchanan, "Lives on the Line," 45–72; emphasis mine.

37. Oxford Business Group, "The Philippines: BPO's Rising Potential" (London: Oxford Business Group, April 24, 2012).

38. Tholons Consulting, "Top 50 Emerging Global Outsourcing Cities" (San Jose, CA: Tholons Consulting, 2009), 27.

39. McKinsey Global Institute, "The Emerging Global Labor Market" (San Francisco: McKinsey, 2005).

40. Michael Heric and Bhanu Singh, "Seizing the Strategic High Ground in Capability Sourcing" (Boston: Bain, April 19, 2010).

41. McKinsey Global Institute, "Emerging Global Labor Market," 14.

42. Ibid., 14.

43. Ibid., 7; emphasis mine.

44. Ibid., 11–12.

45. Paul Laudicina, Johan Gott, and Erik Peterson, "The 2014 A.T. Kearney Global Services Location Index" (New York: A. T. Kearney, 2014).

46. Trestle Group Consulting, "Sourcing Destination Snapshot" (New York: Trestle Group, 2013).

47. Laudicina et al., "2014 A.T. Kearney Global Services Location Index," 1; emphasis mine.

48. McKinsey Global Institute, "Emerging Global Labor Market," 45; emphasis mine.

49. Rene Martel, "Marcos Media Nemesis Joins BPO Wave," *Manila Times*, May 20, 2008,   http://www.manilatimes.net/national/2008/may/20/yehey/business/20080520bus14.html, emphasis mine.

50. Rosemarie Francisco and Jason Szep, "Philippines Tries New Tack: Healthy Man of Asia," *Reuters*, February 20, 2012, http://www.reuters.com/article/2012/02/20/us-philippines-idUSTRE81J0I820120220, emphasis mine.

51. Heric and Singh, "Seizing the Strategic High Ground," 6; emphasis mine.

52. Tholons Consulting, "Top 50 Emerging Global Outsourcing Cities."

53. McKinsey Global Institute, "Emerging Global Labor Market," 56.

54. Laudicina et al., "2014 A.T. Kearney Global Services Location Index," 2; emphasis mine.

55. ABS-CBN, "PH Is Best Outsourcing Destination in Asia: CBRE," *ABS-CBN NEWS*, November 9, 2011, http://news.abs-cbn.com/business/11/09/11/ph-best-outsourcing-destination-asia-cbre; emphasis mine.

56. McKinsey Global Institute, "Emerging Global Labor Market."

57. Ibid., 44; none of the reports I analyzed attempted to quantify costs associated with attrition.

58. Laudicina et al., "2014 A.T. Kearney Global Services Location Index."

59. McKinsey Global Institute, "Emerging Global Labor Market," 51.

60. Ketaki Gokhale, "Infosys Net Climbs 27% as Customers Outsource More Work," *Business Week*, April 4, 2012, http://www.businessweek.com/news/2012-04-12/infosys-net-climbs-27-percent-as-customers-outsource-more-work; Tholons Consulting, "2014 Tholons Top 100 Outsourcing Destination Rankings" (San Jose, CA: Tholons Consulting, 2013); Ilan Oshri, Julian Kotlarsky, and Leslie P. Wilcocks, *The Handbook of Global Outsourcing and Offshoring: The Definitive Guide to Strategy and Operations*, 3rd ed. (New York: Palgrave Macmillan, 2015).

61. Ching Kwan Lee, *Gender and the South China Miracle: Two Worlds of Factory Women* (Berkeley: University of California Press, 1998); Lu Zhang, *Inside China's Automobile Factories* (New York: Cambridge University Press, 2014).

62. McKinsey Global Institute, "Emerging Global Labor Market," 36.

63. Tholons Consulting, "Top 50 Emerging Global Outsourcing Cities," 25.

64. Mohan Munasinghe, *Computers and Informatics in Developing Countries* (Oxford: Butterworth-Heinemann, 2014).

65. McKinsey Global Institute, "Emerging Global Labor Market," 6.

66. Tholons Consulting, "2014 Tholons Top 100 Outsourcing Destination Rankings."

67. GlobalEnglish Corporation, "The Business English Index 2012 Report" (Brisbane, CA: GlobalEnglish, 2012), 3.

68. Ibid., 6.

69. Laudicina et al., "2014 A.T. Kearney Global Services Location Index," 4.

70. McKinsey and Co., "Rethinking the Model of Offshoring Services" (San Francisco: McKinsey, 2009), 9, http://www.mckinsey.com/insights/business_technology/rethinking_the_model_for_offshoring_services.

71. Trestle Group Consulting, "Sourcing Destination Snapshot."

72. Laudicina et al., "2014 A.T. Kearney Global Services Location Index."

73. As quoted in Paolo G. Montecillo, "BPO Sector in Philippines Not Just about Call Centers," *Philippine Daily Inquirer*, July 10, 2011sec. Business, https://business.inquirer.net/6592/bpo-sector-in-philippines-not-just-about-call-centers

74. Tholons Consulting, "2014 Tholons Top 100 Outsourcing Destination Rankings."

75. Xiang Biao, *Global "Body Shopping": An Indian Labor System in the Information Technology Industry* (Princeton, NJ: Princeton University Press, 2006), 10; emphasis mine.

76. Shehzad Nadeem, *Dead Ringers* (Princeton, NJ: Princeton University Press, 2010), 34.

77. Patel, *Working the Night Shift*, 41; Phil Taylor and Peter Bain, "'India Calling to the Far Away Towns': The Call Centre Labour Process and Globalization," *Work, Employment and Society* 19, no. 2 (2005): 268; Parthasarathy, "Changing Character of Indian Offshore ICT Services Provision," 387; Miriam Altman, "Industrial Strategy, Offshoring, and Employment Promotion in South Africa," in *The Oxford Handbook of Offshoring and Global Employment* (New York: Oxford University Press, 2013), 630.

78. Nadeem, *Dead Ringers*, 91.

79. By 2001, seven IITs were in operation; see Messenger and Ghosheh, "Offshoring and Working Conditions in Remote Work." By 2016 sixteen more schools had been certified as IITs.

80. AnnaLee Saxenian, *The New Argonauts: Regional Advantage in a Global Economy* (Cambridge, MA: Harvard University Press, 2007).

81. Kiran Mirchandani, *Phone Clones: Authenticity Work in the Transnational Service Economy* (Ithaca, NY: ILR Press, 2012), 20.

82. Xiang Biao, *Global "Body Shopping,"* 25.

83. Ibid., 27.

84. NASSCOM, "India IT-BPM Overview" (Mumbai: NASSCOM, 2016), http://www.nasscom.in/indian-itbpo-industry.

85. Mirchandani, *Phone Clones*, 19.

86. Nadeem, *Dead Ringers*, 3; emphasis mine.

87. Vandana Nath, "Aesthetic and Emotional Labour through Stigma: National Identity Management and Racial Abuse in Offshored Indian Call Centres," *Work, Employment and Society* 25, no. 4 (2011): 709–725.

88. Aneesh, *Neutral Accent*, 5.

89. N. Gupta, "Rethinking the Relationship between Gender and Technology: A Study of the Indian Example," *Work, Employment & Society* 29, no. 4 (August 1, 2015): 661–672.

90. A. Aneesh, *Virtual Migration: The Programming of Globalization* (Durham, NC: Duke University Press, 2006), 97.

91. Patel, *Working the Night Shift*, 51.

92. Ibid., 73.

93. Nadeem, *Dead Ringers*, 64.

94. Taylor and Bain, "'India Calling to the Far Away Towns,'" 272; Raka Ray and Seemin Qayum, *Cultures of Servitude: Modernity, Domesticity, and Class in India* (Stanford, CA: Stanford University Press, 2009).

95. Mirchandani, *Phone Clones*, 127.

96. International Labour Organization, "Key Indicators of the Labour Market," The World Bank, 2014, http://data.worldbank.org/indicator/SL.TLF.CACT.FE.ZS.

97. Nadeem, *Dead Ringers*, 92.

98. Taylor and Bain, " 'India Calling to the Far Away Towns,' " 271.

99. Winifred R. Poster, "Who's on the Line? Indian Call Center Agents Pose as Americans for U.S.-Outsourced Firms," *Industrial Relations* 46, no. 2 (2007): 293.

100. Patel, *Working the Night Shift*, 34.

101. Ibid., 44.

102. Xiang Biao, *Global "Body Shopping*," 97.

103. Nadeem, *Dead Ringers*, 67.

104. Xiang Biao, *Global "Body Shopping*." It appears as though the Indian government and NASSCOM have not acted so as to counter the various stigmas associated with call center work in India. Their game is to move more and more investment into the IT-BPO sector, and so having only a modest call center industry to provide remedial training is in their interest.

105. Patel, *Working the Night Shift*, 44.

106. Extreme forms of location masking, such as the requirement that offshore call center agents adopt American names, were for the most part been abandoned by 2015.

107. Diya Das, Ravi Dharwadkar, and Pamela Brandes, "The Importance of Being 'Indian': Identity Centrality and Work Outcomes in an Off-Shored Call Center in India," *Human Relations* 61, no. 11 (November 1, 2008): 1499–1530; Stephen Deery, Vandana Nath, and Janet Walsh, "Why Do Offshored Indian Call Centre Workers Want to Leave Their Jobs?," *New Technology, Work and Employment* 28, no. 3 (November 1, 2013): 212–226.

108. Vandana Nath, "Aesthetic and Emotional Labour through Stigma: National Identity Management and Racial Abuse in Offshored Indian Call Centres," *Work, Employment and Society* 25, no. 4 (2011): 716.

109. Nadeem, *Dead Ringers*, 186.

110. Patel, *Working the Night Shift*, 56; Nadeem, *Dead Ringers*, 192.

111. Aneesh, *Neutral Accent*, 37.

112. Taylor and Bain, " 'India Calling to the Far Away Towns,' "; Nadeem, *Dead Ringers*; Rosemary Batt and Alexander J. S. Colvin, "An Employment Systems Approach to Turnover: Human Resources Practices, Quits, Dismissals, and Performance," *Academy of Management Journal* 54, no. 4 (2011): 695–717; Virginia Doellgast, *Disintegrating Democracy at Work: Labor Unions and the Future of Good Jobs in the Service Economy* (Ithaca, NY: Cornell University Press, 2012).

CHAPTER 4

1. Rob Vos and Josef T. Yap, *The Philippine Economy: Stray Cat of East Asia?: Finance, Adjustment and Structure* (New York: Palgrave Macmillan, 1996).

2. Laudicina et al., "2014 A.T. Kearney Global Services Location Index," 8.

3. For readings on postcolonial legacies and the state, see: Peter B. Evans, *Embedded Autonomy: States and Industrial Transformation* (Princeton, NJ: Princeton

University Press, 1995); Mahmood Mamdani, *Citizen and Subject: Contemporary Africa and the Legacy of Late Colonialism* (Princeton, NJ: Princeton University Press, 1996); Jean Comaroff and John L. Comaroff, *Law and Disorder in the Postcolony* (Chicago: University of Chicago Press, 2008); Jeffrey J. Sallaz, "Deep Plays: A Comparative Ethnography of Gambling Contests in Two Post-Colonies," *Ethnography* 9, no. 1 (March 1, 2008): 5–33.

4. Walden Bello et al., *The Anti-Development State: The Political Economy of Permanent Crisis in the Philippines* (London: Zed, 2006).

5. Fenella Cannell, *Power and Intimacy in the Christian Philippines* (New York: Cambridge University Press, 1999), 5.

6. Dennis O. Flynn, Arturo Giraldez, and James Sobredo, *European Entry into the Pacific: Spain and the Acapulco-Manila Galleons* (New York: Routledge, 2017).

7. Filomeno V. Aguilar, *Clash of Spirits: The History of Power and Sugar Planter Hegemony on a Visayan Island* (Honolulu: University of Hawaii Press, 1998), 23.

8. John Leddy Phelan, *The Hispanization of the Philippines: Spanish Aims and Filipino Responses, 1565–1700* (Madison: University of Wisconsin Press, 2010).

9. Pew Research Center, "Five Facts about Catholicism in the Philippines," Pew Research Center, January 9, 2015, http://www.pewresearch.org/fact-tank/2015/01/09/5-facts-about-catholicism-in-the-philippines/.

10. Jee Y. Geronimo, "Sex Education in PH Schools Still Lacking," *Rappler*, July 9, 2016, http://www.rappler.com/nation/139118-sex-education-philippines-unfpa.

11. Carolina S Ruiz Austria, "The Church, the State and Women's Bodies in the Context of Religious Fundamentalism in the Philippines," *Reproductive Health Matters* 12, no. 24 (November 2004): 96.

12. Data in this paragraph derive from the following: Asean Secretariat, *ASEAN Statistical Yearbook 2005* (Jakarta: ASEAN, 2005); United Nations Population Division, "Household Size and Composition Around the World 2017" (New York: United Nations, 2017); United Nations Population Division, "World Population Prospects: 2017 Revision" (New York: United Nations, 2017).

13. David Brody, *Visualizing American Empire: Orientalism and Imperialism in the Philippines* (Chicago: University of Chicago Press, 2010).

14. McKay, *Satanic Mills or Silicon Islands?*, 54.

15. Stanley Karnow, *In Our Image: America's Empire in the Philippines* (New York: Ballantine, 1989).

16. McKay, *Satanic Mills or Silicon Islands?*, 54.

17. Julian Go, "Global Perspectives on the U.S. Colonial Presence in the Philippines," in *The American Colonial State in the Philippines: Global Perspectives*, ed. Julian Go and Anne L. Foster (Durham, NC: Duke University Press, 2003), 4.

18. Gary Hawes, "United States Support for the Marcos Administration and the Pressures That Made for Change," *Contemporary Southeast Asia* 8, no. 1 (1986): 18–36.

19. Yeganeh Torbati, "U.S. Announces Ramped-up Military Presence in Philippines," *Reuters*, April 14, 2016, http://www.reuters.com/article/us-southchinasea-philippines-carter-idUSKCN0XB0QY.

20. Christopher Erickson et al., *Employment Relations in the Philippines* (Ithaca, NY: Cornell University ILR School, 2001); Anna Romina Guevarra, *Marketing Dreams, Manufacturing Heroes: The Transnational Labor Brokering of Filipino Workers* (New Brunswick, NJ: Rutgers University Press, 2009); Victoria Reyes, "Global Borderlands: A Case Study of the Subic Bay Freeport Zone, Philippines," *Theory and Society* 44, no. 4 (July 1, 2015): 355–384.

21. Bello et al., *The Anti-Development State*, 2; see also: Marco Garrido, "Why the Poor Support Populism: The Politics of Sincerity in Metro Manila," *American Journal of Sociology* 123, no. 3 (November 1, 2017): 647–685.

22. Evans, *Embedded Autonomy*; Philip S. Golub, *East Asia's Reemergence* (Malden, MA: Polity, 2016).

23. Bello et al., *Anti-Development State*.

24. See: Yen Le Espiritu, *Home Bound: Filipino American Lives across Cultures, Communities, and Countries* (Berkeley: University of California Press, 2003); Catherine Ceniza Choy, *Empire of Care: Nursing and Migration in Filipino American History* (Durham, NC: Duke University Press, 2003); Dorothy B. Fujita Rony, *American Workers, Colonial Power: Philippine Seattle and the Transpacific West, 1919–1941* (Berkeley: University of California Press, 2003); Guevarra, *Marketing Dreams, Manufacturing Heroes*; Linda España-Maram, *Creating Masculinity in Los Angeles's Little Manila: Working-Class Filipinos and Popular Culture in the United States* (New York: Columbia University Press, 2013).

25. Robyn Magalit Rodriguez, *Migrants for Export: How the Philippine State Brokers Labor to the World* (Minneapolis: University of Minnesota Press, 2010), 12.

26. Guevarra, *Marketing Dreams, Manufacturing Heroes*, 10.

27. Rodriguez, *Migrants for Export*, x; see also: Vincente L. Rafael, *White Love: And Other Events in Filipino History* (Durham, NC: Duke University Press, 2000), 9.

28. Guevarra, *Marketing Dreams, Manufacturing Heroes*, 2.

29. Rodriguez, *Migrants for Export*, 85.

30. Anna Romina Guevarra, *Marketing Dreams, Manufacturing Heroes: The Transnational Labor Brokering of Filipino Workers* (New Brunswick, NJ: Rutgers University Press, 2009), 2.

31. Benito Veragara, *Pinoy Capital* (Philadelphia, PA: Temple University Press), 3.

32. ABS-CBN, "PH Is Best Outsourcing Destination in Asia: CBRE," *ABS-CBN NEWS*, November 9, 2011, http://news.abs-cbn.com/business/11/09/11/ph-best-outsourcing-destination-asia-cbre.

33. Mike Davis, *Planet of Slums* (London: Verso, 2007).

34. Greg Bankoff, "Constructing Vulnerability: The Historical, Natural and Social Generation of Flooding in Metropolitan Manila" *Disasters* 27, no. 3 (September 2003): 224–238; Gavin Shatkin, "Planning to Forget: Informal Settlements

as 'Forgotten Places' in Globalising Metro Manila," *Urban Studies* 41, no. 12 (November 1, 2004): 2469–2484.

35. Davis, *Planet of Slums*, 27.

36. Emma Porio and Christine Crisol, "Property Rights, Security of Tenure and the Urban Poor in Metro Manila," *Habitat International* 28, no. 2 (June 2004): 203–219.

37. See: University of the Philippines Diliman website, section on history of university. https://upd.edu.ph/about/history/.

38. Figures in this paragraph can be found in: Commission on Higher Education, "Infographics on Philippine Higher Education" (Manila: Commission on Higher Education, 2014).

39. Philippine Statistics Authority, *Survey on Overseas Filipinos* (Manila: Philippine Statistics Authority, 2017).

40. Ibid.

41. Anju Mary Paul, *Multinational Maids: Stepwise Migration in a Global Labor Market* (Cambridge: Cambridge University Press, 2017).

42. Earnings for Filipino overseas workers vary based on qualifications, destination country, and other factors. My estimate of a monthly salary of US$1000 derives from my respondents' reports and existing studies. See: Kathleen Weekley, "Saving Pennies for the State. A New Role for Filipino Migrant Workers?," *Journal of Contemporary Asia* 34, no. 3 (January 1, 2004): 349–363; Guevarra, *Marketing Dreams, Manufacturing Heroes*; Rodriguez, *Migrants for Export*.

43. Nicole Constable, *Maid to Order in Hong Kong: Stories of Migrant Workers*, 2nd ed. (Ithaca, NY: Cornell University Press, 2007).

44. Rhacel Parreñas, *Illicit Flirtations: Labor, Migration, and Sex Trafficking in Tokyo* (Stanford, CA: Stanford University Press, 2011); Nicole Constable, *Born Out of Place: Migrant Mothers and the Politics of International Labor* (Berkeley: University of California Press, 2014).

45. Guevarra, *Marketing Dreams, Manufacturing Heroes*; Rodriguez, *Migrants for Export*.

46. McGeown, "Nursing Dream Turns Sour in the Philippines"; Pei-Chia Lan, "Legal Servitude and Free Illegality, 253–278; Rodriguez, *Migrants for Export*; Parreñas, *Illicit Flirtations*.

47. Pei-Chia Lan, "Legal Servitude and Free Illegality: Migrant 'Guest' Workers in Taiwan," in *Asian Diasporas*, ed. Rhacel Parreñas and Lok C. D. Siu (Stanford, CA: Stanford University Press, 2007), 253–278; Robyn Magalit Rodriguez, *Migrants for Export: How the Philippine State Brokers Labor to the World*; Rhacel Parreñas, *Illicit Flirtations: Labor, Migration, and Sex Trafficking in Tokyo*.

48. Porio, "Global Householding, Gender, and Filipino Migration," 211–242; Guevarra, *Marketing Dreams, Manufacturing Heroes*; Arlie Russell Hochschild, "Love and Gold," *Scholar and Feminist Online* 8, no. 1 (2009), http://sfonline.barnard.edu/work/hochschild_01.htm.

49. Raul Pertierra, *The Anthropology of New Media in the Philippines* (Quezon City: Institute of Philippine Culture, 2010), 68.

50. Erickson et al., *Employment Relations in the Philippines*.

CHAPTER 5

1. Chris Rowthorn and Greg Bloom, *Philippines* (Melbourne: Lonely Planet, 2006), 87.

2. U.S. Bureau of Labor Statistics, *International Labor Comparisons* (Washington, DC: U.S. Department of Labor, 2011).

3. Xiang Biao, *Global "Body Shopping."*

4. Theo spoke these words to me in Tagalog. I have translated his use of the pronoun *siya* as "he or she," as the term is not sex specific. I think in this context the translation is correct given that the field of nursing is not characterized by an extreme sex imbalance.

5. McGeown, "Nursing Dream Turns Sour in the Philippines."

6. Philippines Commission on Higher Education, "Philippine Higher Education," 2013, http://www.ched.gov.ph/wp-content/uploads/2013/02/Infographics-on-Philippine-Higher-Education-v1.pdf.

7. It was because of this sex and gender imbalance in the industry that I oversampled gay and straight male employees as respondents; the implications of this sampling strategy for interpreting my findings are discussed in the methodological appendix.

8. Because my sample of call center agents in Manila was stratified (I overrecruited gay workers and straight male workers), these figures should not be taken to apply to the overall population of call center agents in metro Manila.

9. An important distinction is often made between inbound call centers (wherein agents receive calls from clients, such as billing inquiries or complaints) and outbound ones (wherein agents place calls—for instance, to administer a survey or sell a product). The idea is that interactions may be more problematic in outbound situations because the client has not requested to be contacted and may perceive the call as an interruption. I did not screen for inbound or outbound accounts when I was assembling my sample, yet the large majority (53 of 60) of my respondents worked for inbound accounts. The seven who did work on outbound accounts were as likely to consider their calls as courteous as were the other respondents, though with my low number of respondents it is not possible to make any definitive comparison between the two groups.

10. Michael Greenacre, *Correspondence Analysis in Practice*, 2nd ed. (Boca Raton, FL: Chapman and Hall/CRC, 2007), 1.

11. Sten-Erik Clausen, *Applied Correspondence Analysis* (Thousand Oaks, CA: Sage, 1988), 2.

12. Pierre Bourdieu, *Distinction: A Social Critique of the Judgment of Taste* (Cambridge, MA: Harvard University Press, 1984).

13. Ronald L. Breiger, "A Tool Kit for Practice Theory," *Poetics* 27 (2000): 91–115; Bernard E. Harcourt, *Language of the Gun: Youth, Crime, and Public Policy* (Chicago: University of Chicago Press, 2006).

14. Pierre Bourdieu and Loïc Wacquant, *An Invitation to Reflexive Sociology* (Chicago: University of Chicago Press, 1992), 227.

15. This map captures 46% of the overall variation in the contingency table; refer to the methodological appendix for further details on how this map was generated.

16. Clausen, *Applied Correspondence Analysis*, 2.

CHAPTER 6

1. Guevarra, *Marketing Dreams, Manufacturing Heroes*; Rodriguez, *Migrants for Export*.

2. C. Berghammer, "The Return of the Male Breadwinner Model? Educational Effects on Parents' Work Arrangements in Austria, 1980–2009," *Work, Employment & Society* 28, no. 4 (August 1, 2014): 611.

3. Shelly Errington, "Recasting Sex, Gender, and Power: A Theoretical and Regional Overview," in *Power and Difference: Gender in Island Southeast Asia*, ed. Jane Monning Atkinson and Shelly Errington (Stanford, CA: Stanford University Press, 1990), 48.

4. Ibid., 48.

5. Jiping Zuo and Shengming Tang, "Breadwinner Status and Gender Ideologies of Men and Women Regarding Family Roles," *Sociological Perspectives* 43, no. 1 (April 2000): 29–43.

6. Cristina Blanc-Szanton, "Collision of Cultures: Historical Reformulations of Gender in the Lowland Visayas, Philippines," in *Power and Difference: Gender in Island Southeast Asia*, ed. Jane Monning Atkinson and Shelly Errington (Stanford, CA: Stanford University Press, 1990), 351.

7. Errington, "Recasting Sex, Gender, and Power"; Blanc-Szanton, "Collision of Cultures"; Jane A. Margold, "Narratives of Masculinity and Transnational Migration: Filipino Workers in the Middle East," in *Bewitching Women, Pious Men: Gender and Body Politics in Southeast Asia*, ed. Aihwa Ong and Michael G. Peletz (Berkeley: University of California Press, 1995), 274–298; Belen T. G. Medina, "The Family in the Philippines," in *Families in a Global Context*, ed. Charles B. Hennon and Stephan M. Wilson (New York: Routledge, 2008), 365.

8. Elizabeth King and Lita Domino, "The Changing Status of Filipino Women Across Family Generations," *Philippine Population Journal* 2, no. 1 (1986): 1–22, 8.

9. David Brady, *Rich Democracies, Poor People: How Politics Explain Poverty* (New York: Oxford University Press, 2009).

10. Yih-Jiunn Lee and Yeun-wen Ku, "East Asian Welfare Regimes: Testing the Hypothesis of the Developmental Welfare State," *Social Policy & Administration* 41, no. 2 (April 2007): 197–212.

11. A Filipina who looks like a typical breadwinner in the West—that is, she works, has a working spouse, and has one or two children—might very well *not* consider herself a breadwinner.

12. Medina, "The Family in the Philippines"; Rhacel Salazar Parreñas, *Children of Global Migration: Transnational Families and Gendered Woes* (Stanford, CA: Stanford University Press, 2005); Blanc-Szanton, "Collision of Cultures."

13. I think it is safe to assume that non-breadwinning women are less attached to the industry (i.e., more likely to go abroad or to pursue professional domestic jobs) than are female breadwinners. It is easier to give up smoking than it is to deny one's younger siblings grocery money.

CHAPTER 7

1. Asian Development Bank, "Gender Equality in the Labor Market in the Philippines" (Manila: Asian Development Bank, 2013).

2. Bobby Benedicto, "The Haunting of Gay Manila: Global Space-Time and the Specter of Kabaklaan," *GLQ: A Journal of Lesbian and Gay Studies* 14, no. 2–3 (January 1, 2008): 321.

3. Boarding houses in the Philippines nearly always cater to one sex or the other: "Male bed-spacers wanted" or "Female bed-spacers wanted." With the rapid growth of the call center industry in metro Manila, some "male" boarding houses are catering (via word of mouth) to gay call center agents, even those who cross-dress. Boi and his roommates lived in a more standard boarding house, and reported no problems or tensions with the straight men who lived there.

4. Maragtas S. V. Amante, "Outsourced Work in Philippine BPOs: A Country Case Study" (Quezon City: UP SOLAIR, 2008).

5. UNDP and USAID, "Being LGBT in Asia: The Philippines Country Report" (Bangkok: USAID, 2014).

6. Susan Stryker, "We Who Are Sexy: Christine Jorgensen's Transsexual Whiteness in the Postcolonial Philippines," *Social Semiotics* 19, no. 1 (2009): 79–91.

7. E. David, "Purple-Collar Labor: Transgender Workers and Queer Value at Global Call Centers in the Philippines," *Gender & Society* 29, no. 2 (April 1, 2015): 174.

8. Martin F. Manalansan IV, *Global Divas: Filipino Gay Men in the Diaspora* (Durham, NC: Duke University Press, 2003), 1.

9. Ryan Thoreson, "Capably Queer: Exploring the Intersections of Queerness and Poverty in the Urban Philippines," *Journal of Human Development and Capabilities* 12, no. 4 (November 2011): 493–510.

10. Manalansan, *Global Divas*, 25.

11. Fenella Cannell, *Power and Intimacy in the Christian Philippines* (New York: Cambridge University Press, 1999); Benedicto, " Haunting of Gay Manila."

12. Manalansan, *Global Divas*, ix.

13. J. Neil C. Garcia, *Philippine Gay Culture: Binabae to Bakla, Silahis to MSM*, 2nd ed. (Quezon City: University of the Philippines Press, 2008), 1.

14. Sam Winter, Sass Rogando-Sasot, and Mark King, "Transgendered Women of the Philippines," *International Journal of Transgenderism* 10, no. 2 (November 2007): 79–90.

15. Manalansan, *Global Divas*, 28.

16. Donn Hart and Harriett Hart, "Visayan Swardspeak: The Language of a Gay Community in the Philippines," *Crossroads: An Interdisciplinary Journal of Southeast Asian Studies* 5, no. 2 (1990): 27–49.

17. Manalansan, *Global Divas*, vii.

18. Gwenola Ricordeau, "Review of "Philipine Gay Culture: Binabae to Bakla, Silahis to MSM," *Intersections: Gender and Sexuality in Asia and the Pacific*, no. 19 (2009): 19.

19. Benedicto, "Haunting of Gay Manila."

20. Manalansan, *Global Divas*, 60.

21. Thomas M. Keck, "Beyond Backlash: Assessing the Impact of Judicial Decisions on LGBT Rights," *Law & Society Review* 43, no. 1 (March 1, 2009): 151–186.

22. Amin Ghaziani, *There Goes the Gayborhood?* (Princeton, NJ: Princeton University Press, 2015).

23. The honors awarded to recent films such as *Moonlight* and *Dallas Buyer's Club*, it is hoped, portend a change in the entertainment industry's depiction of LGBT persons and issues.

24. UNDP and USAID, "Being LGBT in Asia," 21.

25. Ibid., 22.

26. Dominique Mosbergen, "The Dangers of Being LGBT in 'Tolerant' Philippines," *World Post*, October 12, 2015, http://www.huffingtonpost.com/entry/lgbtphilippines_us_5614f92fe4b021e856d2d870.

27. Garcia, *Philippine Gay Culture*, xvi.

28. UNDP and USAID, "Being LGBT in Asia," 19, 48, 59.

29. Michael L. Tan, "Survival Through Pluralism: Emerging Gay Communities in the Philippines," in *Gay and Lesbian Asia: Culture, Identity, Community*, ed. Gerard Sullivan and Peter A. Jackson (New York: Routledge, 2013), 120.

30. Ibid.

31. Winter et al., "Transgendered Women of the Philippines," 80.

32. Philip C. Tubeza, "PH Ranks Among Most Gay-Friendly in the World," *Philippine Daily Inquirer*, June 8, 2013, 4, http://globalnation.inquirer.net/76977/ph-ranks-among-most-gay-friendly-in-the-world.

33. Pew Research Center, "The Global Divide on Homosexuality: Greater Acceptance in More Secular and Affluent Countries" (Washington, DC: Pew Research Center, 2013), 4.

34. Garcia, *Philippine Gay Culture*, 64; emphasis mine.

35. Cannell, *Power and Intimacy in the Christian Philippines*, 214.

36. Emmanuel David, "The Sexual Fields of Empire: On the Ethnosexual Frontiers of Global Outsourcing," *Radical History Review* 2015, no. 123 (October 2015): 115–143.

37. Winter et al., "Transgendered Women of the Philippines."

38. UNDP and USAID, "Being LGBT in Asia," 41.

39. Garcia, *Philippine Gay Culture*, 87.

40. Parreñas, *Illicit Flirtations*.

41. UNDP and USAID, "Being LGBT in Asia," 37.

42. David, "Purple-Collar Labor," 174.

43. Ibid., 184.

44. Ibid., 183.

45. Donald Roy, "'Banana Time': Job Satisfaction and Informal Interaction," *Human Organization* 18, no. 4 (1959): 158–168; Burawoy, *Manufacturing Consent*.

46. UNDP and USAID, "Being LGBT in Asia," 37.

47. Benedicto, "Haunting of Gay Manila," 322.

48. Manalansan, *Global Divas*, 26.

49. Mark Johnson, "Global Desirings and Translocal Loves: Transgendering and Same-Sex Sexualities in the Southern Philippines," *American Ethnologist* 25, no. 4 (November 1998): 695–711; Johnson provides an insightful account of how straight men maintain their macho identities while engaging in physical relationships with gay-identified men. As he writes "[M]en do not deny the sexual pleasure they receive at the hands of the *bantut* [the local term for *bakla* in the region he was studying], but stress that they never actively reciprocate the *bantut*, either materially or sexually, particularly in anal intercourse. In short, men present themselves as tricksters capable of successfully playing off the vanity, petty jealousies, and potentially dangerous sexual appetites of the *bantut* in order both to enhance their own masculinity and to turn a profit" (700–701).

CHAPTER 8

1. See: Charles Tilly, *Durable Inequality* (Berkeley: University of California Press, 1999); C. L. Ridgeway, "Why Status Matters for Inequality," *American Sociological Review* 79, no. 1 (February 1, 2014): 1–16; April Sutton, Amanda Bosky, and Chandra Muller, "Manufacturing Gender Inequality in the New Economy: High School Training for Work in Blue-Collar Communities," *American Sociological Review*, 81, no. 4 (2016): 720–748.

2. Louise Marie Roth, *Selling Women Short: Gender and Money on Wall Street* (Princeton, NJ: Princeton University Press, 2006); D. Laurison and S. Friedman, "The Class Pay Gap in Higher Professional and Managerial Occupations," *American Sociological Review*, 81, no. 4 (2016): 668–695.

3. Christine L. Williams, *Gender Differences at Work: Women and Men in Non-Traditional Occupations* (Berkeley: University of California Press, 1989); Ruth

Milkman, *On Gender, Labor, and Inequality* (Chicago: University of Illinois Press, 2016).

4. Joan Acker, "Hierarchies, Jobs, Bodies: A Theory of Gendered Organizations," *Gender & Society* 4, no. 2 (June 1, 1990): 139–158; Juliet Webster, *Shaping Women's Work: Gender, Employment and Information Technology* (New York: Routledge, 2014).

5. Hochschild, *Managed Heart*.

6. Winifred R. Poster, "Dangerous Places and Nimble Fingers: Discourses of Gender Discrimination and Rights in Global Corporations," *International Journal of Politics, Culture, and Society* 15, no. 1 (September 2001): 77–105; Leslie Salzinger, *Genders in Production* (Berkeley: University of California Press, 2003); McKay, *Satanic Mills or Silicon Islands?*; Melissa W. Wright, *Disposable Women and Other Myths of Global Capitalism* (New York: Routledge, 2006); Aihwa Ong, *Spirits of Resistance and Capitalist Discipline: Factory Women in Malaysia*, 2nd. ed. (Albany: State University of New York Press, 2010).

7. Pearson Education Inc., "Versant Test," https://www.versanttest.com/solutions/callCenters.jsp# accessed on June 1, 2016; emphasis mine.

8. Medina, "Family in the Philippines," 368.

9. Jane A. Margold, "Narratives of Masculinity and Transnational Migration: Filipino Workers in the Middle East," in *Bewitching Women, Pious Men: Gender and Body Politics in Southeast Asia*, ed. Aihwa Ong and Michael G. Peletz (Berkeley: University of California Press, 1995), 274–298; Steven C. McKay, "Filipino Sea Men: Identity and Masculinity in a Global Labor Niche," in *Asian Diasporas*, ed. Rhacel Parreñas and Lok C. D. Siu (Stanford, CA: Stanford University Press, 2007), 63–83; Rodriguez, *Migrants for Export*; Steven C. McKay and Don Eliseo Lucero-Prisno III, "Masculinities Afloat: Filipino Seafarers and the Situational Performance of Manhood," in *Men and Masculinities in Southeast Asia*, ed. Michele Ford and Lenore Lyons (London: Routledge, 2011), 20–37; Parreñas, *Illicit Flirtations*.

10. Rodriguez, *Migrants for Export*, 36.

11. McKay, "Filipino Sea Men," 75; emphasis mine.

12. Ibid., 75, 76.

13. Linda España-Maram, *Creating Masculinity in Los Angeles's Little Manila: Working-Class Filipinos and Popular Culture in the United States* (New York: Columbia University Press, 2013).

14. Errington, "Recasting Sex, Gender, and Power," 4.

15. Medina, "Family in the Philippines," 364.

16. Errington, "Recasting Sex, Gender, and Power," 6.

17. Blanc-Szanton, "Collision of Cultures," 378.

18. Ibid., 378.

19. Wallace et al., "Sacrificial HR Strategy in Call Centers," 174–184; Sallaz, "Exit Tales," 573–599.

CHAPTER 9

1. Harry Braverman, *Labor and Monopoly Capital: The Degradation of Work in the Twentieth Century* (New York: Monthly Review Press, 1974); David H. Autor, "Why Are There Still So Many Jobs? The History and Future of Workplace Automation," *Journal of Economic Perspectives* 29, no. 3 (August 2015): 3–30; Martin Ford, *Rise of the Robots: Technology and the Threat of a Jobless Future* (New York: Basic, 2015).

2. Steven Henry Lopez, *Reorganizing the Rust Belt: An Inside Study of the American Labor Movement* (Berkeley: University of California Press, 2004); B. Western and J. Rosenfeld, "Unions, Norms, and the Rise in U.S. Wage Inequality," *American Sociological Review* 76, no. 4 (August 1, 2011): 513–537.

3. Scholarly opinion is much more divided on the issue. Some argue that the specter of offshoring has been vastly overstated; others contend that the rapid development of technologies facilitating the trade of services across national boundaries portend the "next industrial revolution." See: Alan S. Blinder, "Offshoring: The Next Industrial Revolution?," *Foreign Affairs* 85, no. 2 (2006): 113–128; Susskind and Susskind, *Future of the Professions*.

4. Jeffrey J. Sallaz and Michael Gibson, "What Is Outsourcing?: How the New Industrial Revolution Has Been Framed in Newspapers," presentation at American Sociological Association Annual Meeting, New York, 2013.

5. Helene Cooper and Ashley Parker, "Obama Calls Romney Potential 'Outsourcer in Chief,'" *New York Times*, June 26, 2012, http://www.nytimes.com/2012/06/27/us/politics/obama-calls-romney-potential-outsourcer-in-chief.html; Adrienne Roberts and John D. Stoll, "Donald Trump's Promise of Bringing Back Jobs Worked With Many Michigan Voters," *Wall Street Journal*, November 9, 2016, sec. Politics, http://www.wsj.com/articles/donald-trumps-promise-of-bringing-back-jobs-worked-with-many-michigan-voters-1478728229.

6. Michael Sainato, "'They're Liquidating Us': AT&T Continues Layoffs and Outsourcing despite Profits," *The Guardian*, August 28, 2018, https://www.theguardian.com/us-news/2018/aug/28/att-earns-record-profits-layoffs-outsourcing-continue.

7. Jenny Chan, Ngai Pun, and Mark Selden, "The Politics of Global Production: Apple, Foxconn and China's New Working Class," *New Technology, Work and Employment* 28, no. 2 (July 2013): 100–115; Jamie Fullerton, "Suicide at Chinese iPhone Factory Reignites Concern over Working Conditions," *The Telegraph*, January 7, 2018, https://www.telegraph.co.uk/news/2018/01/07/suicide-chinese-iphone-factory-reignites-concern-working-conditions/.

8. Wharton and Blair-Loy, "Use of Formal and Informal Work–Family Policies," 327–350; Bain and Taylor, "Entrapped by the 'Electronic Panopticon,'" 2–18.

9. The phrase "golden chains" was used by Karl Marx in his 1847 essay, "Wage Labor and Capital." The idea that Western workers were essentially tied to capitalist firms by wage premiums and other incentives was developed in late twentieth-century theories of work and industry. See: Karl Marx, "Wage Labor

and Capital," in *The Marx-Engels Reader*, ed. Robert C. Tucker (New York: W. W. Norton, 1978); Ely Chinoy, *Automobile Workers and the American Dream* (Garden City, NY: Doubleday, 1955); Burawoy, *Manufacturing Consent*; Ruth Milkman, *Farewell to the Factory* (Berkeley: University of California Press, 1997); Sanford M. Jacoby, *Employing Bureaucracy: Managers, Unions, and the Transformation of Work in the 20th Century*, rev. ed. (Mahway, NJ: Psychology Press, 2004).

10. Erik Olin Wright, "Working-Class Power, Capitalist-Class Interests, and Class Compromise," *American Journal of Sociology* 105, no. 4 (2000): 957–1002.

11. John N. Schacht, *The Making of Telephone Unionism, 1920–1947* (New Brunswick, NJ: Rutgers University Press, 1985); Stuart Tannock, *Youth at Work: The Unionized Fast-Food and Grocery Workplace* (Philadelphia: Temple University Press, 2001).

12. Rosemary Batt, "Explaining Intra-Occupational Wage Inequality in Telecommunications Services," *Industrial and Labor Relations* 54, no. 2 (2001): 425–449.; Doellgast, *Disintegrating Democracy at Work*.

CHAPTER 10

1. There is an ongoing push by the government to redirect call center investment into provincial areas. But given Manila's large and ever-growing population, and the difficulty in physically accessing much of the rest of the country, it is hard to see such decentralization being feasible on a large scale.

2. Lin Pan, *English as a Global Language in China: Deconstructing the Ideological Discourses of English in Language Education* (New York: Springer, 2015), 3.

3. Laudicina et al., "2014 A.T. Kearney Global Services Location Index," 1.

4. David J. Bier, "America Is Rejecting More Legal Immigrants Than Ever Before," *New York Times*, November 15, 2018, sec. Opinion, https://www.nytimes.com/2018/11/15/opinion/trump-legal-immigrants-reject.html.

5. Bureau of Labor Relations, *What Are the Types of Unions in the Philippines?* (Manila: Department of Labor and Employment, 2016).

6. Doellgast, *Disintegrating Democracy at Work*; McKay, *Satanic Mills or Silicon Islands?*.

ACKNOWLEDGMENTS

1. Teddy Wayne, "At the Tone, Leave a What?," *New York Times*, June 13, 2014, https://www.nytimes.com/2014/06/15/fashion/millennials-shy-away-from-voice-mail.html.

APPENDIX

1. Sallaz, "Permanent Pedagogy," 3–34.
2. +xit Tales," 573–599.
3. Pertierra, *Anthropology of New Media in the Philippines*.
4. Harvey Russell Bernard, *Social Research Methods: Qualitative and Quantitative Approaches* (Thousand Oaks, CA: Sage, 2000), 346.
5. For a sampling of these debates across time and field, see: Robert Aunger, "On Ethnography: Storytelling or Science?," *Current Anthropology* 36, no. 1 (February 1, 1995): 97–130; Jack Katz, "Ethnography's Warrants," *Sociological Methods & Research* 25, no. 4 (1997): 391–423; Steven Lubet, *Interrogating Ethnography: Why Evidence Matters* (New York: Oxford University Press, 2017); Jessica Smartt Gullion, *Diffractive Ethnography: Social Sciences and the Ontological Turn* (New York: Routledge, 2018).
6. Burawoy, "Extended Case Method," 11.

Index